EVANGELISM EXPLOSION

EVANGELISM EXPLOSION

*Equipping Churches for
Friendship, Evangelism, Discipleship,
and Healthy Growth*

BY D. JAMES KENNEDY

FOURTH EDITION

Foreword by Billy Graham
Revised by D. James Kennedy and Thomas H. Stebbins

Tyndale House Publishers, Inc.
Wheaton, Illinois

This book is affectionately dedicated to
the thousands of laymen and laywomen
of the Coral Ridge Presbyterian Church
and to the hundreds of thousands
of others throughout the world
who have faithfully over the years put into practice
the principles and methods of this ministry.

Library of Congress Catalog Card Number 71-116480
ISBN 0-8423-0764-8

Printed in the United States of America
03 02 01 00 99 98 97 96
8   7   6   5   4   3   2   1

TRANSLATION OF EVANGELISM EXPLOSION

It has been properly said that language is the matrix of culture. To move from one language to another is to move from one culture to another. One of the reasons God became man in the person of Jesus Christ in the Jewish culture was to communicate to man as completely as possible. Since the purpose of Evangelism Explosion is to equip churches worldwide for friendship, evangelism, discipleship, and explosive growth, we feel it is imperative that translations be culturally relevant. Straight, literal, wooden translations have a limited capacity for communicating.

Furthermore, there is a personal dimension to Evangelism Explosion ministry that cannot be placed on paper. For these reasons, we have some very specific requirements for anyone desiring to undertake the translation of this work.

Concerning the translator:

1. We need to know his relationship to the evangelical community in his country.
2. We need to know his background in the language and culture of his people and his understanding of the English language.

Regarding the translation:

1. Copies of the translated portions, as they are completed, along with the English equivalent indicating any cultural adaptations, are to be provided to the International Center.
2. Initial production is to be in small quantities so field testing can be adequately done before much money is invested.
3. After approximately a year of field testing, the material may be produced in larger quantities for use in local churches.
4. We need to know where the book will be printed, in what quantity, how it will be distributed to the churches, and whether or not the distributor is willing to work

with Evangelism Explosion International to promote solid, local church-based ministries of evangelism in conjunction with the book.

All these things must be agreed upon before permission will be granted for translation.

Continuous dialogue is expected during the translation period and field testing. When the final manuscript has been completed, a full copy, along with the English equivalent showing any cultural adaptations, must be submitted to E.E. International.

Final permission for printing and distribution of the translation will be granted if the manuscript is linguistically correct, the content is true to the fundamental concepts of E.E., and there has been proper cultural adaptation.

If you are interested in making a translation or assisting the funding of a translation, write to E.E. International, P. O. Box 23820, Fort Lauderdale, Florida 33307.

TABLE OF CONTENTS

FOREWORD
BY DR. BILLY GRAHAM

The Reverend Dr. D. James Kennedy is minister of the Coral Ridge Presbyterian Church of Fort Lauderdale, Florida, and I have known him for many years and followed his ministry closely. So enthusiastic have I become over his program for evangelizing a parish that I have asked him to come regularly and address our Crusade School of Evangelism, where he has been before many thousands of theological students, ordinands, young clergy, and other Christian workers.

Dr. Kennedy was not always a preacher. Indeed, he was a dancing instructor, par excellence, with the Arthur Murray Dancing School and rapidly rising into prominence in that profession. Then one day his clock radio brought him a disturbing question from Dr. Donald Grey Barnhouse, the Philadelphia preacher, concerning where he would spend his eternal destiny. He could turn off his radio, but he could not turn off the eternal implication of this all-important question. The result was a revolutionary conversion. He subjected himself to the disciplines of being trained for and ordained into the ministry.

Christianity Today magazine correctly describes his congregation as the fastest-growing Presbyterian church in the U.S. and this at a time when churches everywhere are complaining of dwindling memberships. There are doubtless a number of reasons for this phenomenal growth, but I would like to cite two. The first is the unwavering devotion of Dr. Kennedy, as a man, to Jesus Christ his Lord, a devotion that counts no sacrifice too great, no cost too high to pay to give Jesus Christ his best. The second is the fact that Pastor Kennedy has recaptured the biblical concept that the church's primary task is "every-member evangelism." The church, having come to Christ, is to go for Christ.

In this book, Dr. Kennedy outlines how a whole congregation can be motivated and mobilized to perform this task of evangelism. The pastor himself must provide the example and leadership in this task. He chooses trainees and in 13 weeks of engaging them an evening a week, trains them in the science and art of house-to-house evangelism. He teaches them the course. He goes with them and demonstrates how it is done. Then the trainees graduate into trainers and, in turn, train others.

In the words of a Canadian pastor who saw 103 members added to his church in the first eight months of implementing this ministry, this plan of Dr. Kennedy's is "the most revolutionary technique for personal evangelism to mobilize the sleeping giant of our laity to be discovered in the twentieth century."

Unworthy as I may feel at times, it has been my privilege to see many of the world's largest stadiums crowded to hear the claims of Christ presented from the Bible. Equally important in New Testament evangelism, however, is this basic principle of one-to-one evangelism.

June 1970

PREFACE TO THE FOURTH EDITION

Something new is happening in the Christian church today! It is the "evangelism explosion."

In recent years we have heard much about the "population explosion"—masses of people burgeoning at rates hitherto undreamed of. But the population has been increasing at a far greater rate than the church. The reason is simple: while people have been multiplying, we have merely been making additions. Obviously, if the Church adds while the world multiplies, we have no hope of ever catching up. The only answer to this dilemma, humanly speaking, is spiritual multiplication. This must involve the laity and, in fact, everyone who bears the name of Christ.

An evangelism explosion is God's answer to the population explosion. The fissionable material is the thousands of laymen and ministers equipped to build loving relationships and graciously, effectively share the Gospel of Christ with their friends, relatives, associates, and neighbors. The explosive power is the Holy Spirit working through the Gospel, which is the *dunameis,* or "dynamite," of God. The result, furthermore, is not chaos but the creation of a vast host of new Christians.

For ages, such an explosion of friendship, evangelism, and discipleship seemed more dream than reality. Today, that dream is increasingly taking on the contours of reality, for the worldwide church of Jesus Christ is growing at an unprecedented rate. This is largely due to the growing number of laypeople who realize their responsibility and privilege to witness for Christ. Each year thousands more believers become equipped and trained to share their faith. The Church is truly beginning to look like "a mighty army."

The most exciting fact, however, is that, as the Church grows and more Christians are trained, the growth rate actually becomes faster. We are now actually beginning to see the results of an explosion of friendship, evangelism, and discipleship, but the best is yet to come! It is estimated at this date that approximately 100,000 churches in 211 countries are training their laypeople to witness using the principles and methods of the Evangelism Explosion (E.E.) ministry.

There are four phases of the Evangelism Explosion ministry:

I. FRIENDSHIP

Effective evangelism requires friendly relationships. It is therefore crucial that we spend the time and effort necessary to befriend those with whom we want to share our faith. By showing an interest in them, listening to them, getting to know them, and cultivating a warm, caring relationship with them, we can earn the right to ask personal questions and share with them the Gospel, which addresses their very personal needs. Hence, in reaching people for Christ, E.E. seeks first and always to establish friendships, be it in brief onetime encounters or over extended periods of time.

Every believer is the center of several networks of relationships. By birth he is related to his family, and by marriage, to family and various in-laws. Employment enables him to interact with coworkers. At home he relates to neighbors, and he builds friendships in schools, clubs, and other social spots. In the normal course of a day or week, he develops ongoing relationships with many others—barbers, beauticians, doctors, dentists, nurses, service station attendants, mail persons, clerks, insurance agents, and other casual acquaintances. It is important that he cultivate these contacts into friendships and develop new ones as bridges to reach people around him with the Good News of God's gift of eternal life through Jesus Christ. The history of the E.E. ministry is replete with stories of people around the globe, men and women who have led to Christ many friends from their networks of relationships.

II. EVANGELISM

Too often "friendship evangelism" never gets beyond friendship. Ofttimes the believer is content to "witness" with his exemplary lifestyle, assuming that someday, somehow, his friend will ask him how to come to Christ. Or he gets so caught up in the friendship that he fears threatening it by broaching the subject of the Gospel.

Because of this, after training Christians to build friendships with unbelievers, E.E. then equips them to lead naturally and inoffensively into the Gospel itself. This could be during a onetime encounter with a fellow airline passenger or through a series of conversations with a longtime friend. E.E. equips believers with the content of the Gospel and with the skills to communicate it effectively.

From the beginning of E.E., it was clear that evangelism was not an end in itself, but a beginning. Though the basic purpose of E.E. was (and still is) evangelism, we realized that this could best take place in a loving, discipling relationship. And we know that new believers cannot be left to themselves; they need concerned follow-up and . . .

III. DISCIPLESHIP

The more E.E. worked in evangelism, the more evident it became that effective evangelism best takes place within the context of three levels of discipleship.

A. NEW BELIEVERS AND SPIRITUAL PARENTS

In His great commission, Christ did not instruct His disciples to go and make conversions, but to "go and make disciples." While conversions are important and necessary, they must be followed by thorough, biblical disciple-making. In order to properly disciple new believers, it is not enough merely to know the content of the Gospel; one must share one's life with them. Spiritually, functionally mature Christians should take responsibility for discipling their spiritual children into mature believers.

Evangelism Explosion trains lay evangelists to do "immediate follow-up" first—that is, to help the new believer to start growing immediately after his or her profession of faith. Then we give practical suggestions for how to do "continuing follow-up" for many months until the spiritual babe matures into a responsible, reproducing disciple and is assimilated as a functioning member of a local church.

B. E.E. PARTICIPANTS AND OTHER MEMBERS IN THE CHURCH

Through E.E.'s prayer-partner ministry, many members of the church family are discipled. E.E. participants each ask two adult members to uphold them in prayer during the semester of training. Needs are shared and prayed for each week as participants and prayer partners bring the evangelism contacts before the Lord. This results in more people in the church becoming involved in the evangelism ministry. In their relationship with others in the church and in E.E. directly, participants soon learn that bringing people to Christ is only the beginning. Also, they realize that teachers and leaders in the church can greatly help them build up the new Christians.

Every congregation has a high percentage of people who merely attend. But when attenders enter into prayer-partner relationships with E.E. participants or E.E. trainers/trainees, they tend to grow and begin wanting to become spiritual reproducers. The discipling that takes place through the prayer-partner ministry also prevents any pharisaical elitism among those in Evangelism Explosion. It provides a means for developing stronger disciples throughout the church.

C. TRAINER AND TRAINEE

When Jesus enlisted His first disciples He said, "Follow me and I will make you become fishers of men." His first discipleship training course was in evangelism, and that course included on-the-job training.

In Evangelism Explosion's on-the-job training, experienced lay evangelists take less experienced people with them as they share the Gospel. Over several months, the trainees are gradually drawn into the presentation until the novice is finally able to lead the entire conversation. On-the-job training makes more and better lay evangelists.

IV. Healthy Growth

Evangelism Explosion was born in the church and has always been a church-based ministry. Lay evangelists are enlisted in the church, equipped at the church, sent out from the church, share without apology about the church, fold new believers into the church, and continue to nurture those believers in the church. The church that properly applies E.E.'s equipping ministry will therefore experience three kinds of healthy growth.

A. SPIRITUAL GROWTH

As the family of God on earth, the local church is composed of believers who are physically young or old and spiritually mature or immature. For disciples to grow into proper functional maturity, they need to learn how to interact with mature disciples, with those who are not mature, and with non-Christians in the world. Evangelism Explosion fosters this interaction.

When a church equips its members through E.E., it will grow spiritually in several ways. Paul wrote to his dear friend and fellow worker Philemon that if he would be active in sharing his faith, he would come to a full understanding of everything good that he had in Christ. One church participated in E.E. and doubled in active membership, but its pastor testified that if no one had been added to the church, it would still have been worth the effort because his leaders and congregation had grown so much spiritually!

One reason Christians involved in E.E. grow spiritually is that by witnessing and discipling others they are clearly obeying their Lord's command to do so, and we are told in Acts 5:32 that the Holy Spirit fills those who obey Him. In Acts 1:8 Jesus stated that when we are filled with the Spirit we will receive power and be witnesses for Christ. Hence, it is inconceivable to me that any believer who is not actively and regularly seeking to share his faith can claim to be filled with the Spirit.

Another reason Christians who are involved in E.E. experience spiritual growth is that in learning and sharing the E.E. presentation, they are rooted and grounded in soteriology—the doctrine of salvation. Learning a logical presentation of the Gospel, memorizing basic Scripture verses, and mastering the use of a number of lucid illustrations about grace, man, God, Christ, and faith—they can't help but grow! In developing their own personal testimony, they apply these truths to their own life and thus discover a strong security, a deep assurance of eternal life, and this security and assurance have an unmistakable impact on their spiritual growth.

Through on-the-job training, E.E. participants see sinners transformed into believers. As the training semester progresses, they begin to share the Gospel themselves and experience the immeasurable joy of leading others to Christ. Then they begin to share the Good News as a way of life with their friends, relatives, associates, and neighbors and see some of them come to Christ. Few of them have ever before experienced anything so eternally significant! And this unmistakable significance adds a whole new purpose and meaning to their lives and brings them easily recognized, unprecedented spiritual growth!

E.E. is an interdenominational international ministry that de-emphasizes divisive issues that plague many believers and churches. Jesus said, "By this shall all men know that ye are my disciples, if ye have love one to another." As we affirm and express in living reality our oneness in Christ, the world will know that God has sent Him. The loving unity of God's people in E.E. demonstrates to the world the power and truth of the Gospel and has a tremendous impact for spiritual growth in the life of each believer. And such a spiritually healthy, united, witnessing body of believers can't help but experience, in turn . . .

B. NUMERICAL GROWTH

Numerical growth, of course, was evident in the first-century church as the number of Christ's followers literally exploded from 12 to 70 to 500 to 3,000 to 5,000 and then to such great numbers that they could no longer be counted! The number of churches also multiplied and spread beyond Jerusalem to Judea, Samaria, and on to the ends of the earth!

As lay evangelists in E.E. win people to Christ, disciple them, and fold them into a local congregation, the church will grow in number. The church I pastor, Coral Ridge Presbyterian Church, in 1962 averaged 246 worshipers on Sunday morning. In 1972 the average number of worshipers had exploded to 2,512—over ten times the size. And the church's growth has continued through the ensuing years. This amazing phenomenon has been experienced in church after church across the land and on every continent of the world!

In Hong Kong one church grew from 60 to 350 within two years of implementing E.E. In Wales, where churches are often in a state of decline, one pastor applying E.E.'s strategy has seen his congregation grow by 600 percent. In Minsk, Belarus (former Soviet Union), one church reports that after 16 weeks of E.E. ministry 790 persons had professed faith in Christ. You also can experience this same growth in your local church!

C. ORGANIZATIONAL GROWTH

As local churches grow spiritually and numerically, they will also need to grow organizationally. New leaders will emerge, new ministries will be started, and additional staff will be called to cultivate and conserve the fruit of evangelism. These additions are necessary to maintain the momentum and continue the expanding ministry that God the Holy Spirit graciously engenders.

Within three years of the first E.E. leadership clinic in 1967, attendance had grown so dramatically that it became necessary to encourage churches elsewhere in the U.S. to begin hosting their own clinics. Then leaders from other countries expressed interest in this work, and those with cross-cultural sensitivity who functioned in basically healthy churches benefited greatly. Now we have established an international center for this ministry that maintains regular communication with ministries around the globe. Praise God—today national directors and advisory boards lead indigenous Evangelism Explosion ministries on every continent; and in the not-too-distant future, every nation will have its own leaders at the helm of their E.E. ministries!

ACKNOWLEDGMENTS

I would like to express my gratitude to the many long-forgotten or untraceable friends who, nevertheless, have been the source of numerous thoughts and illustrations in this book. I also thank Rev. Kennedy Smartt, who patiently took me with him on home visitation, and instructed me in the fine art of personal evangelism. In addition, I would like to acknowledge my indebtedness and appreciation to many who have helped to make this book a reality: Rev. Harry Miller, who first gathered our materials into notebook form; the dedicated group of men and women in our church, who, again and again over the years, put the notebook together for use in the church and clinics; the Reverend T. M. Moore, who assisted me with the third revision; and the Reverend Thomas H. Stebbins, who helped me with this fourth revision. Many thanks are due my personal secretary, Mrs. Mary Anne Bunker, for her constant assistance; and a very special word of appreciation to Mrs. Ruth Rohm, our publications secretary, for her faithful labors in typing, retyping, and editing the work.

This new edition goes forth with heartfelt prayer and hope that God, the Lord of the harvest, will continue to be pleased to use this ministry for the salvation of vast multitudes of people around the world.

Soli Deo Gloria
D. James Kennedy, Ph.D.
   Founder and President
   Evangelism Explosion International
   April 1, 1996

One

EQUIPPING LAYPEOPLE

This is not theory, but fact! These are not the idle speculations of the ivory tower, but the tested results of hard experience. First in the congregation of the Coral Ridge Presbyterian Church of Fort Lauderdale, Florida, and then in thousands of other churches throughout the United States and much of the rest of the world, these principles and procedures have brought new life and vitality and have resulted in the conversion of multitudes of people.

This ministry of training laymen for the task of friendship, evangelism, and discipleship based on New Testament principles grew out of the specific problems and opportunities faced by our congregation. Yet the ministry contains readily transferable techniques which have been used by numerous other congregations in cities and towns, in ghettos and rural areas, and in many languages and cultures throughout the world. We believe that the principles contained in the ministry represent some of the basic principles of the New Testament concerning the matter of evangelism, though by no means does this ministry exhaust all of the biblical teaching and possibilities. This is a ministry of friendship and personal evangelism and does not begin to encompass many of the other sound and biblical methods of evangelism, such as crusade evangelism, pulpit evangelism, literature evangelism, etc.

Realizing that laymen are the most strategic and also the most unused key to the evangelization of the world, we have endeavored to build a ministry which will motivate, recruit, and train men and women and boys and girls to do the job of friendship evangelism and then *keep* them doing it! This, of course, is not an easy task, as most pastors can testify. And yet it would seem that the basic principles of New Testament evangelism require that this mobilization of the laity takes place. We are not talking about the "flash and ash" type of program of which there have been numerous examples on the evangelical scene, but we are talking about a type of mobilization and recruitment that will ensure an ongoing ministry of lay evangelism year after year in the local church. Let us look at some of the *biblical* principles through which this may take place.

I. First Biblical Principle: Every Christian a Witness

A. CHRIST'S FIRST INSTRUCTIONS

Christ's first instructions to His new followers in the first chapter of Mark were, "Come ye after me, and I will make you to become fishers of men." His last instructions on this earth to His disciples were, "But ye shall receive power, after that the Holy Ghost is come upon you: and ye shall be witnesses unto me both in Jerusalem, and in all Judea, and in Samaria, and unto the uttermost part of the earth" (Acts 1:8). Christ thus began and ended His ministry with the command to be witnesses and fishers of men! This thrust of His teaching is summed up in the great commission, where Jesus commands His followers to go into all the world and preach the Gospel to every creature. The first and most obvious principle, then, is that the Church is a body under orders by Christ to share the Gospel with the whole world. But the question then arises, how is this to be done and by whom?

B. THE WILES OF SATAN

The apostle Paul said that we are not ignorant of the wiles of the devil. But I wonder how true that is today. I wonder how many times we have been deceived by him. I am sure it has been often. What is the greatest strategic victory Satan has ever achieved? What would you suppose it to be? The most signal victory for Satan would obviously be the worst defeat for the Church. What might it be?

C. SATAN'S GREATEST VICTORY

Surely a number of his devious stratagems leap to mind. I would like to suggest one thing which, in my opinion, is his greatest victory. Let me present it to you in the way of an analogy. Suppose that in our modern, secular world, the center for propaganda in Moscow dreamed up a new idea. They polished it very carefully and then began to spread it abroad. It would appear first of all in some avant-garde publications, coming to the surface in magazine and newspaper articles. Perhaps a play would be made out of it, then a motion picture, and finally a television production. Groups would be formed to push the movement, protests would be made, and finally the idea would prevail and be accepted by the American people almost unanimously. What is the idea? It is this: that wars are very dangerous, complicated operations, and ordinary persons could get hurt needlessly; therefore, they should go home and let the generals and admirals fight wars. I don't think there is any doubt in our minds as to what would be the outcome of the cold—or not so cold—war in which we would be engaged.

D. LET THE GENERALS FIGHT THE WAR

Right away we say, That is ridiculous! Such a ludicrous idea could never be put over

on any people. Yet in the church this, in essence, is exactly what Satan has done! I am certain that for the vast majority of Christian church members the idea has firmly taken root in their minds that it is primarily the task of the minister to fight the battles of Christ—especially for the souls of men. In the minds of most, the work of evangelism is the work of professionally trained men. After all, they say, I'm just a butcher, baker, or candlestick maker, and what do I know about theology? I've never been to seminary; leave it to the trained ecclesiastical generals! This, I believe, has been the greatest tragedy that has befallen the Church of Jesus Christ. Its results are so far-reaching, so vast in scope, that we have little concept of what damage has been done.

E. THE EARLY CHURCH

But it wasn't this way in the early church! Examine again that passage in Acts 8:1-4. It says, "They were all scattered abroad. . . . They that were scattered abroad went every where preaching the word." That is a great text to preach. But some people might say, "Well, just a minute, Preacher, not so fast. You have turned the corner a little too rapidly. You see, the people that went everywhere spreading and preaching the Word were the apostles. You remember, Jesus chose those twelve, trained them, and they went out and spread the Word."

F. EVERYONE EVANGELIZING

Well, we all know that a standard exegetical axiom is, "A text without a context is a pretext," and it has been a pretext long enough to let ecclesiastical George do it! The significant context of that verse is found in Acts 8:1, where we read that "they were all scattered abroad . . . except the apostles," and "they that were scattered abroad went every where preaching the word" (Acts 8:4). The word translated "preaching the word" is the Greek word *euangelizo,* which means "evangelizing." That is, everybody except the apostles went everywhere evangelizing! Now we know that the apostles did their share. But the point the inspired writer is emphasizing here is that everyone besides the apostles also went and evangelized.

G. EARLY RESULTS OF LAY EVANGELISM

That is how the Church of Jesus Christ in 300 years accomplished the most amazing results. The whole pagan Roman Empire was undercut and overthrown by the power of the Gospel of Christ, which, on the lips of Christ-conquered disciples, crossed seas and deserts, pierced the darkest jungles, seeped into every city and town, and finally into the senate and the very palace of Rome itself—until a Christian caesar was placed upon the throne. How? By *everyone* taking part in evangelizing.

The Christian church was burgeoning with such rapidity that by the middle of the second century one of the great apologists could say, "We are everywhere. We are in your towns and in your cities; we are in your country; we are in your army and navy; we are in your palaces; we are in the senate; we are more numerous than anyone." Constantine knew very well (whether or not he was truly converted, I will leave for the historians) that he had no chance of unifying the Roman Empire or holding power in that empire without the help of the Christians.

H. CLERGY-LAITY SPLIT

By A.D. 300 the church had shown such tremendous strength and virility and was spreading so swiftly that it appeared the entire civilized world could be evangelized by A.D. 500. But something happened. Emperor Constantine, in the year 313, issued the Edict of Toleration, by which the long agonizing persecution of the Christians was at last brought to a halt. In the following decades numerous other edicts favoring the Christians were passed, until at last the whole Roman Empire was declared by fiat to be Christian. Thus, millions of barbarians flooded into the church, bringing with them all of their pagan superstitions and heresies. They didn't even know the Gospel. They had never experienced its transforming power, and, of course, they could not go out and tell others about it. So, little by little, the idea arose that there was a division between the clergy and the laity and that this task of evangelism was the job of the professionally trained individuals. So they decided to let ecclesiastical George do it. The Dark Ages followed! With only a few bright spots in the history of the church since that time, this deplorable condition has continued down to our day.

I. LET CLERICAL GEORGE DO IT

So successful has Satan been with this stratagem, it has been estimated that probably 95 percent of American church members have never led anyone to Christ. Thus, the army of Christ has been more than decimated, and the response from the pew has been, "Let clerical George do it." I am thankful that today there is an obvious reversal of this trend, as more and more laymen and churches are realizing and accepting their responsibility to witness.

J. EVANGELISM AS A WAY OF LIFE

Not only did all the early Christians witness, but they witnessed daily and to everyone they met—especially to those who were in their network of friends, relatives, associates, and neighbors. In the New Testament it is very evident that evangelism was not a special activity to be undertaken at a prescribed time, such as a once-a-year crusade or a once-a-week visitation effort, but it was the constant overflow of individual and corporate experiences and knowledge of Christ. Each Christian assumed responsibility for sharing the Gospel in the natural context of daily life. Christ at the well (John 4), Andrew with his brother Peter (John 1), Philip with Nathanael (John 1), Peter at the temple gate (Acts 3), and Paul in the Philippian jail (Acts 16:22-34) are clear examples of how Christ and early believers used their relationships as bridges through which to share the Gospel.

In Evangelism Explosion we seek to equip laypeople to witness not just in the once-a-week ministry of visitation and on-the-job training but throughout the week as a way of life to the people with whom they have developed trusting relationships. We encourage our laypeople to develop new relationships through which they can share Christ. And then we train them to articulate their faith effectively so that when the opportunity presents itself, they are ready to share the Gospel with the people whom God the Holy Spirit has prepared.

II. Second Biblical Principle: Pastors Must Equip Their Laypeople

A. LAYPEOPLE NEED TO BE TRAINED

It is the task of ministers to train their laypeople to evangelize. Over 99 percent of the church is made up of laypeople. If they are AWOL (absent without official leave) there is little doubt that the battle will be lost. If the laity has been deceived, I think it is equally true that the ministers have also been deceived by the subtlety of Satan concerning the basic purpose of their ministry.

B. PURPOSE OF MINISTERS

In the fourth chapter of Ephesians we read that Christ has given to the church "some, apostles; and some, prophets; and some, evangelists; and some, pastors and teachers; for the perfecting of the saints, for the work of the ministry, for the edifying of the body of Christ." This is the way it reads in the King James translation. This, however, is not a very accurate rendering of the Greek text. Instead of the preposition "for" being repeated three times, the Greek would be better rendered: "for," "unto," "unto." A more literal translation, then, would be that Christ has given pastors and teachers to the church "for the equipping of the saints unto the work of ministry, unto the upbuilding of the body of Christ."

C. REVOLUTIONARY CONCEPT

Such a concept, once grasped, would completely revolutionize many ministries. A basic criterion for determining the successfulness of a pastorate would then become: "How many saints have I equipped to do the work of ministry?" As ministers, then, we need to see ourselves not as the star performers or virtuosos but rather as the coaches of well-trained and well-coordinated teams of personal evangelists!

We have seen what needs to be done and by whom; now let us ask: How are we going to get them to do it?

III. Third Biblical Principle: On-the-Job Training

There have been hundreds of thousands of messages preached on the responsibility of Christians to witness, and yet there is a striking absence of any formidable army of lay witnesses. Something, therefore, must be missing. This brings us to an important biblical principle, namely, on-the-job training. It has been accurately observed that "Evangelism is more *caught* than *taught*." This oft-repeated cliché rather accurately describes what is missing in most attempts at teaching laymen to evangelize, and it also describes fairly well the method Christ used to teach his followers.

I have asked thousands of ministers whether they have preached sermons on the need to witness and have taught classes on this subject. Most of them have raised their hands. But when I have asked how many of them make a habit of taking their people with them when they go out to evangelize, only 3 or 4 percent will usually respond. I questioned a group of ministers, missionaries, and teachers and found that only 12 percent of their members were regularly engaged in leading people to Christ, and only three of these people took their laymen with them when they went to evangelize.

The average person can no more learn to evangelize in a classroom than he can learn to fly an airplane in the living room. The missing link of modern evangelistic training, which was so thoroughly provided by Christ, is "on-the-job" training.

IV. FOURTH BIBLICAL PRINCIPLE: TRAINING SOUL WINNERS MORE IMPORTANT

The fourth biblical principle may surprise you. Simply stated, it is that you will make a far greater impact for eternity by training soul winners than by just winning souls. Spiritual multiplication will not take place unless converts are turned into evangelists, disciples into disciplers. Since about 95 percent of converts never win anyone to Christ because they are not equipped to do so, it is obvious that training a person to evangelize effectively will be more fruitful than merely winning someone to Christ.

The Lord Jesus did not say to go and make converts, but to go and make disciples. It is because winning a person to Christ is so important that training someone to win 10 or 100 or 1,000 people to Christ is so much more important. One of the wonderful parts of this ministry is that these two tasks are combined, and people are trained to evangelize by observing others being evangelized. Thus, one is not done to the exclusion of the other.

These are the basic principles we feel need to be understood and accepted if a church is to have an effective ministry of evangelism.

V. REVIEWING THE HISTORY

A. FEAR OF WITNESSING

This ministry grew out of the experiences I had in the Coral Ridge Church, which started as a home mission project in 1960. I came directly to this work from seminary, and though I preached evangelistically, and I had taken all the courses offered at seminary on evangelism and read many books, I found that the sophisticated people of Fort Lauderdale did not respond to my message from the pulpit. I was totally lacking in both confidence and know-how in regard to confronting individuals face-to-face with the Gospel. After eight or ten months of my preaching, the congregation had dwindled from forty-five to seventeen, and I was a most discouraged young minister. About that time I was invited to Decatur, Georgia, to preach ten days of evangelistic services. Happy to get away for a while from my Fort Lauderdale fiasco, I accepted the invitation.

B. LIFE-CHANGING EXPERIENCE

When I arrived, the pastor told me I would be preaching each night, but more important, he said we would be visiting in homes each day—morning, noon, and night—to present the Gospel to people individually. I was petrified, for I knew I had no ability whatsoever to do this. However, the next morning we went out. After about a half hour of my stumbling attempts at evangelism, the pastor took over the conversation and in about fifteen or twenty minutes led the man to Christ. I was astonished but did not realize even then the impact this was to have on my life. For ten days I watched this pastor lead one person after another to Christ, for a total of fifty-four individuals during those ten days.

I went back to Fort Lauderdale a new man, and I began to do just what I had seen done. People responded in the same way. Soon dozens, scores, and then hundreds accepted Christ. The principle of "on-the-job" training had been applied to my life and had produced its results.

C. FAILURE OF CLASSES

I then realized there was a definite limit to the number of people I, myself, could see, and that I ought to train others to do what I was doing. What I then foolishly did is the same thing thousands of others no doubt have done: I organized a class on witnessing. I gave the class six lessons and sent them out. They all went home terrified! I waited a few months and tried again. This time I gave them twelve lessons. Again, no success. A few more months and another series—more elaborate, more complex. Fifteen weeks. Again, no results! I do not know of one single adult who was brought to Christ by any one of those laymen as a result of the witnessing classes.

D. THE MISSING LINK

Finally it struck me like a bolt of lightning—I had taken classes for three years and had not learned how to witness. It was not until someone who knew how had taken me out into people's homes that I finally got the confidence to do it myself. Thus I began a ministry that has continued for over thirty years. It started by my taking out one individual until he had confidence to witness to others, and then another, and another. And so it has grown. After the people are trained, they in turn can train others.

VI. RECRUITING THE WORKERS

A. PROBLEMS OF MASS RECRUITMENT

Often, when an evangelism ministry is envisioned, a pastor will begin by preaching on the subject and then inviting everyone who is willing to take part to come on a specified night to begin the evangelism ministry. This is the way we tried at first to motivate people and recruit them, but we found it was not very successful. The basic motivation will no doubt begin from the pulpit with sermons on the responsibility, privilege, and necessity of witnessing for Christ. The great texts already mentioned, and others, should certainly be preached with clarity and forcefulness. However, our experience teaches us that the actual recruiting should not be done from the pulpit but rather should be done on a person-to-person basis, first by the pastor and then by the trained laymen.

B. INDIVIDUAL INVITATION

When Christ called His apostles, He first prayed all night and then called them specifically by name. Now an apostle *(apostolos)* was "one sent forth with a commission." The term has both a narrow and a wide meaning. In its narrow sense it refers only to the twelve apostles whom Christ first called. In its broader sense it refers to every Christian who has been sent forth by Christ with the great commission. We would, therefore, recommend that after much prayer the pastor select several people he would like to take with him to teach them how to evangelize.

C. RAPID MULTIPLICATION

I did not want to begin a ministry in this small way, with only one or two individuals, but wanted, rather, to train a whole class of evangelists at one time. The result was that I ended up with none. However, if you begin with a few, you can grow, in not too much time, into a large body of witnesses. At the end of the four-month training semester, each of these four trained individuals will recruit two more workers, and the minister also will recruit four more. Now there will be the original four plus their eight, making twelve, plus the minister's new four, making sixteen, plus the minister, for a total of seventeen. After the next semester the sixteen laymen will get thirty-two more, making forty-eight, plus the minister's four, which makes fifty-two, plus the minister, making fifty-three. Soon it could grow to a hundred, two hundred, etc.

D. NOT THREE MEN

I would suggest that the pastor begin by selecting two people for one morning visitation and two others for one night visitation. As long as we do not have three men together, which seems a bit heavy, we have not found that three individuals constitute much of a problem. One reason for going out in teams of three was that women were involved in the ministry from the start. Someone might say, "But doesn't the Bible tell us that we should go out two-by-two?" Well, let us take a closer look at that passage.

There is no doubt that Christ sent out the seventy, two-by-two. But the question arises, "Whom did he send out?" I believe there is little doubt that he sent out seventy men. If, however, he had thirty-five men and thirty-five women, what would he have done then? This, of course, was not feasible in that day. Today it is. In our time, to send out two women into a modern metropolis at night is exceedingly dangerous. To send out a woman with somebody else's husband can also be dangerous. Sending them out by threes has the double advantage of including women in the ministry and also doubling the speed of training. Someone might ask, "Can't you send out a husband and wife together?" Yes, you can, but this is a dead-end street, for the whole purpose of this training is to continually expand the number of people trained, and you cannot do this without dividing the husband-and-wife team.

E. RECRUITMENT BANQUETS

The people are recruited by personal visits, at which time the ministry is explained in detail by the trained individual, and they are invited to a dinner where there will be a fuller explanation of the goals, principles, and reasons for the training, plus testimonies of what has been accomplished. They are asked at the banquet or rally to commit themselves to the entire four-month training semester or else not to start. The ministry may grow in a church until it reaches a point at which a dinner is no longer feasible, in which case a rally may be held. This is what has happened at Coral Ridge. These rallies are generally held on Friday nights.

VII. Training the Evangelists

We have two training semesters a year, the first beginning early in September and running through December—about 13 weeks. Then we begin our next training semester, which runs till the middle of May. All of these details will vary according to local customs and circumstances. We offer four basic types of training:

A. CLASS INSTRUCTION

These classes, lasting about sixty minutes each, are held on the day the people come to the church for visitation. They meet together for class instruction and then go out into the field. During this class instruction, there is a brief lecture on the topic of the week, assignments are given for study during the following week, and the class is divided into three-person teams in which they practice what has been learned during the previous week. Details for the class instruction and the homework assignments are given in the Training Notebooks.

B. PREPARATION FOR CLASS

The detailed Training Notebooks contain instructions on how to present the Gospel logically and interestingly. Assignments are given each week consisting of the portions of the Gospel presentation to be learned at home. These are checked and recited each week at the class.

C. ON-THE-JOB TRAINING

The third and most important part of the training is "on the job." Each trainee goes out with a trained individual and listens as this trained person presents the Gospel in an endeavor to lead someone to Christ. This is the vital, almost indispensable, element of training.

It is here that the trainee overcomes the greatest obstacle he faces in learning to witness—the fear of what others will say. During the 13 weeks of training, he will see the Gospel presented many times and see a number of people come to profess their faith in Christ. This will have a transforming effect upon him and will do more than anything else to assuage his fears.

An important principle to keep in mind here is the gradual transferal of responsibility. In the same way that a student learning to fly an airplane would gradually assume more responsibility for the overall task of taking off, flying, and landing, so the evangelistic trainee gradually assumes increasing responsibilities.

The three parts of flying, namely, takeoff, flight, and landing, may be likened to the three parts of a Gospel presentation, namely, introduction, Gospel, and commitment. Just as a student of flying first handles the plane in the air, so the trainee begins by handling increasingly larger parts of the Gospel. Then he includes the introduction and the commitment.

In this way the overall task is broken down into manageable assignments for the student. The part of the Gospel presentation the student is to give on a particular night has been assigned the week before, studied by the student, and first recited in class before he goes out.

In the home, the trainer, when he reaches that point, will say something such as: "Well, John, I've been doing most of the talking so far. Why don't I let Mary share with you something about the grace of God and what it means to her."

Mary will then pick up the presentation at the assigned point and present as much as she has learned, and when she hesitates, the trainer will pick up the conversation again by saying something such as, "Thank you, Mary, that was very well said." Then the trainer will conclude the presentation.

D. REPORT-BACK SESSIONS

We have selected Wednesday mornings from 10 to 12 and Wednesday and Thursday evenings from 7:30 to 9:30 as our times of visitation. After visitation we have a report-back meeting—which I feel is quite important to prevent discouragement. During these sessions we provide decaffeinated coffee and doughnuts. At these times we hear the reports of the on-the-job training visits. A person from each team gives a report of their visit. This not only encourages those who are listening but also gives the trainees additional opportunities to speak, thus encouraging them in their ability to speak before others. A results form is filled out. Statistical results of the day's calling are also indicated on a specially prepared chalkboard. Problems or objections encountered during the visit may be brought up at this time, and the teacher/trainer may wish to make some comment about them, thus helping the entire group to more effectively deal with the obstacles confronted in the homes. These report sessions help reduce dropouts due to discouragement, as evangelists have an opportunity to have their spirits lifted by returning to hear others whom God has blessed that night or morning.

How the report sessions are conducted is described in detail later in this book (see chapter 10, Folding into the Church).

VIII. POWER OF THE HOLY SPIRIT

The essence of the evangelical faith is: "Salvation is of the Lord" (Jonah 2:9). Salvation is thus seen to be the supernatural work of the divine Trinity—of the Father who elects, of the Son who redeems, and of the Holy Spirit who applies the salvation of Christ to the hearts of men. Hence it is seen that conversion is not obtained by salesmanship, by persuasion, by rhetoric, by argumentation, or by any other human endeavor, for "Salvation is of the Lord."

I have often told my people that the lost men and women to whom they are sent with the Gospel have a slight impediment. They are deaf, blind, and dead; other than that, they are in fairly good shape. The modern witness for Christ should never lose sight of the statement of the apostle Paul: "The natural man receiveth not the things of the Spirit of God: for they are foolishness unto him: neither can he know them, because they are spiritually discerned" (1 Corinthians 2:14).

This means that our witnessing must always be a "trialogue" rather than a dialogue. It means that we are speaking not only to the lost persons before us but also to the Holy Spirit above us and within us, that He might open their eyes and enlighten their minds to understand what we are saying in order that they might be saved. The witness should be taught from the very beginning to depend not on his own persuasiveness but upon the power of the Holy Spirit, or else he is witnessing in the flesh and not in the Spirit.

If "salvation is of the Lord," then why should we witness at all, much less try to do it in the best possible manner? I have often used an illustration which I think speaks to this point.

A riveter is placing rivets in the side of a steel ship. With one hand he holds up a rivet to the side of the ship; with the other he places a pneumatic gun to the rivet and drives it into the ship.

There are four elements involved in this illustration. First, the steel ship; second, the rivet; third, the riveter; and fourth, the pneumatic gun. Each plays a part. If the man could simply place the rivet to the steel ship and push it in with his thumb, he could then say, "What a strong fellow I am!" But, of course, he cannot do this. He must rely on the pneumatic gun.

This is analogous to the situation in witnessing. The steel ship represents the stony hearts and adamantine minds of unbelievers; the rivet represents the Gospel; the riveter represents the witness; and the pneumatic gun represents the Holy Spirit—an appropriate illustration, since "pneumatic" comes from the Greek word for Spirit, *neumatikos.*

If we could, by our own persuasiveness, argumentation, salesmanship, or logic, press the Gospel into somebody's heart and mind, then we could say, "What a wonderful evangelist I am!" But this we cannot do. Therefore, we must depend entirely upon the power of the Holy Spirit to drive the Gospel home to the hearts of men.

If, however, we did not at least hold up the rivet, then the pneumatic gun would only make holes in the side of the ship. Thus God allows us the marvelous privilege of being involved in the greatest work in the world. Dr. John Gerstner put it this way: "We can save no one, but unless we proclaim to them the Gospel, God will save no one."

IX. THE LAWS OF PERSUASION

Having examined the divine or supernatural aspects of salvation, let us consider for a few minutes the human side. Someone has well said, "You can't sell the Gospel; in fact, most Christians can't even give it away." This points out two truths: One, there is something involved far beyond salesmanship—namely, the supernatural work of the Holy Spirit; and two, from the human standpoint, most Christians need a better understanding of the laws of persuasion or salesmanship.

A. JESUS' USE OF THE "FIVE LAWS OF PERSUASION"

There are five great laws of selling or persuading: attention, interest, desire, conviction, and close. It does not matter whether you are selling a refrigerator or persuading men to accept a new idea or philosophy, the same basic laws of persuasion hold true. Did salesmen invent these? No, they just extracted them. They learned that that is the way the human mind and heart reach conclusions and take action. This is what Jesus did, for example, with the woman at the well in John 4.

1. **Attention:** He began where she was and got her attention. "Give Me to drink."
"How is it You ask me? We have nothing to do with each other."

2. **Interest:** "If you knew who was asking you for water, you would ask Me and I would give you living water." Now she was really interested.
"Where would You get living water? The well is deep and You have nothing to draw with. Are You greater than Jacob who gave us this well?"

3. **Desire:** "He who drinks of this water will thirst again, but whoever drinks of the water I give will never thirst." Now she desired ardently what Jesus offered.
"Give me this water so I will never thirst again or have to come here to draw."
Here she was, a woman of ill repute, having to go to the well at noon when no one else was there. Everyone else came in the cool of the day. She seems more interested in not going to the well to draw than in not thirsting again. "Give it to me."

4. **Conviction of sin** (truthfulness of claims): "Go call your husband." He put His finger on her sin. Did she have to have her husband to be saved? No. That was to pinpoint her sin.
"I have no husband."

"You're right. You have had five husbands, and the man you live with now isn't your husband." He drove home the evidence of her sinfulness.

(Diversion:) She tried to avoid the issue. "Our fathers worship in this mountain; You worship in that mountain. . . . When Messiah comes, He will tell us about these matters."

5. Commitment: Jesus used something from her digression to get back on the main subject and confront her with the decision she must make: "I who speak to you am He."

Now she confronts the living Christ. She must either accept or reject Him.

There you see a beautiful piece of workmanship by the Master Workman, who says we should copy Him in dealing with people. He made a smooth transition from where she was to where He wanted her to be.

We should familiarize ourselves with these laws of persuasion and use them to critique our presentation of the Gospel to help detect places of weakness. We should ask ourselves such questions as: Did I fail to get their attention or to hold their interest? If so, why, and what can I do to change this? How much desire was created for knowing Christ and being a part of His kingdom? How can this be increased? Was the person convicted concerning his sins and his need for forgiveness? If not, why not? Did I confront the person clearly with his need to make a decision for Christ and to commit his life to Him in repentance and faith? If not, how can I do this better next time? Such questions as these will help both trainees and trainers better evaluate their progress in the presentation of the Gospel of Christ.

X. Obtaining the Prospects

It is important if we are going to effectively train our people that we provide them with the best possible source of prospects. To deal consistently with only the most difficult type of individuals is most certainly going to discourage the average beginner. We have found from our experience that the best sources of prospects are the following:

A. CHURCH VISITORS

People who have visited our worship services, I would say, are the easiest people with whom to deal. Their hearts are further prepared by a few weeks of sitting under the ministry of the Word.

Some will say, however, "We do not have many visitors come to our church." This objection was raised by a minister in one of the evangelism schools I was conducting. I asked him how many visitors he did have. He said, "We may have two or three on any given Sunday." I then asked him how many people he had going out to present the Gospel to them. He said, "Oh, I have no one doing that," to which I responded, "Well, then, you already have two or three visitors too many."

There was a time when we had only a handful of people coming to church and very few visitors, but you can begin with the visitors you do have. We have found that the number of visitors has increased as the enthusiasm engendered by this ministry has increased. In seeking to increase the number of visitors coming to church, we may ask ourselves the question, What causes people to visit a church? In a survey conducted at our church we asked about one thousand people why they came to our church the first time. The overwhelming majority said that some member of the church had invited them. This, then, is one of the big secrets of getting people to come to church—encouraging your members to invite them.

Periodic "Visitors' Sundays" with perhaps some coffee served afterward and a special emphasis on inviting friends for several weeks beforehand is a fruitful source of prospects. An enthusiastic congregation will provide more than enough people to talk to about Christ.

B. RELATIVES AND FRIENDS

After those who come to your church, the second most responsive source is the relatives and friends of new believers. Each of us is the center of a network of relationships. The longer you are a Christian, the fewer non-Christians remain in your "network." The new Christian usually has many non-Christian friends and relatives. As the Lord begins to change the new Christian's life, those near him notice. The witnessing team can be of great assistance in sharing the Gospel. Relational evangelism will be discussed later in this book.

C. SUNDAY SCHOOL

Another good source of prospects would be the parents of children who attend Sunday school. This source, however, will not prove very fruitful unless Sunday school teachers have had an active program of visiting in the homes and showing an interest in the children's progress in their Christian education. If this has been done the parents will generally be open to the Gospel.

D. NEW RESIDENTS

A fourth source of prospects is the weekly or biweekly or monthly listing of those who have bought new homes in the area. This can be obtained from some source in almost every city. Any real estate salesman in the congregation can usually tell you where to obtain it. In Fort Lauderdale it costs seventy-five dollars per year, but it is worth many times that to any church.

We begin by sending a friendly letter to these people, welcoming them into the community and offering our services in any way possible. We conclude the letter by stating that someone from the church will drop by in the near future and welcome them personally to our area and to our church. A card is then made out for the visitation team showing the date the letter was mailed and indicating that the people are new residents in the area. They are then processed in our visitation ministry.

E. RELIGIOUS QUESTIONNAIRES

A fifth source of prospects, if the others fail to provide an adequate number, is a religious questionnaire. For some time we have worked with "assurance questionnaires" and "religious questionnaires." They can be used in residential and public places. Five to seven questions are raised that let you know whether the person contacted is responsive or resistant. The questionnaires must be used wisely with no "blitzing," or you will generate resistance. How to use the questionnaires is discussed later in this book.

The questionnaires will sift the general population and help you find the people who have a genuine interest in spiritual matters. As has been said many times, "There is no sense in tugging at green fruit."

XI. Presenting the Gospel

A. POSITIVE APPROACH

Our basic approach is neither apologetic, defensive, nor negative. It is a simple, positive statement of the good news of the Gospel. We have found that most Christians do not know how to make an intelligible, forceful, and interesting presentation of the Gospel. This is basically what we are trying to teach them to do.

B. WRITTEN PRESENTATION

We feel that a very useful tool that is often omitted from texts on evangelism is an actual presentation of the Gospel itself. Such a presentation is included in chapter three and in the training materials. E.E. trainees are encouraged to learn it and use it as a guide as they begin to present the Gospel of Christ. Later it is adapted to the individual personality with many additions or subtractions, as the case may require. But most people need something with which to start.

C. BASIC TRAINING

The essential things we are trying to teach our people are how to get into the Gospel and find out where the person is spiritually, how to present the Gospel itself, how to bring the person to a commitment to Jesus Christ at the conclusion, and how to vitally relate the new convert to the family of God.

D. THREE ELEMENTS OF THE PRESENTATION

In teaching the trainees the presentation of the Gospel, we proceed in the following manner. First, we have them learn the outline of the Gospel, which might be considered the *skeleton*. Second, we have them learn Scripture verses that give *muscle*, so to speak, to the outline. Third, we have them learn illustrations which *flesh out* and make clear and understandable the outline of the Gospel.

E. BUILD ON THE OUTLINE

In having the trainees learn the Gospel, we do not have them memorize the entire presentation, but rather have them learn the outline and then gradually build on to it. First we have them learn just enough so the "bones" of the outline don't rattle. Next we have them give a three-minute presentation of the Gospel. And then we enlarge it to five minutes and then to eight. We continue to enlarge the presentation until they are able to present the Gospel in one minute or one hour, depending on what the particular situation warrants. We provide them with the short presentation of the Gospel, as well as the long one, to use as resource material for building their presentation on the basic outline.

F. *MAKE IT THEIR OWN*

In this way it becomes their own. We encourage them to work on it, practice it, and give it until, indeed, they own it and can give it with authority.

G. *NOT A "CANNED" APPROACH*

This raises the question of our basic philosophy of training others to present the Gospel. A careful study of the New Testament will show that Jesus used a different method in presenting the Gospel Himself than He did in training His followers. When He sent them out He told them where to go, what to do, what to take with them, and what to say upon entering and leaving the home.

In teaching a large group of people anything, it is inevitable that a certain degree of stereotyping will take place. However, we have tried to avoid the two extremes that exist in training others to present the Gospel. One extreme is the completely "canned" approach whereby the person memorizes a presentation, or reads it to someone, or gives him a tract, a tape, or a book. In every instance the layman has simply taken the product of the "expert"—that is, the clergyman—and is passing it on mechanically to others. We reject this method because of its "canned" flavor and also because it short-circuits the creativity of the layman.

The other extreme is called the "spontaneous expansion of the church." Under this theory all we need to do is get people soundly converted and filled with the Spirit, and they will go out and just naturally win the world for Christ. Unfortunately, it doesn't seem to work this way. Christ obviously didn't think too highly of this method, for He spent three and a half years training His apostles.

We have tried to select a method intermediate between these two. We give the layman some help, some guidance, some direction, but also allow him to express his own creativity. We do this by giving him an outline, plus some Scriptures and illustrative material. But we urge him to continually add to this his own illustrations that he discovers in his own reading or from his own experience, as well as other Scriptures that speak strongly to him concerning one of the points of the Gospel. In this way he builds his own Gospel presentation on the skeleton we provide for him and continually personalizes it more and more until it becomes "his own."

XII. PRESERVING THE FRUIT

A. *IMPORTANCE OF FOLLOW-UP*

A ministry of evangelism such as this generates a tremendous need for follow-up. It has produced a need for a follow-up secretary and a follow-up minister on our staff. However, the main responsibility for follow-up rests with the individual who has led the person to

Christ. In this training workbook we have a rather elaborate section on follow-up principles and procedures. In essence, the follow-up procedure involves the spiritual parent using the total services of the local family of God. In the past we have used a variety of printed materials. Now we have produced our own materials for following up new converts. These materials are listed and their uses described later in this book. They are tailored to the local church and the context of the Evangelism Explosion Discipleship Training.

The first week of the new convert's life is the most critical. Therefore, I have prepared a series of six cassettes, which are loaned to the convert the day he makes a profession or are brought to him as soon as possible. He is encouraged to listen to one of these messages each day for the first week of his Christian life. The subjects covered are: Knowing You Are Going to Heaven; Staying Right with God; Getting into the Bible; Practicing the Art of Prayer; Continuing in Fellowship *(Koinonia)*; Transforming the World. A study booklet has also been prepared to go with these so that they may be used in a classroom session, as well. This has been very profitably done in some churches.

The first Sunday after one professes faith, he should be encouraged to attend a Sunday school class. The best arrangement is to have a three-week class on three basic elements of Christian living—Feeding on the Word of God, Cleansing, and Relating to the Forever Family of God. Each unit should be self-contained so a new believer can start with any one of the topics. This helps get him off to a good start.

After the new believer completes these three classes, he should start in the six "This Is the Life" classes. With these nine weeks of study behind him, he can go into almost any class in your adult education program.

B. SPIRITUAL GRANDCHILDREN

Follow-up procedures are not completed until the convert has been taught to study God's Word, to pray, to live the Christian life, and to walk with Christ. Then he is encouraged to come into the evangelism training to learn how to win others to Christ. Yet, at this point the follow-up still is not complete, for he must be taught not only how to reproduce, but also how to disciple his new convert until he has matured to the place where he also is able to bring someone else to Christ. This emphasis on spiritual multiplication, looking past the first generation to the second, third, and fourth, is the secret to an expanding and multiplying evangelistic ministry. In just a few years this has produced instances of great-, great-, great-, great-, great-, great-, great-grandchildren in the faith. The acid test of any follow-up procedure will ultimately be: Is it producing spiritual grandchildren and great-grandchildren? If not, then something is amiss, and somewhere the process is breaking down.

XIII. MULTIPLYING THE RESULTS

A. A VISION OF THE WORLD

Christ said, "The field is the world." I believe our field should be the world; that every church, every individual, has a worldwide responsibility. I do not believe any church can settle for anything less than worldwide evangelism as its own responsibility. Is it utterly unrealistic? I think not. Eleven men, indeed a very small church, succeeded in carrying the Gospel to most every nation on the earth. And the march of those eleven men goes on today.

I do not believe, however, that it necessarily must take hundreds or thousands of years for the impact of the Gospel to spread around the world. The process of spiritual multiplication can grow with the rapidity of the physical population explosion we are seeing today. Our goal, then, is to reach the world for Christ. How can this be done?

B. MULTIPLYING YOUR MINISTRY

First we must realize that our responsibility extends beyond our church, our city, our state, or our country. But how are we to meet this responsibility? We have proceeded in this manner. In addition to training an increasing number of people in our own church, we have also trained a good many other churches in the city and in the immediate area.

In 1967 we began having clinics for church leaders. Only thirty-six attended that first clinic. However, in 1970 attendance leaped to 350, and we had to turn away an additional 1,500 because we could not accommodate them. We tried to increase to five leadership clinics per year at Coral Ridge Church, but this was too disruptive to the local church life.

We encouraged other churches to have similar clinics. A few were able to do this well, but most were not successful at conducting leadership clinics. I spoke to many church leaders, and our minister of evangelism conducted numerous small area clinics. The more we became involved, the more we understood the ingredients necessary for successful leadership clinics. The emphasis in the clinics is very properly on evangelism technique. But evangelism is for the purpose of producing disciples, and healthy disciples are produced only in reasonably healthy churches.

Therefore, to ensure maximum responsible multiplication of this ministry, the process of certification was established. Certification gives uniform minimum standards of excellence with maximum potential for communication and multiplication. We feel it is an essential element in strategy for effective evangelization of the world. As a result of years of experience, we now are seeing very effective certified-leadership clinics conducted throughout the United States, Canada, and on every continent of the world. Culturally relevant equivalents of this ministry are in operation, and our goal is to see them become totally indigenous national fellowships.

Because of wide interest in this ministry, Evangelism Explosion International was established as a nonprofit corporation. Its ministry is interdenominational and international.

Laypeople certified as trainers in their churches can function as missionary trainers on short- or long-term bases in other churches in different parts of the world. A mighty army is being mobilized. The very gates of hell are being stormed, and Christ is building His church!

Soli deo gloria!

Two

WITNESSING
AS A WAY
OF LIFE

Witnessing should be a way of life for every Christian! This is one of the primary goals of Evangelism Explosion Discipleship Training. It follows from the clear teaching of both the Old and New Testaments. In Deuteronomy 6:7 the Israelites were commanded to teach the truths of God's redeeming love "when thou sittest in thine house, and when thou walkest by the way, and when thou liest down, and when thou risest up." And in the great commission, Matthew 28:18-20, Jesus commanded that as we are going about our tasks each day, in whatever situation we may find ourselves, we are to "teach all nations . . . to observe all things whatsoever I have commanded you." In fact, almost without exception, the evangelism that is recorded as taking place in the New Testament occurred not as the result of some organized program or sophisticated campaign but as individual believers took it upon themselves to bring their evangelistic efforts into their everyday lives. If we follow the example of Christ and His apostles, we will discover an opportunity to bear witness in almost every situation.

Christ used the most ordinary things to lead people to Himself in order that they might have life. At a well, He spoke of Himself as the Water of Life that quenches deep thirst. To the hungry, He presented Himself as the Bread of Life. To the crippled and the sick, He presented Himself as the one who could make men whole.

There are opportunities to witness all around us. Our responsibility is to develop the alertness of mind and the zeal for sharing God's love that will enable us to take advantage of every opportunity the Lord leads us into, day in and day out. We must study to develop a witnessing mind-set, ever asking God to give us the ability to see the opportunities for lifestyle evangelism that He brings into our path each day. And we must ask God for a heart that is bold enough to use these opportunities for His glory.

I. RELATIONAL EVANGELISM

Undoubtedly, the first place to begin looking for evangelistic opportunities in our everyday lives is in the numerous relationships the Lord has enabled us to develop and enjoy. As the phrase "relational evangelism" is used here, it means using existing relationships and developing new ones as bridges through which to communicate the message that in Jesus Christ, God has done all that is necessary to reestablish man in a right relationship with God and His people.

A. A NETWORK OF RELATIONSHIPS

Every human being is the center of a network of relationships. For instance, consider yourself. You were born into a family and thus are related to your mother and father, brothers and sisters, grandparents, aunts and uncles, cousins, nephews and nieces. When you marry, this network is enlarged. Not only are you related to your new husband or wife and the children, and possibly grandchildren, that will come from your union, but marriage also brings you into your spouse's family. You then have a whole network of in-laws. As you encounter these *family members* in the normal course of your life, ask God to embolden you to tell them of His love for them in Jesus Christ.

My wife, Anne's, mother had been a church organist since age eleven; she became her pastor's aid and was always in church. She married a Christian who never talked about his faith. He was one of those secret agents! The couple took their family to church seven days a week and observed family devotions daily. Anne's mother did all the good works Christians are supposed to do, but never expressed any interest in heaven or hope of going there. As an adult, Anne trusted Christ for eternal life and began to wonder about her mother, who never talked to Anne about Christ or any personal relationship with Him.

Her mother was about sixty-five years of age at the time, and one night before going to bed, Anne asked her if she knew for certain she was going to heaven. Her mother said she didn't, but she "sure would like to!" Anne shared the simple Gospel with her mother, knelt with her by the bed, and right there led her in prayer to trust Christ for eternal life. Anne's dad noticed a dramatic change in his wife. Before she put her trust in Christ she had been a "worry wart" who worried about everything. After she put her trust in Christ she didn't worry about things but trusted Christ completely. Anne's father testified later that the last ten years they lived together before the Lord took her home were like a ten-year honeymoon!

Anne also experienced the joy of leading her sister Carolyn to Christ. When Carolyn married, she and her husband dropped out of church, claiming they "just didn't have time for that." One day Anne asked Carolyn the same question she had asked her mother. Carolyn didn't know for sure she was going to heaven but wanted to! Hence, Anne had the joy of explaining the Gospel to her sister and leading her in a prayer to trust Christ. Since then Carolyn has grown much in her faith and has become an active worker in her church and a faithful supporter of our worldwide E.E. and TV ministries.

Many relationships develop from your work. You are an employer or an employee. A number of people are your fellow workers. Many of them will be people who need to hear the Gospel from you. Years ago I managed an Arthur Murray Dance Studio. The owner of the studio was a stunning woman, a tremendous salesperson and businesswoman, who, because she was pretty hard-nosed, could scare the daylights out of you and "lay you flat."

After I came to Christ I left the studio. When I was leaving, or had just left, I shared the Gospel with her, and she made a profession of faith. I talked to her by phone every now and then and realized she wasn't growing much in her faith. Hence, I invited her to come to our church for an E.E. clinic. The clinic training really turned her on! She returned to her church in St. Petersburg, got involved in E.E., and before a year had passed was teaching the course. Later, when the minister of evangelism resigned, she took over the whole department and through the ensuing years, directly or indirectly, led a great many people to Christ.

When you select a place to live, the residence comes with a set of neighbors. Denise Ostrom, whose husband, Tom, is on our E.E. International staff, was jogging through her neighborhood with Sheryl, a friend who lived nearby. "Denise, what is it that is so different about you?" Sheryl asked. "You have something I don't have."

Denise wasn't able to clearly explain the difference, so she went home and told Tom that she was going to sign up for the next semester of E.E. training. One day several weeks later, having learned to share her faith adequately, she invited her fellow jogger to sit down on the curb, and right there Denise led her neighbor Sheryl to the Lord.

Meanwhile, Joe and Nancy moved into the neighborhood and met Tom in the middle of their cul-de-sac. Noticing on Tom's lapel E.E.'s two-question-mark pin, the couple asked what it meant. After getting further acquainted with Joe and Nancy, Tom asked them the two questions and shared the Gospel—up to the subject of faith. At that point, the couple clearly didn't want to hear more and changed the subject. Tom, well trained not to exert undue pressure upon people, backed off and waited for God to present another opportunity to complete his presentation.

Joe and Nancy developed problems in their marriage, and this became very evident to others in the neighborhood. For over a year the couple was too embarrassed to share their troubles with Tom and Denise. Instead, they visited church after church searching for help. Finally, one Sunday night they spied Tom coming home from church and pulling into his driveway. "Tom," they called across the street, "what are you doing? Could you do us a favor and come over and tell us about eternal life?" They hadn't forgotten what Tom had shared earlier, and having encountered marriage difficulties, they were now very receptive to Tom's witness. Both Joe and Nancy gave their lives to Christ, started coming to Tom and Denise's church, joined their Sunday school class, and grew rapidly in their newfound faith!

Over the years you will develop some special friendships. And, during the normal course of a day or week, there are many, many other people—doctors, service station attendants, mail persons, clerks, sports associates, and other casual acquaintances—for whom you may be the means of their gaining eternal life. Recently, I was speaking up north when a young man came up to thank me for my message. Then he asked, "Incidentally, how's your backhand? You don't recognize me, do you?"

"I'm trying real hard," I replied.

"You were at Lake Tahoe Camp," he explained. "After the lesson, you came up to the net, shared the Gospel, and led me to Christ."

Then I remembered that after that encounter, we invited him and his wife out to dinner so we could present the Gospel to his wife. She was very emotional and started crying, so we weren't able to consummate the witness that night. I was so excited to meet the couple again and to learn that she had accepted the Lord just two weeks after her husband. When I asked him if he was still teaching tennis, he replied, "No, I'm going to school to become a Christian counselor so I can proclaim the Gospel to people."

The history of the Evangelism Explosion Discipleship Training Ministry is literally strewn with testimonies from men and women all over the globe of how they have been able to lead people in the network of their relationships to a saving knowledge of our Lord.

When God the Son became a man in the person of Jesus of Nazareth, He entered into most of the same relationships you and everyone else has. Mary was His mother. Joseph was His stepfather. He had brothers and sisters, cousins and uncles. He worked in the carpenter shop in Nazareth. He, too, developed a network of relationships. He loved his family. Even as He died on the cross He made arrangements for John, His special friend, to take care of His mother. While Jesus loved his earthly family and friends, He was most concerned that they be in God's heavenly family. Evidently, He led John the Baptist, His cousin; Mary, His mother; and James, His brother, into a saving relationship with Himself.

B. RELATIONSHIPS AS BRIDGES

God desires to use your relationships as bridges to reach those close to you, so that they may be brought into His forever family. You are the salt of the earth and the light of the world. Salt prevents corruption. It adds taste. It makes one thirsty. Light helps people see where they are going. God wants to use your life to show others the way, to cause others to thirst for Him, to add taste to life, and to curtail the corruption of sin that is in the world.

Most Christians can trace their spiritual roots to either a relative or a friend. That is because the Gospel is shared by someone the prospect trusts rather than by a stranger. The Gospel is also usually shared in an unhurried and natural context. The lifestyle of the well-known witness adds credibility to his or her message. The witness, being a friend, is then a natural source for nurture. And the witness's church provides effective help in follow-up and assimilation into the body of Christ.

At this point I need to give you a word of caution about a paradoxical situation that can develop. The longer you are a believer, the more opportunity you have for spiritual growth. The more you grow spiritually, the more involved you become in the life of the church. As you become increasingly involved in the church, you will find that you have less opportunity to be involved with your unbelieving friends, relatives, associates, and neighbors. In fact, if you're not careful, you can be lifted right out of your normal contact with them and lose your witness to them.

So how do you build bridges back to unbelievers? You must discover creative ways to become reinvolved with your unbelieving friends, relatives, and neighbors. You also need to explore your existing network of relationships systematically, because in every Christian's network of relationships, there is at least one person who is ready to take the next step toward Christ.

One way to do this is to help those you lead to Christ share the Gospel with their non-Christian friends. First, encourage them to become involved with you in the Evangelism Explosion Discipleship Training Ministry of your church. Then, be available to share the Gospel with the people who constitute their network of relationships. It has been wisely stated, "Lead me to a new Christian, and we will discover a whole nest of sinner prospects." Isn't that what happened when the Samaritan woman found Christ at the well and then brought her friends in Samaria to her Savior?

One of our E.E. clinic teachers, Scott Smith, experienced this networking principle when he presented the Gospel to Sharon. She trusted Christ as Savior and then introduced Scott to Don and Jean, who also professed faith in Christ. Then Don and Jean invited their friends, Karen and Kirby, to come over and meet Scott, who shared the Gospel with them and led them to Christ as well.

Another way to develop relationships with unbelievers is by joining a club or becoming involved in a community activity. Take time to develop relationships with your hairdresser, insurance salesman, grocery clerk, or auto mechanic. Work at getting to know the neighbors around you.

Eleven-year-old Brandon Smith spent the last three years of his life battling leukemia. Many celebrities, including baseball great Joe DiMaggio, Governor Lawton Chiles, and members of the Miami Heat basketball team, visited him while he was in the hospital. People all over the state kept in contact with him. He was "everybody's child" and a wonderful little boy. His father said, "He was a forty-year-old evangelist in the body of an eleven-year-old." Brandon took time to build a relationship with his nurse, and just three days before he died he came out of a semiconscious state and led her to Christ. As soon as this was completed he went back into a semiconscious state.

To develop an effective witness with those people in your network of relationships, you need to develop a personal profile for each person. Our new booklet, *Partners in*

Friendship, will provide you a place to keep a detailed record of and valuable information about each of your friends, relatives, associates, and neighbors. It will also serve as a reminder to help you pray regularly for their salvation and a tool where you can monitor the progress you make in developing a caring relationship with them.

It is crucial that you pray regularly for the people in your network of relationships, remembering that God is the one who opens hearts to the Gospel (Acts 16:14; Colossians 4:2-4). It takes time for fruit to ripen, and all fruit doesn't ripen in the same season. The Holy Spirit is working at His own pace, so be patient and persevere in prayer.

C. SENSITIVITY TO NEEDS

When you don't have anything in common with certain people, you need to build a special bridge. The best way to do this is to find a need and meet it, find a hurt and heal it. People around you are like pendulums, constantly moving back and forth between times of crisis and calm, responsiveness and resistance. Those who have recently experienced a high degree of change in their lives are generally more receptive to the Gospel.

God evidently uses difficulties as opportunities through which to communicate to us. Job 36:15 says, "He delivereth the poor in his affliction, and openeth their ears in oppression."

Therefore, we need to be alert and express loving concern to people at such times of need. Too many Christians suffer from a spiritual malady called "people blindness"; that is, there are hurting people all around them, but they don't see them and are insensitive to their needs. If we are alert, times of need may prove to be divine appointments for sharing the comforting and saving message of Christ's Gospel.

D. VERBALIZING THE GOSPEL

Sometimes, however, an opportunity won't present itself for you to naturally share the Gospel with a friend, relative, associate, or neighbor. At such times, if you still feel the time is right and ripe for a verbal presentation of the Gospel, you might take the following steps.

First, invite the person(s) out to a meal, explaining that you have something exciting in your life that you would like to share. You will have his or her undivided attention for at least an hour without interruptions or opportunities for your friend to "escape." Remember, people, like fish, can at times be pretty slippery!

Next, begin with your E.E. personal testimony, modifying the details, as needed, to identify with your prospect. Ask for permission to ask the first diagnostic question. Before asking the second question, be sure to share 1 John 5:13 and ask for permission (don't forget this very important step!) to share the Gospel.

Then share the E.E. Gospel presentation, making necessary adaptations to meet your friend's needs and circumstances.

Finally, ask for a commitment, and if your friend receives the gift of eternal life, follow up with John 6:47 and *Partners in Growing* or the immediate follow-up steps in the E.E. tract *Do You Know for Sure?*

Gladys Israels was one of the first persons I was privileged to lead to Christ. She was also one of my first E.E. trainees. Today she serves as secretary of our International Board of Directors. An active witness for Christ, Gladys grew concerned when her son Frank started dating Denise, an unbeliever he had met while sharing an interest in the same sport. As the couple continued to date for two years, the concerned mother prayed that she might have an opportunity to introduce Denise to Christ and that Denise would trust Christ as her Savior.

Faithfully each Sunday, Frank picked up his "best girl" and brought her to church. But just as consistently, Denise would come out of the service commenting, "That was awful. You go to church and he makes you feel bad—just terrible!" One of those Sundays, Gladys and her husband, Roger, brought the couple home for the noon meal. As they visited over dinner, Denise suddenly opened up and told Gladys about a team of three who had visited her that week. "I told them their visit came at a very inconvenient time, but I'm dating Frank Israels, so whatever you were going to tell me, I'll just ask his mom and she can explain it to me.

"Now," Denise added, "I want you to tell me what it was they came to my house to share." While Frank was out on the patio and Roger was reading his paper, Gladys spent about an hour presenting the Gospel. Denise's heart was so ready that she prayed to invite Christ into her heart right then and there. Within a week, at the dermatologist's office where Denise worked, people were saying, "Denise, what happened to you? You act so different!" Now Gladys claims that Denise is not just a wonderful daughter-in-law, she's a spiritual daughter!

One thing is certain: As relational evangelism increasingly becomes a way of life, you will discover a rich source of many new and ripe evangelistic prospects!

II. THE OCCASIONAL WITNESSING SITUATION

Maximizing the evangelistic opportunities that exist within your network of relationships is a matter of being alert to occasions that lend themselves to introducing the Gospel into the conversation. Some of these occasional witnessing situations may come about very naturally as divine appointments. You may be able to create others by being alert to the circumstances in which you are involved with another individual. If you are alert, you can find, in almost any situation, some type of "springboard" into the Gospel presentation.

A. THE OCCASIONAL INTRODUCTION

The occasional introduction has three parts:

1. **The occasion:** that is, the specific situation you use to raise the question of eternal life.

2. The two diagnostic questions: the assurance question and God's "Why?" They help you diagnose the person's spiritual condition.

3. Permission to share the Gospel. Permission should always be sought. If it is granted, this usually means the person you have contacted is open and willing to listen.

B. DEATH AND BAD NEWS

A person's conversation about a recent close call with death may, depending upon the circumstances, lead you to tactfully ask them whether, if they had in fact left this life, they would be certain that they would happily find themselves enjoying eternal life in the place the Bible calls "heaven."

Another person's conversation about a tragic news headline might open the way for you to talk about the prevalence of bad news being communicated in the media. This, in turn, might lead you to introduce the most wonderful news the world has ever heard!

C. QUESTIONS ABOUT E.E.

Someone may ask you about your Evangelism Explosion training. You might respond by telling him that you've been learning the answers to two fascinating questions. Often this will cause him to ask what the questions are. When he does ask, don't just hastily blurt out the questions. Rather, say to him, "Before I tell you what the two questions are, will you promise to give me your answers?" If you don't obtain a commitment that he will answer the questions before you ask them, he may simply chuckle and say: "Those really are cute questions," and walk away.

Several years ago at an E.E. clinic in Walden, New York, one of the clinicians accidentally left his keys locked in his car. Seeing a car dealership next door to the church, the clinician asked a mechanic for help. "This isn't Sunday. What are all these cars doing here?" asked the mechanic. "Oh, we're having an E.E. clinic," responded the clinician. "Okay, but what is E.E.?" asked the mechanic further. The clinician told him it was one of the most exciting things he had ever discovered in life and apologized that he had to get back to class. Before leaving, however, he asked what time the mechanic would get off work. Then the clinician made an appointment to meet him at his car to explain E.E. Before the afternoon had passed, the clinician had led his mechanic friend to Christ!

D. PRAYER REQUESTS

When people ask you to pray about something, such as a job, a sick relative, or a marriage relationship, they are giving evidence of an interest in spiritual matters. Listen to the need and then ask, "Are you on praying ground?" That will probably cause them to ask, "What do you mean?" Then you can reply, "It's important when we pray to be in a right place spiritually with God. I'd be interested to know, have you come to the place in your spiritual life where you know for certain that if you were to die today, you would go to heaven?"

Likewise, when people come to you for counsel, ask them about their "spiritual foundation." For instance, you might say to someone having marriage difficulties, "It's been well said that the family that prays together stays together. Have you and your wife come to the place in your spiritual lives where you know for certain," etc. Hundreds of couples have been led to Christ after such a transition!

E. PERSONS' NAMES

Sometimes you can use a person's name as a springboard into the Gospel. To a woman named Grace, you can say, "With a name like Grace, you probably know for sure that you are going to heaven. Am I correct?" Whether she says yes or no, ask God's "Why?" and then proceed to share the Gospel. The name Irene means "peace." Timothy and Dorothy mean "a gift from God." The names of any of the saints of Scripture can be used to spring into the Gospel. To a man named Jim, you can say, "You know you have the same name as one of the apostles—James. He is in heaven now. Do you know for sure that you will go there, too?" With someone named Christopher you might comment, "Did you know that you have *Christ* in your name? The question I'd like to ask you is—Have you ever invited Christ into your heart?" Then you can show him Christ's invitation in Revelation 3:20 and share with him how he can do just that.

F. ELEVATORS AND INSURANCE

Elevators can be used to get into the Gospel. I once stood outside an elevator with a friend. When another person approached, my friend reached for the button to call the elevator and said to the woman, "Are you going up?"

"Yes," she responded.

"Are you going all the way up?" he inquired.

"No, just to the third floor," she said.

"I mean, when God's sweet chariot swings down low to take His people home to heaven, do you know for sure that you are going all the way up to heaven?" he continued.

Her response was, "No, I'm not sure of that," and as we entered the elevator, he began sharing the Gospel with her.

I know an insurance man who shares the Gospel with his customers. After he has finalized a policy he says, "This will take care of you until you die, but what's going to happen to you then? Do you know for sure that you are going to heaven?" With that introduction, he has had numerous opportunities to share the Gospel.

G. SEASONS AND HOLIDAYS

The seasons of the year can be used to spread the Good News. In the fall, as things are dying, you can use death in nature around you as a springboard into the topic of death. In spring, as new life buds out of the deadness of winter, this can be used to speak of eternal life that even death cannot overcome.

Special holidays can be used, especially Christmas and Easter.

There are so many opportunities to which we are oblivious. We must ask God to give us eyes to see them and boldness to use them wisely.

H. E.E. CERTIFIED-TRAINER PIN

Pins are available through the certification department of Evangelism Explosion International to all trainers who fulfill the requirements of certification specified for the training. The special pin presented to all certified E.E. trainers is given with the express purpose of providing to them possible opportunities to witness. Its two question marks, of course, symbolize the two diagnostic questions.

When you wear the pin, people will ask what it means or what the two question marks stand for. Reply with something like this: "There is a great deal of uncertainty in the world today. People have so many questions. But when certain key questions are correctly answered, things come into focus. Two key questions have helped me greatly. Before I found the answers to these questions, my life was . . . (personal testimony). Now that I have found the answers to these key questions, my life is . . . (personal testimony). Would you like to know what the questions are, and will you promise to give me your answers?"

If the answer is yes, raise the questions and proceed according to the person's need and response.

If the answer is no, you may want to back away from the situation with a very abbreviated presentation of the Gospel. Your testimony can bring eternal life into the conversation. The person contacted may not want to talk religion. So say, "One thing I've always appreciated about God is His patience with us. He knows we are sinners and can't save ourselves. And even though He came into the world in the person of Christ, died for our sins, and came out of the grave alive, He said, 'I stand at the door, and knock: if any man hear my voice, and open the door, I will come in to him.' He doesn't knock the door down. Since He doesn't force Himself on us, I don't feel I can force Him on someone either, but if some day you change your mind, pray to Him in faith and ask Him to give you His gift of eternal life. It's been nice meeting you. I hope I'll meet you again in heaven." Then give him the tract *Do You Know for Sure?* and be on your way. Pray that God will use your brief encounter to draw the person to Christ.

After speaking at a church in Pennsylvania, Tom Stebbins, executive vice president of E.E. International, was greeting worshipers as they departed. Two young men, Bryan and Joe, thanked Tom for the message. Then Joe added, "What's the significance of your pin and the two question marks?" In responding, Tom followed the steps suggested above. Bryan answered both questions correctly, while Joe answered the second with, "I'm not on drugs and I live a clean life." Tom commended Joe that in a society riddled with drugs he could stay "clean," then added: "Joe, if you have a few minutes, I have something fantastic to share with you about your answers to those questions." The three men stepped into the pastor's study where they could avoid interruption, and about half an hour later Joe committed his life to Christ.

Before the two men left, Bryan said to Tom, "I've been praying for Joe for one whole year and brought him to church today hoping he'd find Christ. Thanks so much, Pastor Tom!" Joe added, "And thank you, Pastor, for wearing those question marks. That's what caught my attention and interest!"

I. DEVELOPING A WITNESSING WAY OF LIFE

Bringing evangelism into the whole of your life is not something that will happen automatically. Each person must work consciously, determinedly, and daily to develop a witnessing way of life.

The effort begins in prayer. Each morning, survey before the Lord, in prayer, the things you have to do that day and the people you are likely to meet. Ask God to begin preparing them to hear the Good News. Ask Him to give you boldness to share, as the occasion permits.

As you go about your daily tasks, stay mindful of the people around you. Look carefully for springboard opportunities to initiate a conversation about eternal life. Be sure you carry a New Testament and materials to leave with someone when the situation does not allow for a complete presentation of the Gospel.

Also, be ever alert to individuals who, because they already know the Lord Jesus Christ, are involved in a network of relationships in which they can become effective witnesses for Christ. Offer to share the Gospel with their friends and acquaintances, making sure the person with whom you are talking sets up the appointment and is present when you make the presentation. And seek to enlist these individuals into the Evangelism Explosion Training Ministry in your church. You will greatly increase your effectiveness as a lifestyle evangelist if you cooperate with those whose network of relationships reaches people far beyond those whom you as an individual might be able to reach.

J. A LIFESTYLE, NOT A PROGRAM

The purpose of the Evangelism Explosion Discipleship Training Ministry is to train lifestyle evangelists who will be able to witness to people in the natural context of their daily lives. If the only thing happening in a local church is that a group of people come together at a given time to study Evangelism Explosion and then go out on calls, that church is only partly successful in training soul winners.

For that reason, beginning with the first week of E.E. training, all trainees and trainers should seek outside opportunities to share the Gospel with friends, relatives, associates, and neighbors. It would also be wise to offer an advanced-level course in E.E. specially focusing on witnessing as a way of life. A good textbook for such a course is *Friendship Evangelism by the Book,* by Tom Stebbins. It can be ordered through our E.E. International office. The book offers biblical illustrations and practical suggestions, as well as discussion questions at the end of each chapter, which will stimulate you and your congregation to become excited about winning people in your network of relationships to Christ.

In the report session of your church's training time, be sure every week to give your trainers and trainees opportunity to share with the class their outside opportunities to present the Gospel. Make note of the occasions others report. This will suggest to you new opportunities and increase your alertness and effectiveness in using them. It is, after all, the lifestyle of evangelism we are most concerned to develop through the E.E. training.

When, through the E.E. training, growing numbers of people in the local church witness to the Lord Jesus Christ as a way of life, you will discover a whole new enthusiasm and excitement in your ministry, and you will know that the ministry's real purpose is being realized.

Three

SHARING
GOOD NEWS

ABBREVIATED OUTLINE OF THE GOSPEL PRESENTATION

I. The introduction

   A. Their secular life

   B. Their church background

   C. Our church (their impressions)

   D. Testimony: personal and/or church

   E. Two diagnostic questions:

      1. Have you come to a place in your spiritual life where you know for certain that if you were to die today you would go to heaven, or is that something you would say you're still working on?

      2. Suppose that you were to die today and stand before God and He were to say to you, "Why should I let you into my heaven?" What would you say?

II. The Gospel

   A. Grace

      1. Heaven is a free gift

      2. It is not earned or deserved

   B. Man

      1. Is a sinner

      2. Cannot save himself

   C. God

      1. Is merciful—therefore doesn't want to punish us

      2. Is just—therefore must punish sin

   D. Christ

      1. Who He is—the infinite God-Man

      2. What He did—He died on the cross and rose from the dead to pay the penalty for our sins and to purchase a place in heaven for us, which He offers as a gift.

    E. Faith
       1. What it is not—mere intellectual assent or mere temporal faith
       2. What it is—trusting in Jesus Christ alone for eternal life
III. The commitment
    A. The Qualifying question: "Does this make sense to you?"
    B. The Commitment question: "Would you like to receive the gift of eternal life?"
    C. The Clarification of commitment: "Let me clarify this . . ."
    D. The Prayer of commitment
    E. The Assurance of salvation
IV. The immediate follow-up
    A. Welcome to the family of God!
    B. *Partners in Growing* booklet
    C. The means of growth
       1. Bible (seven-day callback appointment)
       2. Prayer
       3. Worship
       4. Fellowship
       5. Witness
    D. Appointment for church
    E. Closing prayer

A Brief Presentation of the Gospel

This is a condensed ten-minute presentation starting with the two diagnostic questions and ending with the commitment question.

I. INTRODUCTION (A–D)

E. Two Diagnostic Questions

Question 1: Well, that's very interesting, Sue. May I ask you a question? Have you come to a place in your spiritual life where you know for certain that if you were to die today you would go to heaven, or is that something you would say you're still working on?

I didn't think anyone could really know that!

I didn't know myself for many years, but then I discovered something wonderful! I discovered it was possible to know for sure! I even discovered that this was the reason the Bible was written. The Scripture says, "These things have I written unto you that believe on the name of the Son of God; that ye may know that ye have eternal life." May I share with you how I came to know for certain that I have eternal life?

Yes, that would be great!

Question 2: Fine! I'll be happy to. First, let me ask you another question which I think really brings this whole matter into focus and which clarifies our thinking about it greatly. Suppose you were to die today and stand before God and He were to say to you, "Why should I let you into My heaven?" What would you say?

I can't think of any answer.

I know you don't have a thesis prepared on the subject, but just offhand what comes to your mind? What do you think you would say?

Well, I've tried to do the best I can, and I've tried to keep the Ten Commandments. I try to live by the Golden Rule.

Good News transition: Well, that's interesting, Sue. Those things are all very commendable.

You know something, Sue—when you answered that first question I thought that I had some really good news for you. And after hearing your answer to the second question, I know that I do. In fact, I would go so far as to say that in the next sixty seconds you are going to hear the greatest news you have ever heard in your whole life! That's quite a statement, isn't it?

It certainly is.

II. THE GOSPEL

A. Grace

1. Heaven is a free gift.

Let me show you a Scripture verse in the New Testament. Here it is. Just read it for yourself. "The wages of sin is death; but the gift of God is eternal life . . ." (Romans 6:23). Isn't that amazing?

2. It is not earned or deserved.

A large part of my life I felt exactly as you do. I thought that if I was ever to get to heaven I'd have to earn it—I'd have to become good enough, and work for it and deserve it. And then I discovered something that amazed me. I discovered that heaven is an absolutely free gift—it is unearned, unmerited, and undeserved. It's free! Isn't that tremendous? The Bible says, "By grace are ye saved through faith . . . not of works, lest any man should boast" (Ephesians 2:8-9). This can be seen more clearly when we understand what the Bible says about man.

B. Man

1. Is a sinner

The Bible teaches that all of us have sinned. "All have sinned, and come short of the glory of God" (Romans 3:23). In our thoughts, in our words, in our deeds—we have all failed to keep His commandments, both by sins of commission and by sins of omission—that is, by the things we have done and the things we have left undone. We have also sinned in word, thought, and deed.

2. Cannot save himself

There is not one of us good enough to get into heaven because God's standard is perfection! If we had to be good enough, Jesus says we would have to be perfect. "Be ye therefore perfect, even as your Father which is in heaven is perfect" (Matthew 5:48). This is the reason none of us can earn his way into heaven. We can't save ourselves. The Bible says, "There is a way which seemeth right unto a man, but the end thereof are the ways of death" (Proverbs 14:12). This comes into sharper focus when we look at what the Bible says about God.

C. God

1. Is merciful—therefore, He does not want to punish us

The Bible says, "God is love" (1 John 4:8). We know that God is merciful and loving, gracious and kind, but the same Bible says that the same God is also just and holy and righteous.

2. Is just—therefore, he must punish sin

The Bible says that He "will by no means clear the guilty" (Exodus 34:7). Of course, we know that the Bible teaches that God is loving and merciful and gracious. He doesn't want to punish us. He must deal with sin, but He doesn't want to punish us because He loves us. Now what is the answer to this dilemma?

God, in His infinite wisdom, devised a solution. God solved this problem in the person of Jesus Christ.

D. Jesus Christ

1. Who He is—the infinite God-Man

Now, who is Jesus Christ? According to the Bible, Jesus Christ is God, the second person of the Trinity, the Creator of the universe. The Bible says, "In the beginning was the Word, and the Word was with God, and the Word was God. . . . the Word was made flesh, and dwelt among us . . ." (John 1:1, 14). God came down into human flesh.

2. What He did—He died on the cross and rose from the dead to pay the penalty for our sins and to purchase a place in heaven for us, which He offers as a gift.

What did He come to do? The whole Bible is about one great transaction. Imagine that this book in my right hand contains a minutely detailed account of my life: everything I've ever done, all of my sins, all of my thoughts, all of my motives—everything I've ever done in secret—are all recorded in this book. The Bible says that someday the books will be opened, and everybody will be judged according to the things recorded in the book.

This (hold up the book) is my problem, you see, my sin. Here is my sin upon me like a great burden. (Place the book on the palm of one hand.) This keeps me out of heaven. This prevents me from rising up to God. What's going to be done with that?

Then Jesus Christ fulfilled the mission that was His. What was it? Simply, it is described in one text: "All we like sheep have gone astray; we have turned every one to his own way; and the Lord hath laid on him the iniquity of us all" (Isaiah 53:6).

Suppose that my other hand here represents Jesus Christ. The Bible says that

God placed all our sins on Jesus. (Transfer the book to the "Jesus" hand.) He has laid to the account of Christ our guilt, our sin—the sin that God hates. God has laid it all upon Christ. Christ bore "our sins in his own body on the tree" (1 Peter 2:24). When He died, He was buried in the grave for three days (put the book on your lap); but He rose from the dead and went to heaven to prepare a place for us. Now He offers heaven—eternal life—to us as a gift. And this gift is received by faith. By His grace He freely offers to give to us this gift of heaven. How do we receive it? We receive the gift by . . .

E. Faith

1. What it is not

Faith is the key that opens the door to heaven. Many people think they have faith, but they really don't know what it is. Let's see what faith is not.

It's not mere intellectual assent. Many people believe in Jesus Christ the same way they believe in Napoleon or George Washington. They believe He actually lived, that He was a real person in history, but they are not trusting Him to do anything for them now. And they suppose that this is faith. But this is merely an intellectual assent to certain historical facts. The Bible teaches us that even the devil believes in God. Did you know that? And even the demons believe in the deity of Christ. But they evidently weren't saved!

It's not mere temporal faith. Other people think they have faith in Christ, but when you ask them what they really mean, they are only trusting in Christ for the temporal things of life, such as health, their finances, protection, or guidance—the things that have to do only with this life and that will pass away.

2. What it is

But what the Bible means by faith is *trusting in Jesus Christ alone for eternal life.*

Christ didn't come down here merely to get us through an appendicitis operation or to get us safely on a plane to New York! Christ came to get us to heaven that we might have eternal life.

The Bible says, "Believe on the Lord Jesus Christ, and thou shalt be saved" (Acts 16:31).

People trust in only one of two things—either in themselves or in Christ. And I was trusting in the same thing you were—in my own efforts to try to live a good enough life. Then I realized that what I needed to do was to cease trusting in myself and start trusting in Jesus Christ.

And so, years ago, I did just that, and I received the gift of eternal life. I didn't deserve it then, and I don't deserve it now, but by His grace I have it! Let me illustrate with this chair. You believe this chair exists, don't you? (Point to empty chair.)

Yes.

Do you believe it would support me if I were to sit on it?

Yes.

But it is not supporting me now for a very simple reason. I'm not sitting on it. How could I prove to you that I truly trust the chair?

By sitting on it.

Let the chair represent Jesus Christ. For a long time I believed He existed and could help me, but I did not have eternal life because I was trusting my own good works to get me into heaven. Remember what you said you would say to God if He asked why He should let you into heaven? You said, "I try to do the best I can. . . ." Who is the only person referred to in your answer?

Me?

Whom were you trusting to get you to heaven when you said that?

Me.

To receive eternal life, you must transfer your trust from yourself to Christ. (Sit on the empty chair.)

Motive for living a godly life: What, then, is the motive for living a godly life? The motive for living a godly life is gratitude for what Christ has given us. The Bible says that "the love of Christ constraineth us."

A former president of Princeton put it this way. He said, "As a young man I accepted Christ and the gift of eternal life. All the rest of my life was simply a P.S. to that day, saying, 'Thank you, Lord, for what You gave to me then.'"

III. COMMITMENT

A. The Qualifying Question

Sue, does this make sense to you?

Oh, yes, that's wonderful!

You've just heard the *greatest story* ever told, about the *greatest offer* ever made, by the *greatest person* who ever lived.

B. The Commitment Question

Now the question God is asking you is this: Would you like to receive this gift of eternal life?

Oh, yes, I would.

An Extended Presentation of the Gospel

(The extended presentation of the Gospel that follows contains many additional illustrations and scriptural texts which may be used as a resource for building short presentations upon the basic outline. It is not an exact presentation that someone is to memorize word for word, but my personalized presentation as I would share with someone when I and my E.E. team call on church visitors.)

I. INTRODUCTION

A. Their Secular Life

(A knock at the door) Good morning, Mrs. Tucker. I'm James Kennedy from the Coral Ridge Presbyterian Church. (Holding up the card that they signed at church) We were happy to have you worshiping with us recently, and we came to repay the visit. May we come in and visit with you a while?

Why, hello. Please do come in.

Thank you. This is Mary Smith and George Simon from our church. We were so happy to have you visit with us and wanted to become better acquainted with you.

That's real nice of you.

May we sit over here?

Fine.

Thank you. This is a lovely home you have. That painting is most interesting. It seems to radiate peacefulness and contentment. Did you paint it yourself?

Oh, no. A friend did it for me just before we moved here. We have enjoyed it.

Where did you move from, Mrs. Tucker?

Virginia.

Virginia! I thought I noticed a bit of Virginia accent.

I don't doubt it.

Do they really say "aboot the hoose" up there?

They surely do.

Do they really? Let me hear you say "about the house."

Look oout, there's a moouse in the hoouse!

That's delightful. I've always enjoyed listening to people with Virginia accents. Tell me a little more about yourself. How did you happen to move down here?

We vacationed in this area several times and just loved it. When my husband retired we came down and looked around one summer and settled in Fort Lauderdale. We just love it here.

It is a beautiful city, isn't it?

Yes, it is.

B. Their Church Background

What church did you attend back in Virginia?

Baptist.

The Baptist church? Well, I knew there was something nice about you. I have many friends who are Baptists.

Thank you. I was a charter member.

You had the joys of seeing a new congregation born and you helped it grow?

Yes, some of those days were pretty trying, but we got our problems ironed out and it is a large church now. I was president of the Women of the Church for two years and taught a Sunday school class for a while.

Wonderful! It's good to meet someone who is really active in the life of her church. We are truly delighted to have you here in Fort Lauderdale with us now.

C. Our Church

How did you happen to attend our church?

We were looking for a church in the neighborhood, and while driving around we saw your building.

How did you like the service, and what were your impressions of our church?

Oh, we liked it very much. The people seemed so friendly and made us feel at home. The singing is just wonderful. You people seem to really enjoy singing. Somehow the spirit was different.

D. Testimony (Use either church testimony or personal testimony)

1. Church testimony (For those who have first visited your church, a church testimony is usually sufficient.)

(If a person does not volunteer something about the service, you can simply ask: Since you have come to a new church, do you have any questions that you would like to ask? Then you can proceed: Well, let me share with you a little bit about our church. . . .)

Jesus Christ came that we might have life and have it abundantly. The Scriptures were written that men and women might know that they have eternal life, and yet we have found that millions of ethical, moral, churchgoing people, even those who have gone to church all of their life, aren't really sure they have this abundant life, and they're not really sure about what will happen to them when they die. They have hopes, but they don't know for sure that they will go to heaven. That's because, historically, we in the church have done a poor job of communicating the message of eternal life to them.

How about you? Have you come to the place in your spiritual life where you know for certain that if you were to die today you would go to heaven, or is that something you are still working on? (Thus you are now into the first of two diagnostic questions.)

2. Personal testimony

There was a time in my life when, although I'd gone to church faithfully, somehow I still didn't know for sure that I had eternal life. Instead, I had a terrifying fear of death and dying. The thought of death terrified me because I had no idea what lay beyond death's door.

When I was in college I was living in a small mobile home. One night a terrible storm arose with wind gusts over fifty miles an hour! The wind was so strong that the rain was blowing horizontally across the ground. Our home was rocking on its concrete-block foundation. A bolt of lightning struck a tall oak tree right next to our home. I was so afraid that I sat on the edge of the sofa holding on, just knowing I was going to die and terrified every moment.

Not many months later a friend shared with me something very wonderful, and I received eternal life. Many things changed in my life.

Now that I have eternal life, the fear of death and dying is gone. Not long after I received eternal life we were driving during an ice storm that put a sheet of glazed ice on the highway. We were easing along at twenty-five miles an hour when we came alongside a semitrailer truck. The wind was blowing very hard, and the trailer began to act like a sail catching the wind. The truck was gradually being pushed across the centerline and steadily toward our car. There was nowhere to go. We couldn't go to the right as we would run into the truck; we couldn't go to the left because we would eventually end up in a ditch with the truck on top of us.

As we waited to see the outcome, death or tragic injury seemed certain. My whole life panned before me, and yet God had given me complete peace in my heart that even in light of this almost certain tragedy, I knew for certain that if I were to die, I would go to heaven. What a joy and difference that made as I faced that danger. And it's the same today. I know that if I were to die right now, I would go to be with God in heaven. May I ask you a question?

E. Two Diagnostic Questions

1. **"Have you come to a place in your spiritual life where you know for certain that if you were to die today you would go to heaven, or is that something you would say you're still working on?"**

Why, I don't think anyone can really know.

You know, that's just the way I felt about it. For many years I didn't know. I wasn't even aware of the fact that anybody knew. But let me tell you some really good news: I discovered that it is possible to know for sure, and there are a great many people who do know.

Really?

That was an amazing discovery to me! In fact, I even learned that that was the reason the Bible was written! The Bible says: "These things have I written . . . that ye may know that ye have eternal life" (1 John 5:13).

Why, I never knew that!

I didn't either. Isn't that a fantastic thing! Think how wonderful it would be if you could go to bed tonight and lay your head on your pillow knowing for certain that if you didn't wake up in your bedroom, you would wake up in heaven with Jesus Christ. Wouldn't that be a wonderful thing to know?

Yes, it really would.

May I share with you how I came to know for certain that I have eternal life and how you can know also?

Yes, please do.

All right, I'll be happy to, for it is the greatest discovery I have ever made. It really has changed my whole life. You know, it's amazing how many people are anxious to know! I talk to people in all strata of society, and everywhere there are men and women eager to know, and yet no one has taken the time to explain these things to them.

I've never heard it.

Before I share with you, let me ask you another question which I think really crystallizes our thinking on the matter. This was a question that was very helpful to me. A minister asked me this one day.

2. Suppose that you were to die today and stand before God and He were to say to you, "Why should I let you into My heaven?" What would you say? That's a pretty good question, isn't it?

It certainly is.

It really makes you think. What would your answer be?

Well, I never thought of anything like that. I've gone to Sunday school and church all my life. And I try to be as good as I know how. Of course, I know that I haven't always been perfect, but I don't think I've ever intentionally hurt anyone. And I try to love my neighbor. I don't think I've been too bad.

All right. Anything else?

Well, I visit the sick, and I do the very best I can to live according to the Golden Rule.

Well, thank you, Mrs. Tucker. It's Rene, isn't it? May I call you that?

Yes.

You would say to God, "I've gone to church all my life. I try to be good. I haven't intentionally hurt anyone. I try to love my neighbor, to visit the sick, and to live according to the Golden Rule." Is that what you would say?

Yes.

Good News: You know, Rene, when I asked you if you knew for sure if you had eternal life, and you said that you didn't, I thought I had some really good news to tell you. And after your answer to that second question, I know that I do! In fact, I would say that I have the greatest news you've ever heard in your whole life. That's quite a statement to make, isn't it?

II. THE GOSPEL

A. Grace

1. Heaven is a free gift.

Well, let me see if I can back it up. You know, all my life I felt exactly like you did. I thought heaven was something I had to earn, something I had to merit by keeping the commandments and following rules, and sometimes I almost despaired of the whole thing. Then I discovered something that absolutely amazed me. I discovered that heaven is not something you earn, or deserve, or work for, but, according to the Scriptures, heaven—eternal life—is an absolutely free gift! The Bible says, "The gift of God is eternal life through Jesus Christ our Lord" (Romans 6:23).

Free?

Absolutely free! Isn't that amazing?

Yes, it is.

You know, Rene, I think the most wonderful sentence I have heard in my life is only three words long: "Heaven is free."

2. It is not earned or deserved.

It's unearned, undeserved, and unmerited. It's free. You know, we sort of think there's nothing in this life that's free. We always look for the price tag. And we are probably right. But thank God that the greatest thing man could ever have—eternal life—is free! Of course, the idea that we have to pay for everything is something which is ingrained in us from our earliest days, isn't it?

Yes, it is.

The Bible says this: "For by grace are ye saved through faith; and that not of yourselves: it is the gift of God: not of works, lest any man should boast" (Ephesians 2:8-9). No amount of personal effort, good works, or religious deeds can earn a place in heaven for you because eternal life, like any genuine gift, is free.

Friend's gift: Suppose your best friend were to surprise you with an expensive gift, and let's suppose your response would be that of immediately digging into your purse or wallet for a couple of bills to help pay for the gift. What an insult that would be!

You must accept gifts freely. If you pay even a penny, it is no longer a gift. It is the same with eternal life. Isn't that amazing, Rene?

That's wonderful!

Why, it's the most wonderful thing I've ever heard in all my life! I'm sure this raises many questions in your mind. "How can these things be? How can God do this and still be just? And who gets the gift, after all? Everybody? How do we get it? And how can we know if we have it?" Now, Rene, let me see if I can answer these questions for you.

Well, the fact that heaven is a free gift and can't be earned or deserved **can be seen more clearly when we understand what the Bible says about man.**

B. Man

1. Is a sinner

The first thing I came to understand was what God says about man in the Bible, that is, what God says about us, you and me. This is a practical place to begin because it brings us face-to-face with the predicament in which we find ourselves—and a real predicament it is! According to God's Word, we have made a colossal mess out of everything we have laid our hands on.

If we were to get away from this planet and look at it objectively, we would appreciate the truth of this statement. We have wars and riots, we have crime and delinquency, we have murder and hatred and envy and strife. According to the Bible, all of these are the results of sin.

This is the fatal malignancy which infects the soul of the entire human race. The Bible says, "All have sinned, and come short of the glory of God" (Romans 3:23). The Bible teaches that all of us have sinned, right?

I know that.

Sin defined: When we think of sin, many times we think only of robbery, murder, adultery, etc., but the Bible tells us that sin is anything that doesn't please God or is a transgression of His law. Anything we do that we shouldn't do, like losing our temper or stealing—these are sins of commission. Anything we should do, but don't, like failing to pray or read the Bible, or to truly love our neighbor—these are sins of omission. There are not only sins in deed but also sins in word and thought, like lying, cursing, lust, pride, and hatred. The Bible says these are all sins.

Three sins a day: Sometimes I wonder just how many times a day the average person sins. I imagine it's fifty to one hundred times or even more. John Calvin said no one knows the one-hundredth part of the sin that clings to his soul. Today a psychologist would tell us that we have forgotten 99 percent of all those things we have ever done wrong. We suppress them because we don't like to think about the unpleasant.

Just suppose that a person sinned only ten times a day, or even five, or even just three. Why, he would practically be a walking angel! Imagine if not more often than three times a day did he think unkind thoughts, lose his temper, or fail to do what he ought toward God and man—he would be a pretty fine person, would he not?

Even if he were this good, he would have more than one thousand transgressions a year! If he lived to the average age of seventy, he would have more than seventy thousand transgressions. Think what would happen to a habitual offender in a criminal court with seventy thousand transgressions on his record!

Did you ever wonder about how good you would have to be to make it, Rene? Well, God has told us how well we would have to do to get into heaven. He has revealed the passing grade in His class of life. Do you know what it is?

No.

All right. Hold on to your chair! Are you ready? Here it comes! Jesus said: "Be ye therefore perfect, even as your Father which is in heaven is *perfect*" (Matthew 5:48).

Perfect?

There it stands! That's the passing grade! The amazing thing I discovered is that God doesn't grade on a curve. God says, "Be ye . . . *perfect*" (Matthew 5:48).

2. Cannot save himself

This impresses us with man's predicament. According to the Bible, he is a sinner. He has broken God's law. The Bible goes on to teach that our predicament is compounded by another factor that is understood by even fewer people. Because man is a sinner, he cannot save himself; he cannot earn his way into heaven. That is, he cannot merit eternal life by doing good things.

Omelet: If I were to prepare an omelet with five good eggs and one rotten egg, I couldn't serve it to company and expect it to be acceptable. Even less can we serve up our lives to God, which may have many things in them that men would call good and yet are filled with deeds and thoughts that are rotten, and expect them to be acceptable to God. Scripture says, "For whosoever shall keep the whole law, and yet offend in one point, he is guilty of all" (James 2:10). If we want to get to heaven by our good works, then all we have to do is be perfect. God's standard is complete obedience to Him for all time. We all fall short of this.

So, trusting in our own efforts to be good obviously will not get us to heaven. Many people have this belief today. In talking of these matters with literally thousands of people, we have found that the vast majority indicate that they intend to enter heaven on the basis of their own good works. The Bible teaches, "There is a way which seemeth right unto a man" (Proverbs 14:12). It would appear that this is the way that seems right unto man, but the Bible continues, "but the end thereof are the ways of death."

Do you see now, Rene, why it is impossible for you to save yourself by going to church, trying to do good, loving your neighbors, visiting the sick, and trying to live by the Golden Rule?

Yes, I do.

Well, Rene, **this all comes into sharper focus when we see what the Bible says about God.**

C. God

1. Is merciful—therefore He doesn't want to punish us

One of the most amazing and most difficult facts to learn about God is that He loves us in spite of what we are. He loves us, not because of what we are, but because of what He is. For the Bible tells us that "God is love" (1 John 4:8). He loves us more than any father or mother loves his or her child, more than any husband loves his wife. How vast! How measureless is this love of God for us!

2. Is just—therefore He must punish sin

But the same Bible that tells us that God is loving and gracious also tells us that this same God, because He is just and righteous, must punish sin. Because He is a just judge, He must punish our sins; His law declares that our sins must be punished and that He "will by no means clear the guilty" (Exodus 34:7). There is no doubt about this!

God is loving, Rene, but wouldn't you view with contempt a judge who was overly lenient with offenders? If one were to "slap the wrist" of his friend who was guilty of a heinous crime, we would cry, "Impeach him! Justice must be preserved."

Bank robber: Suppose I were to rob a bank of five thousand dollars. A hidden camera takes movies of me in the act, and the teller and other eyewitnesses identify me as the robber. When I am brought before the judge, the evidence is undeniable, so I respond, "I am guilty, Your Honor."

Suppose I were then to say to him, "Judge, I am very sorry that I robbed the bank. You have the money, and no one was hurt. I promise you I will never rob another bank if you will just let me go."

Would the judge be just if he let me go? He has a standard of justice that must be satisfied. If he let me go, there would be no safe bank in the land. If a human judge, because of justice, must punish lawbreakers, how much more must a just and holy God punish sin! That's why the Bible says He can by no means leave the guilty unpunished.

The teachings God emphasizes about Himself are that He is holy and just and must punish sin, but He is also loving and merciful and does not wish to punish us. In effect, this creates a problem, which He has solved in Jesus Christ.

D. Jesus Christ

1. Who He is—the infinite God-Man

Now, what is the answer to that problem? God in His infinite wisdom devised a marvelous solution. Jesus Christ is God's answer to our predicament. He sent Him into the world, and, as you know, we celebrate His birth every Christmas. Rene, I would be interested in your opinion about Christ. Who do you think He is? What kind of a being was He?

Well, He was probably the best man that ever lived. He was a wonderful teacher, and I believe He is supposed to have worked miracles.

Fine! Jesus was a great teacher and miracle worker. And He was good. Anything else?

Well, He was the Son of God.

Yes, He was. But I am also a son of God. Is He any different from me?

I don't really know.

The Bible teaches that Jesus Christ—Jesus of Nazareth, the carpenter of Galilee—was and is God! He is the Creator of the world! He is the one who created the whole universe! Jesus is God Almighty, Himself! In fact, the Bible says, "In the beginning was the Word [Jesus Christ], and the Word was with God, and the Word was God. And the Word was made flesh, and dwelt among us, (and we beheld his glory, the glory as of the only begotten of the Father,) full of grace and truth" (John 1:1, 14). And when Jesus Christ, after His death, rose from the grave, one of His followers, named Thomas, was so amazed at His victory over death that He cried out, "My Lord and **my God**" (John 20:28). Up until the time of Christ's resurrection Thomas called Him Lord or Master, but after he put his fingers in the wounds of the resurrected Christ, he acknowledged Him as God!

This comes as a real surprise to many people. They don't realize that He is God the Son—that God is Father, Son, and Holy Spirit, and that the Trinity is one God.

God the Son became man! This is what we mean by incarnation. This is what we celebrate at Christmas. He left His home in glory and was born in the filth of a stable. God became man for a grand and noble purpose.

2. What He did—He died on the cross and rose from the dead to pay the penalty for our sins and to purchase a place in heaven for us, which He offers as a gift.

He lived a perfect and spotless life. He taught the world's greatest teachings! He worked its mightiest deeds. Finally, He came to the end of His life—to that hour for which He had come into the world. In that hour we see the great transaction about which the whole Bible is written—the great transaction which is the central fact of Christianity.

What is it?

Record book: Let's imagine this book in my right hand is a minutely detailed account of my life. Each page details the sin of a particular day, every word I have spoken, every thought that ever crossed my mind, every deed I've ever done. Here, then, in my hand (the book) is the problem—my sin. God loves me (pointing at hand), but He hates my sin (pointing at the book) and must punish it.

To solve this problem, He sent His beloved Son into the world (bringing other hand next to the hand with book). The Bible says, "All we like sheep have gone astray; we have turned every one to his own way; and the Lord hath laid on him (passing the book to the open hand) the iniquity of us all" (Isaiah 53:6). All of my sin which God hates has been placed on His beloved Son.

Christ bore our sin in His body on the cross (1 Peter 2:24). When He died He was buried for three days (putting the book on your lap); but He rose from the dead and went to heaven to prepare a place for us. Now He offers heaven—eternal life—to you and me as a gift.

Tetelestai: Jesus endured the wrath of God on the cross, the infinite wrath of God. Even the sun hid its face as the God-Man descended into hell for us. Finally, when the last sin had been paid for, Jesus said, "It is finished" (John 19:30). This is an interesting word in the original text. It is *tetelestai,* which means finished, completed, or accomplished. It is also a word which was used in commercial transactions. They have recently discovered in Alexandria, Egypt, bills from different merchants which itemize what was owed for various items and then diagonally across the paper, in bold letters, is stamped the word *tetelestai,* which means "it is paid"; the debt is paid. "The wages of sin is death" (Romans 6:23). Jesus said, *"Tetelestai.* It is paid!" It is purchased. With His own passion on the cross Jesus paid the penalty for our sins and purchased a place in heaven for us. Christ then rose triumphantly from the grave.

G-R-A-C-E: The Bible says, "By grace are ye saved . . . not of works, lest any man should boast" (Ephesians 2:8-9). What is the meaning of grace? John Stott, chaplain to the queen of England, once gave this acrostic at a meeting of world leaders: G-R-A-C-E: **G**od's **R**iches **A**t **C**hrist's **E**xpense. God's riches: forgiveness, heaven, eternal life, peace, joy, and a sense of the love of God—at Christ's expense. The expense of the scourge, Gethsemane, the mocking, the plucking of His beard, the crown of thorns, the nailing of His hands, the piercing of His side, the wrath of God, and hell itself. "Jesus paid it all. All to him I owe." He offers us eternal life as a gift by grace.

Who receives this gift? Everybody? No. The Bible says that few find the way to life and that many go to destruction. How then can we have this gift? **This gift is received by faith.**

E. Faith

This brings us to the fifth and last thing we need to understand. We receive the gift of God by faith. The Bible says faith is the key that opens the door to heaven. You know, you could have a key ring with a lot of keys on it, like this (use actual key ring as an object lesson); they all look somewhat alike. But I'll tell you something. If you go to the front door of my home, you could try all of these keys except the right one and they would not open that door. The right key to heaven is called faith, saving faith. That is what will open the door to heaven. Nothing else in the world will open that door.

1. What it is not

Let me tell you what saving faith is not. Many people mistake two things for saving faith. If you were to look at these keys, you would find that several of them look very similar. In fact, you might not be able at first glance to tell which was which. So it is with faith.

Mere intellectual assent: Now, the first thing people mistake for saving faith is this: an intellectual assent to certain historical facts. Some people believe in Jesus Christ the same way they believe in Napoleon or George Washington. They believe He actually lived. He was a real person in history, but they are not trusting Him to do anything for them now. You believe in God, don't you?

Yes, I always have.

You have always believed in God. So have I. But that type of belief is not what the Bible means by saving faith. I believed in God all my life, but for about twenty-four years I was not truly saved.

The Bible says that the devil believes in God. Did you know that? The Bible says, "Thou believest that there is one God; thou doest well: the devils also believe, and tremble" (James 2:19). So believing in God is not what the Bible means by saving faith. The demons in the Gadarene demoniac said, "What have we to do with thee, Jesus, thou Son of God? Art thou come hither to torment us before the time?" (Matthew 8:29). Even the demons believe in the deity of Christ! But they evidently weren't saved! That's one thing people mistake for saving faith—an intellectual assent to the historicity of Christ, but that's not what the Bible means by faith.

Mere temporal faith: Let me give you one other thing that people mistake for saving faith. You have prayed to God many times, haven't you?

Oh, every day.

You've had problems that you've committed to the Lord, right? You've trusted Him for some things.

Oh, yes. I couldn't have gotten through life without prayer.

Rene, for example, what did you trust Him for?

Well, when my children were sick, when our finances were low and our business was bad—why, I've always prayed to the Lord for those things.

You see, you had more than intellectual assent. You have actually trusted Him for some things, right?

Yes.

Your children were sick. Your financial situation and your business were bad. I could probably add other things. You probably trusted him for decisions that you had to make; you probably even prayed that He would keep you safe while you traveled on a long trip. Perhaps you had an operation. You prayed to Him to bring you through that safely. Things like that.

Yes.

Now, all of these are good and you should trust in the Lord for all these things. But, you see, even this is not saving faith. We might say that when you trusted in the Lord for your finances you had a financial-faith. You trusted in the Lord to take care of your family—you could call that family-faith. You trusted in the Lord to help you with your decisions—you might call that deciding-faith. On trips you had traveling-faith.

There is one element all these things have in common. They are temporal, aren't they? They are all the things of this life, things of this world that shall pass away. Now many people, I find, trust the Lord for all these temporal matters. But saving faith is trusting Christ to save you—to save you eternally.

2. What it is

I never thought of it that way.

Why, neither had I. You see, I trusted the Lord for this and that and the other, but to get right down to what I was trusting in for eternal salvation—I was trusting in myself. I tried to live a good life. I tried to keep the Ten Commandments. I tried to live by the Golden Rule. I, I, I, I—you see? It was "I"!

What did I ask you?—"What are you trusting in for eternal life? What are you trusting in to get into heaven?" Do you remember what you said? "I try to do the best I can. I try to live a good life according to the Golden Rule. I try to do all these things." Do you see?

Saving faith is trusting Jesus Christ alone for our salvation. It means resting upon Christ alone and what *He* has done rather than upon what I have done to get me into heaven. As the Scripture says, "Believe [trust] on the Lord Jesus Christ, and thou shalt be saved" (Acts 16:31).

The chair: Let me illustrate. You see this chair here? A lovely chair, isn't it?

Yes.

You believe that chair exists? Do you believe that it would hold me up?

Yes.

But, you see, it's not holding me up for a very simple reason: I'm not sitting on it. Rene, how could I prove to you that I really trust that chair?

You would have to sit on it!

Right! That is the way I was with Christ. I believed Jesus existed. I believed He was divine. I trusted Him for finances, for health, and for travel, as you have done, too. (Put a few objects on the chair like your glasses to represent your health, then your wallet or purse to represent your finances, and also your car keys to represent your travel.) But, you see, saving faith is trusting in Christ for eternal life. Some people will trust the Lord for protection when they go out at night. They wouldn't think of putting out the garbage at night without trusting the Lord to take care of them. But as far as their eternal welfare is concerned, they are trusting in their own efforts because they have never understood what the Bible teaches.

Rene, do you remember what you said you would say to God if He asked why He should let you into heaven?

Yes. I said, I try to be good. I try to love my neighbor. I visit the sick. I do the best I can.

Well, Rene, who is the only person referred to in your answer?

I guess it was "I"!

Whom were you trusting to get you to heaven when you said "I"?

Myself.

Rene, to receive eternal life you must transfer your trust from yourself to Jesus Christ alone for eternal life (sit on the empty chair). *Saving faith* is putting our trust in Jesus Christ alone for eternal life.

Years ago I repented of my sins and transferred my trust from myself to Jesus Christ—from what I had been doing for God to what He has done for me on the cross. By a simple act of faith I transferred my trust from what I had done to what Christ had done for me. Just as I am now transferring my trust from this chair that I have been resting on—representing my good works—to this one representing Christ. Now I'm resting on only one thing: Jesus Christ. No longer am I trusting what I have done; rather, I trust what He has done for me.

Motive for godly living: Let's say that this pen in my right hand represents eternal life. There are only two relationships you can have to it. Either you have it, as this hand does, or you haven't, as my left hand doesn't. Now if you don't have it and you believe it exists, you are going to want to get it. So you do the best you can: You love your neighbor, go to church, read the Bible, pray, give money, and then you say, "Lord, here are all the things I've done. I hope I've done enough to get to heaven."

But you see, in this case it becomes evident that everything that you've done has been for the motive of getting eternal life. There is this selfish motive underlying everything, and so you couldn't possibly get it.

Beggar's hand: We could never earn eternal life. The Bible says that God came to earth and that on the cross, in the person of His Son, He paid for eternal life—an infinite price. By His graciousness He offers it to us freely as a gift. (Move pen in right hand over to the left hand.) It is received by faith: "Faith is the hand of a beggar receiving the gift of a king." (Reach out with left hand and accept the pen from the right hand.)

This beggar reached out an unclean hand forty years ago and received the gift of eternal life. I didn't deserve it then and I don't deserve it now—nor will I ever deserve it. But I have it! By grace!

Why, then, should I try to live a good life? The reason for living a godly life is gratitude. I'm not trying to gain something I don't have by my efforts to be good; rather, I'm saying "thank you" for the gift of eternal life Christ has given me.

A former president of Princeton put it this way in a book. He said that as a young man he accepted Christ and the gift of eternal life. All the rest of his life was simply a P.S. to that day, saying, "Thank You, Lord, for what you gave me then." The motive for all is gratitude for the gift of eternal life.

III. THE COMMITMENT

A. The Qualifying Question

Rene, does that make sense to you?

Oh, yes, that's beautiful!

B. The Commitment Question

Rene, you have just heard the greatest story ever told about the greatest offer ever made by Jesus Christ, the greatest person who ever lived. It's called the Good News, the Gospel of Jesus Christ.

Now, Rene, the question God is asking you is simply this: Do you want to receive this gift of eternal life—His gift that the Son of God left His throne and went to die on the cross to procure for you? Would you like to receive it?

Oh, yes, I would.

C. The Clarification of Commitment

(**Transfer your trust**) Wonderful! Let me clarify just what this involves. It means, first of all, that you are going to transfer your trust, that is, your hope of eternal life, from what you have been doing—going to church, being a good neighbor, living by the Golden Rule, etc.,—to what Jesus Christ has done for you on the cross. He takes our sin and we receive His righteousness. Is that what you want to do, Rene?

Oh, yes.

(**Receive the resurrected and living Christ**) Eternal life becomes yours by receiving the resurrected, living Christ into your life. Do you want to stop trusting in Rene and start trusting in Christ?

Yes, I do.

(**Receive Christ as your Savior**) You receive eternal life by receiving the person of Jesus Christ as your Savior. He rose from the grave and is alive today, and He wants to come into your life! In fact, He says, "Behold, I stand at the door, and knock: if any man hear my voice, and open the door, I will come in to him" (Revelation 3:20). You can receive and know the most exciting person in the history of the world because He is alive! Would you like to do that, Rene?

Yes, I would.

(**Receive Christ as Lord**) Next, you need to receive Christ as Lord of your life. Picture a throne room in the heart. He wants His rightful place on that throne. Are you ready and willing to yield your life to His control as a result of your gratitude for His offer of eternal life?

Yes, I am.

(**Repent**) He also commands us to repent of our sins. Are you willing to repent of your sins and follow Him? That means a willingness to turn from what you have been doing that is not pleasing to Him and follow Him as He reveals His will to you in His Word. Rene, are you willing to repent of your sins and become a responsible member of God's forever family and follow Him and serve Him as a member of His body, the church?

Yes, I am.

All right, if that's what you really want, I can lead us in prayer and we can tell God what you just told me.

D. The Prayer of Commitment:

All right, Rene. The Lord is here right now. We can go to Him now in prayer, and we can tell Him that you want to cease trusting in your own strivings and that you want to put your trust in Christ the Lord for your salvation, to receive Him as your personal Savior and Lord. Is this truly what you want?

Yes.

All right. Let me point out to you, Rene, that the Lord is looking at your heart more than He is listening to your lips. He says, "Ye shall seek me, and find me, when ye shall search for me with all your heart" (Jeremiah 29:13). If this is really what you mean, the Lord will hear your prayer and grant you eternal life. Let us pray.

(**Preparatory prayer**) Father, I pray that Thou would grant to Rene the gift of eternal life. May Thy Holy Spirit draw her unto Thyself and help her to truly understand what You have done for her. Grant her faith to believe Thy promises. Grant her repentance to turn from her sins. Reveal unto her Christ crucified today.

(**Pray together**) (Heads still bowed.) Rene, the Lord has said, "Where two or three are gathered together in my name, there am I in the midst of them" (Matthew 18:20). He is right here. You are not talking to me now but to Him. If you really want eternal life, will you say to Him aloud: (Pray short phrases at a time—bits of the Gospel personalized.)

Lord Jesus, I want You to come in and take over my life right now. (She repeats each phrase.) I am a sinner. I have been trusting in myself and my own good works. But now I place my trust in You. I accept You as my own personal Savior. I believe You died for me. I receive You as Lord and Master of my life. Help me to turn from my sins and to follow You. I accept the free gift of eternal life. I am not worthy of it, but I thank You for it. Amen. (Continuing in prayer with heads bowed.)

(**Assurance of pardon**) Father, You have heard the prayer that Rene has prayed. And I ask that in this quiet moment, the Holy Spirit will grant unto her the assurance of life eternal; grant unto her the certainty that her sins are forgiven. Grant that she may hear in the depths of her soul Thy voice saying, "Thy sins be forgiven thee. Go in peace." Grant, O Christ, that she may hear Thy voice saying, "As far as the east is from the west, so far have I put thy sins from thee, never to remember them against thee anymore. He that believeth on Me shall not come into condemnation. He that trusteth in Me is passed from death unto life. He that believeth on Me shall never perish but has everlasting life" (paraphrased from Psalm 103:12; John 3:18; 5:24; 3:16). In Jesus' name we pray. Amen.

E. The Assurance of Salvation

Rene, you have just prayed the most important prayer you have ever prayed in your life. I want you to see now what Christ says about what you have just done. In John 6:47 the Lord says something very significant. I would like you to read this. (Have her read aloud.) "Verily, verily, I say unto you, he that believeth on me hath everlasting life."

All right, Rene, in our prayer you didn't hear any angel choirs or see any visions. However, by a simple act of faith you have placed your trust in Jesus Christ for your salvation. Is that correct?

Yes, that's right.

In whom are you now trusting, Rene, for your salvation?

Jesus Christ.

He says, "He that believeth," that is, He that trusteth, "in me has eternal life." That doesn't mean an intellectual assent, for you have believed in Christ all your life in that way. This doesn't mean trusting Him for temporal affairs. You've done that all your life. Saving faith means trusting Christ alone for eternal salvation. Is this what you have done today?

Yes.

Jesus says that the person who does that has everlasting life. Do you believe Him?

Yes, I do.

Rene, if you should die in your sleep tonight, where would you wake up?

In heaven.

And if God asked why you should be in heaven, what would you say?

I am trusting Christ for eternal life.

The angels are rejoicing! God said it. That settles it. Rene, if you meant in your heart what you just said with your lips, then you have the promise of Christ that He has forgiven your sins, adopted you into His family, and given you eternal life. Praise the Lord! We may rejoice in it.

Welcome, Rene, to the family of God.

IV. IMMEDIATE FOLLOW-UP

A. Welcome to the Family of God!

Rene, I'm so happy for you and proud of you! Let me be the first to welcome you to the family of God, where we enjoy a relationship with Him and spiritual fellowship with each other.

B. *Partners in Growing* Booklet

Here's a helpful booklet entitled *Partners in Growing.* Its contents will be of special interest to you now that you have eternal life! It reviews some of the things we've been talking about today and tells you where in the Bible you can find some of the Scripture references I've used.

1. This is for you . . .

This is for you! One of the things you will appreciate about this booklet is the . . .

2. Read "My Spiritual Birth Certificate"

Please review the page right inside the front cover for a minute, noting what the card says. Then I would like for you to read it aloud for me. The card and booklet are for you to keep. The birth certificate is not a ticket to heaven or a church membership card.

3. Is this the decision you have made?

Is this the decision you have made? (Response).

4. Prospect signs

I would like for you to sign the birth certificate, and keep it as a reminder of this special day. Then . . .

5. Evangelist's name, address, and phone

I want the privilege of signing the card also. I will give you my telephone number and address so you can contact me whenever you may need to do so.

C. The Means of Growth

Rene, when anyone receives Christ and eternal life, the Bible calls it new birth, or spiritual birth, as physical growth is after physical birth. Let me suggest some good means of spiritual growth that can help you from this moment through the rest of your life! The first one is . . .

1. Bible (seven-day callback appointment)

The Bible will become your spiritual food. You're going to sense a hunger and thirst for spiritual things, and you can find satisfaction for that hunger and thirst in what God has said to you through His Word, the Bible. I'd like to return a week from now and talk more with you about the tremendous helps I've discovered in the Bible. At that time you may have questions or observations about what you have read in the Bible. Is that a good time for you?

Yes, that would be fine.

Here is a copy of the . . .

Gospel of John: There are twenty-one chapters in it. I think it's the best book in all the world about Jesus Christ!

Chapter a day: Please read one chapter a day. In this way, you will have read the world's finest document on Jesus Christ in only three weeks after receiving Him and His gift of eternal life! Another means of growth is . . .

2. Prayer

God has given us the privilege of speaking with Him personally, privately, and publicly! If reading the Bible is how God speaks to us (and it is!), then prayer is how we speak to Him! Just express your thoughts and feelings in natural but reverent words. He has promised to hear and answer our prayers! Another way to grow as Christians is through . . .

3. Worship

Both the Bible and prayer will become basic elements of your worship experiences. You'll want to have private, family, and public worship. Find a good Bible-believing church and become a part of it. I will be available to help you with this if you need me. Another very helpful means of Christian growth is . . .

4. Fellowship

Someone suggested that fellowship is like "two fellows in the same ship." It's so good for fellow believers in Jesus Christ to assist, encourage, and pray for one another amid their struggles, as well as rejoice and celebrate with each other in the midst of their joys and victories! We all need that! And we really grow when we . . .

5. Witness

That's what we do when we tell others what God has done for us! Who is the first person you would like to tell about welcoming Christ into your heart and receiving His gift of eternal life?

My brother, John.

Is John a Christian? Will you tell him before going to bed tonight?

Yes.

This booklet called, *Do You Know for Sure?* follows rather closely the presentation of the Gospel you've heard today. Please study it carefully. It will help you better communicate to your friends and family what has happened to you!

D. Appointment for Church

Rene, one of us would like to come by for you and take you to church next Sunday! May we pick you up at 9:15 Sunday morning?

Yes, of course. I'll be ready!

Wonderful! And if you need anything before then, please phone me. I've written my phone number on your spiritual birth certificate.

E. Closing Prayer

Now, for just a moment before I go, may we thank God again for what He has done in your life today?

Four

MAKING FRIENDS

In flying a plane the two most difficult things are takeoff and landing. In evangelism, getting acquainted and making friends with a person through the introduction is much like takeoff in that it requires very careful training to be done effectively.

Evangelism Explosion employs three different kinds of introductions to get acquainted and make friends with a person with whom you are going to share the Gospel.

The first kind of introduction was covered in chapter 2, "Witnessing As a Way of Life," and is done when witnesses use their existing relationships or develop new ones as bridges to lead into the Gospel.

The second is set forth in this chapter and is generally referred to as the conversational introduction. It assumes that the person has attended your church, so this format should be used whenever there is time to carry on a conversation. If the person you are attempting to reach hasn't attended your church, it can easily be adapted.

The third kind of introduction is the questionnaire approach, discussed at length in chapter 14, "Screening Contacts."

I. THE PURPOSE OF THE INTRODUCTION

The introduction is of great importance and fulfills a number of significant objectives in the overall presentation of the Gospel, the most important of which are:

A. BECOMING A FRIEND

The most important objective of the introduction is establishing friendship. Whether in the conversational introduction, the witnessing-as-a-way-of-life approach, or in questionnaire evangelism, building friendship is essential to effective evangelism.

Hence, great care should be taken to create and cultivate a friendly relationship with the prospect.

B. PRECLUDING COMMON OBJECTIONS

The best way to handle objections is to preclude them, that is, to answer them before they are raised and thus prevent them from coming up. Certain objections occur so frequently that steps have been taken in this presentation to preclude them. A number of such objections and the manner in which they are precluded will be seen in the following purposes of the introduction.

C. CREATING A SMOOTH TRANSITION INTO THE GOSPEL

To grab somebody by the lapels and say, "Brother, are you saved?" is one way to begin a Gospel presentation, but it will probably result in hostility on the part of many who are so accosted. We have found that smooth and gradual transition into the Gospel is by far the more preferable method.

This means that we begin where they are—that is, their secular life—and move gradually into the area of church, and then move easily into the spiritual realm. This avoids the sudden jump from the secular life, where people live, to very personal questions and precludes the objection: "Get lost, buddy, I'm not interested!"

During the introduction, the mood needs to be somewhat light. Often those with whom you share the Gospel are ill at ease and rigid in the initial moments and not very responsive. Humor at this point can help them relax and change their whole attitude. Some approach the Gospel presentation as if they were "friendly undertakers" who have arrived to dispose of the body!

D. EARNING THE RIGHT TO ASK PERSONAL QUESTIONS

I once heard a man walk up to a woman and say, "How are your kidneys today?" That's the truth! I actually heard the man ask that question. Her response? Did she hit him with her purse? No, she said the following: "Oh, they're much better today, thank you, Doctor." I overheard those words in a hospital room. The doctor had earned the right to ask that personal question. If you doubt that, stop the next lady you meet on the street and ask it yourself, and see what happens.

All of which is to say, we need to earn the right to ask personal questions. We can do this by becoming a friend, by getting to know the people, by listening to what they have to say, by showing interest, by hearing them when they talk. This is best accomplished in the section on their secular life, as will be discussed at greater length below.

E. FINDING OUT WHERE THE PERSON IS SPIRITUALLY

A discussion of the person's church background, or lack of it, can help form some understanding of his or her spiritual condition and of any particular spiritual problems that exist. We will probably see if there is a tendency to be more of a Pharisee or a Sadducee, to lean more toward legalism or license, or if there is some peculiar doctrinal hang-up. These things will be revealed as we discuss the person's church background. If some peculiar bias is discovered, the entire presentation can be slanted to help overcome the problem and thus preclude the objection.

F. DISCOVERING IF THE PERSON HAS WHAT YOU ARE OFFERING

We have come to offer him, in the name of Christ, eternal life, the privilege of knowing Christ now and everlastingly. We should ascertain whether or not the person already has this knowledge. This can be done with the first diagnostic question: Have you come to the place in your spiritual life where you know for certain that if you died you would go to heaven? There is, of course, no point in belaboring the Gospel with a person who is already saved.

G. CREATING A DESIRE TO HEAR THE GOSPEL

I have seen many people try to witness to others who quite obviously had no desire to hear what was being said. Such a desire, however, is essential before a person will ever commit himself to Christ.

To create such a desire, we should pinpoint some particular need we might sense in the person and show how Christ can fulfill that need. There are many such needs: loneliness, lack of purpose, guilt, hostilities, depression, anger, etc. Everyone has a need in life. Christ came that we might have life and have it abundantly and eternally. The need should be strongly emphasized, and its fulfillment in Christ should be demonstrated.

It has been said, "You can lead a horse to water, but you can't make him drink." But I think, with a little creativity, I could make any horse drink. Just place a salt tablet inside his lower lip! What I am saying is that though we can't make him drink, we can make him thirsty and he will want to drink. The Bible says we are the salt of the earth. We ought, therefore, to be able to make people thirsty for the Water of Life. One way to do this is simply to tell them about the wonders of the eternal life which Christ gives and dwell upon that for a while. The very frequent result is that a spiritual thirst will develop.

This can be done either in a personal testimony in the introduction or after you have asked the first diagnostic question and discovered that the person does not have eternal life. At this point you can share that at one time you did not have eternal life but now you do, and it is the most wonderful thing you have ever discovered, and you then explain.

If such a desire is not created, the objections may take numerous forms, such as "I'll have to think it over," or "Thank you, but I don't think I'm ready yet to make that decision." Perhaps it will appear as some form of theological objection, which is only masking the true fact that the person doesn't want what you are offering him. Therefore, it is very important to create desire by showing needs and explaining that Christ can meet those needs.

H. ASKING PERMISSION TO SHARE THE GOSPEL

I used to say to people, "Would you like for me to tell you how you can know this?" This, however, indicated a teacher-student relationship and gave the impression of an air of superiority on my part, and I found it definitely did not work.

I then changed the question to the following: "May I share with you how you can know this?" This worked much better, but still, a small percentage of people would smile and say, "I don't think that will be necessary."

I finally found that by "adding a rider to the bill" I could eliminate all objections at this point. Therefore, I would suggest the following wording, "May I share with you how I made this discovery and how you could know it, too?"

Thus far I have never had a person say no to this question. It should be remembered, however, that this is built upon the preceding preparatory work, especially in the discussion of their secular life, where I have asked questions and listened to them tell me about themselves. It would be a little bit difficult for them to say, "No, I don't want you to tell me how you made any discovery. I just want to talk about myself some more."

The obvious objection precluded by getting permission to share the Gospel in this way is, "I don't like people shoving religion down my throat."

I. DETERMINING WHAT THE PERSON IS NOW TRUSTING IN FOR SALVATION

This is accomplished through the second diagnostic question. "Suppose you were to die tonight and stand before God and He were to say to you, 'Why should I let you into my heaven?' What would you say?" It is vitally important to find out what they are trusting in for salvation, since probably the most common objection we run into with people who are at all church related is, "Oh, I have always believed that."

To preclude this objection, therefore, it is *vitally important* before sharing the Gospel with them to find out what it is, precisely, that they are trusting in for their salvation and to confirm to them that you heard their answer correctly.

J. TELLING THE PERSON HE IS WRONG WITHOUT MAKING HIM ANGRY

If the person gives you a wrong answer to the diagnostic questions, how can you inoffensively tell him he is wrong? How can you preclude the person thinking or stating openly, "I don't like people telling me I am wrong"? Such a response is usually not stated but appears in the form of anger and hostility, which, of course, makes a successful presentation of the Gospel extraordinarily difficult.

I have found that it is possible to tell someone he is wrong—even make him happy to hear it—if we use the vehicle of good news to tell him. Our response to a person's wrong answer to the second diagnostic question would be as follows: "When I heard your answer to that first question, I thought I had some good news for you. And after hearing your answer to this question, I *know* I have some good news for you. In fact, I would go so far as to say that you're going to hear the best news you've ever heard in your life! That's quite a claim, isn't it? Let's see if I can back it up. For years I thought the same way you did. If ever I were to get to heaven, I had to follow all of the commandments and keep all of the rules and do so many things that I almost despaired of ever making it. And then I made the most wonderful discovery of my life. I discovered that, according to the Scriptures, according to the historic Christian faith, eternal life—heaven itself—is absolutely a free gift. It is not earned, deserved, or worked for. It is absolutely free. Isn't that amazing?"

Telling a person he is wrong via good news is like saying to a person who has just declared that his Aunt Sarah has died and left him $10,000, "No, you're wrong! Your Aunt Sarah did not leave you $10,000. I have seen the will, and she left you $10 million." That's not the kind of statement likely to make anyone very unhappy, and yet you did tell him he was wrong.

You will notice that the blow of telling the person he is wrong is softened in a second way by shifting the discussion to myself and actually stating that I was wrong: "For years I thought the same thing. If ever I were to get to heaven, I had to keep all of the commandments and follow all of the rules, and then I made the most wonderful discovery of my life." I am identifying myself with him in the discovery that I was wrong and also telling him that it was a wonderful discovery.

The introduction to the Gospel has been designed to fulfill all of the objectives outlined above and to preclude all of the objections indicated. If the introduction is handled well, the rest of the presentation is vastly easier than it otherwise would be. Now let us move systematically through the introduction in order to analyze more fully and understand more clearly just what we are trying to do.

II. THE FIRST THREE STEPS OF THE INTRODUCTION

A. THE PERSON'S SECULAR LIFE

Upon entering the home the first thing you will deal with is the person's secular life. This covers a lot of things. It will include the basic amenities of the day—where the person is from and what he does, his family and his hobbies. At this point we will do four things:

1. Observe carefully and search the room for some indication of your host's interests—a specially placed and lighted painting; a group of portraits of children; trophies from golf, swimming, or bowling all furnish materials for saying, "Tell me something about yourself."

2. Ask questions that move toward the core of his life (like peeling an onion). We will not ask merely about things on the periphery of his interest. Avoid questions which solicit only a yes or no answer. Rather, ask: What? When? Where? Who? How? and Why? or say: "Tell us . . ." By the use of such questions, you will discover important facts about your prospect. You will better understand where he is coming from, properly relate to him, and more appropriately share the Gospel. After asking questions . . .

3. Be quiet and listen to him talk for five minutes. People usually are most interested in what they themselves have to say. By listening, we earn the right to be heard and also demonstrate Christian love. Remember, listening is not just waiting your turn to speak or thinking of what you're going to say next. It is responding with your whole person, being careful to hear all that the prospect is saying, both verbally and nonverbally. Look the prospect in the eye, move your head up and down, echo what he says by repeating his words and voice inflection. Be sensitive to his felt needs and respond appropriately. Remember and use his name often in the conversation. Then you will want to . . .

4. Pay a sincere compliment. In order to do this, you will have to listen to what he is saying. Everyone has something you can compliment if you observe and listen carefully.

B. THE PERSON'S CHURCH BACKGROUND

Assuming you are visiting from the church, it is natural for you to talk about his previous church experiences. Note his views on the church: Emotional? Negative? Has he been regular in attendance? Begin to qualify the person. Whom do you have—a Pharisee, a Sadducee, or a libertine? Learn more about the person—how he views the church, and what his relationship was to the church back home. Don't criticize or agree with him when he criticizes his denomination, his congregation, or his minister. You are not there as a judge or jury but as a witness for Christ. Keep in mind that you have come to make a friendly visit and to show your interest and concern for him.

C. OUR CHURCH—THE PERSON'S IMPRESSIONS

It is logical to move from discussing his previous church activity to his visit to your church. Find out if his impression of your church is negative or positive, hostile or friendly. It will be helpful at this point if your service was meaningful and encouraging to him. Ask him if he noted any unique aspects of your worship and your people. Such questions as these will be helpful:

"How did you happen to come to our church?" "Do you know any of the members of our congregation?" "How did you enjoy the service?" "Did you notice anything different about the service or the people?"

The best preparation for an evangelistic call is a vital worship service for the visitors and a friendly, helpful congregation to greet the visitors and assist them in finding the nursery, rest rooms, etc., according to their needs. A positive experience causes them to want to know what creates such an environment. Discussing their impressions of your church gives you a natural and smooth transition into your impressions of the church, which is your testimony.

While the conversational introduction properly includes testimony and diagnostic questions, for the sake of clarity, I will treat them separately in the two chapters that follow. Before I conclude this chapter, I need to give you some . . .

III. GUIDELINES FOR VISITATION

A. WHEN SHOULD YOU CALL FOR APPOINTMENTS?

If you have to drive a long distance, you should call to save gas and time. If you have more people to visit than teams to do the visiting, call to be sure all your church visitors are at least contacted by phone.

If you have fewer people to be visited than teams doing the visitation, don't call. Experience indicates that out of ten phone calls, eight or nine will respond that it's not convenient, that they already have a church, that they were just visiting with a friend, etc. It is much better, if possible, to visit unannounced. If it turns out to be inconvenient, make an appointment at the door to come back when it is convenient.

B. WHAT IS THE BEST WAY TO MAKE APPOINTMENTS?

Following the Sunday-morning worship service, a church, no matter how large or small, should have a visitor reception. The purpose for such a reception, of course, is to extend warm hospitality to church visitors.

At our church our greeters give visitors a "visitor" tag as they enter the sanctuary. The tag is long and rectangular and says "guest." If the visitor is a local resident, the greeter will give him a tag that is cut off diagonally at the bottom. (The visitor doesn't notice that.)

When that visitor comes to our reception we know by the tag that he is a local resident. After becoming acquainted and chatting for a while, you can say to him, "It has been such a pleasure to meet you. I would love to come to your home sometime to get better acquainted. Would that be all right? . . . Well, wonderful, how about this Thursday evening? Super! Is eight o'clock all right? Wonderful! I have a couple of church friends I think you would love to meet, and if it's okay, I will bring them with me. Let me get your address." Write down their address and be sure to check with the visitation secretary so another team doesn't show up at the door right after you get there.

In this way you don't have to drive all over town knocking on darkened houses or apartments, and you have an opportunity to visit someone you've already met. Much of the tension is removed because the visitor is now a friend and much more open to the Gospel. I virtually never go out without an appointment, and I find that people visited in this manner are very responsive.

C. WHAT SHOULD TAKE PLACE EN ROUTE TO THE VISIT?

Before leaving the church, each team member should pray a few sentence prayers. Travel time should be spent in meaningful conversation about E.E. or related subjects. The trainer should prepare his team members for their participation and what to do at the door. Avoid parking in driveways or walking on lawns. While approaching the house, keep conversation limited and subdued. All team members should be visible, but not too close to the door, with the lady member, who is the least "threatening" member of the team, most visible.

D. WHAT ABOUT TEAM MEMBERS' APPEARANCE?

Team members should be modest, clean, and neat. Each church should establish its own dress code that is appropriate for the community or type of on-the-job training. Small New Testaments in the purse or pocket are preferred, and visitation packets should be carried in the lady's purse, if possible. Keep hands out of your pockets; this might be threatening to some people.

E. WHAT SHOULD BE SAID AT THE DOOR?

The leader may say, "Hello, Mr. Smith? I'm Jim, and this is Gladys and Jerry. We're from First Community Church. It was good to have you worship with us last Sunday. We have come to repay your visit. May we come in?" Don't ask if it's convenient; it never really is, and the question gives them an "out." If the response is, "Please come in!" enter for a visit. If the response is, "It's not a convenient time," make an appointment for a visit at a later time or day.

F. HOW SHOULD THE TEAM SIT IN THE PROSPECT'S HOME?

The presenter should be the first member of the E.E. team to select a seat in order to have the best position for communication. Think of the visit as four friends sharing, rather than three talking to one. In fact, if possible, avoid having the team of three all sitting on the couch facing the prospect, who may feel as though he is being placed before a firing squad!

G. WHAT SHOULD OTHER TEAM MEMBERS DO DURING THE PRESENTATION?

Watch! Look at whoever is speaking. Pray (with eyes open) for the prospect, the one presenting the Gospel, and specific needs. Handle distractions, such as children, household pets, and interruptions. The entire team should participate in the conversation during "their secular life," "their church background," and "our church." But no one team member should monopolize the conversation.

As the training semester progresses, trainees will participate in the presentation on an increasing scale. The trainer should be sure to give his trainees the opportunity to share the parts of the presentation assigned. At times, faced with an opportunity to lead someone to Christ, the trainer will be tempted to do it all alone, but should trust that the Holy Spirit will help the trainees communicate effectively. If necessary, when the trainee is finished, the trainer can "flesh out" whatever parts of the presentation may need further clarification.

IV. DO'S AND DON'TS

After several years of hitting our heads against stone walls and finding that in many cases the same stone walls bruised our heads in the same way, we have searched for ways of avoiding the collision. Following is a list of some practical do's and don'ts that help contribute to the success of our lay evangelism ministry.

Don't carry a large Bible on your visit! A New Testament in your pocket or purse will furnish all the Scriptures you will need. A large Bible in your lap can have the same effect as a .45 revolver. Your prospect will wonder, "What's he going to do with that?" Never show your "weapon" until you are ready to use it. At the right time you can "draw and shoot him alive!"

Don't give the reference when you quote Scripture. You need to know the reference, but giving the location of each verse you use can interrupt your prospect's train of thought.

Do quote just the relevant portion of the verse. For example, we use 1 John 5:13 when we affirm that the Bible was written that men might know they have eternal life. We quote only: "These things have I written . . . that ye may know that ye have eternal life." The rest of the verse would introduce matters not germane to the discussion at that point. People do not get all the meaning in a long verse. They can be easily lost. Concentrate on the portion of the verse that bears on the discussion at the moment.

Do anticipate objections and preclude them, if possible. When an objection arises, deal with it in a manner that indicates that you are not threatened by it. Handle objections in a straightforward, matter-of-fact manner and return to the main course of the discussion.

Do stress the positive benefits of the Gospel. Some indicate by their manner of presentation that coming to Christ is one of the greatest disasters of life. Certainly this is not the case.

Don't use leading questions. If you know just a little psychology, you can get your prospect to say yes to anything. However, you cannot manipulate a person into the kingdom of God.

Don't use misleading questions. For example, "Tell me, Mr. Jones, what do you think you have to do to earn your way to heaven?" Such a question misleads your prospect. He may be trusting in Christ, but you come with a voice of authority implying that he can do something to save himself. You have misled him. He may give you information he does not truly believe, and the rest of your conversation would be in vain.

Do start where the person is. Do not assume that people today know very much about the contents of the Bible.

Do dangle your bait in front of the prospect. Do not shove the hook down his throat.

Do ask permission to ask questions. It is wise also, occasionally, to ask your prospect's permission to continue discussing the matters at hand, particularly if you sense some reticence on his part to continue. His simple "Yes" to "Would you like me to share with you what I learned about how to get to heaven?" will preclude his seething with rage as you proceed.

Do ask your prospect's opinion. He will feel more kindly toward you if you indicate that you are an intelligent person who values his opinion.

Do listen to your prospect talk so you can intelligently refer to statements he has made as you make your presentation.

Do be conservative in your estimation of what happens on your visit. You may see a profession of faith. Only time will tell whether your prospect was born again and has really accepted the Lord and been converted.

Don't feel you have to secure a profession regardless of what you might have to do to get it. High-pressure tactics are to be abhorred.

Do be overly modest as you talk about your church. Do not convey the idea that yours is the only church that presents the Gospel.

Do avoid critical comments about other congregations, ministers, and denominations. It is true that many are unfaithful to the Lord, but you will lose your prospect's confidence if he feels you try to build your flock by tearing others down.

Do smile, especially as you ask the two commitment questions. If you are too intense, your prospect may feel he is being pinned down and resent it.

Do make your exit sweet—even if the Gospel is rejected. Remember: It is the Gospel—not you—that has been rejected. The harvest is not until the end of the world—the prospect may yet be drawn to Christ.

Do watch your grooming and manner of dress. Sloppy shoes and unpressed suits do not speak well of the King you represent. Skirts that are too short can be distracting. Neatness is most important. A good rule: Dress in a way that will not draw attention away from your message.

Do ask a friend if you have bad breath, and encourage an honest answer. If you have it, do something to get rid of it or your prospect will be thinking of ways to get rid of you! The only thing worse than bad breath is no breath at all!

Don't sit in the car at the prospect's house and pray before you go to the door. Pray before you get to your prospect's residence.

Don't laugh outside the home en route to your car. He may misunderstand your reasons for laughing. Wait until you are on your way back to the church to discuss the prospect and your visit (see Appendix B for contact analysis).

Five

SHARING
YOUR
TESTIMONY

Testimony is commonly used in the secular world. Advertisers regularly utilize satisfied customers to attest to the value of their products. Television commercials pay top sports figures thousands of dollars to recommend everything from deodorants to tennis shoes, beverages, and breakfast cereals. Various diet programs set forth in living color the "before and after" of their most successful clients.

Likewise, giving a testimony is the first aspect of witnessing. When Jesus healed the demoniac in the Gadarenes He said, "Go home to thy friends, and tell them how great things the Lord hath done for thee."

Three times in the book of Acts, the apostle Paul gave his testimony. Notice in Acts 22 that he set forth the three essential elements of a good testimony:

1. What I was before I received eternal life (vv. 3-5)
2. How I received eternal life (vv. 6-11)
3. What eternal life meant to me (vv. 12-21).

A testimony may take either of two forms. It may be a church testimony, or it may be a personal testimony—your own or that of another.

I. CHURCH TESTIMONY

A church testimony is used in order to establish the mission of the church, i.e., to proclaim the Gospel that men and women may have eternal life. It also precludes the objection, "I want eternal life, but I don't want to go to church."

You may want to point out that the purpose of the church is twofold: First, to *show* the reality of eternal life in and through the loving care of your local church. You may want to give an example. Second, it is to *share* the message of eternal life with all who are interested.

A church testimony may be introduced in one of two ways. If the person is enthusiastic about the service he attended and indicates that the people were unusually friendly or enthusiastic, then you could introduce the church testimony in this way: "Would you like for me to share with you why I think the people at the church are so enthusiastic? It's because the people have found something in their lives that is really exciting and has given their lives new meaning. You know, Jesus came into the world that people might have life and have it abundantly and eternally. . . ."

If, however, the person does not seem enthusiastic over the service or did not notice anything particularly unusual about it, then you can introduce a church testimony in the following manner: (This means the church should work on the morning service and the friendliness and enthusiasm of the congregation.) "Since you are a visitor to our church and, as yet, do not know much about it, I would like to share with you some things we're trying to do that I think you will find interesting. You know, Jesus Christ came into the world that men might have life and have it abundantly and eternally. . . ." (See full church testimony in extended presentation of chapter 3.)

II. Personal Testimony

To be an effective witness for our Savior, the first tool needed is a clear, forceful personal testimony. It is the most original contribution toward an effective witness and the first thing shared because it is familiar and it is the thing easiest to share. It also creates a desire to hear the Gospel. Christians are the "salt of the earth," and their salty testimonies can make non-Christians thirsty for the Water of Life.

If you have met God in Jesus Christ in your own life, you have found Him working according to His promises. Your experience of God's faithfulness is the substance of your testimony. As you prepare your testimony, realize that you are fashioning an evangelistic tool so you will be a more proficient witness.

Some Christians give admirable testimonies—testimonies with zip and life—testimonies devoid of rough spots and trite platitudes. However, others stumble and bumble in a disorganized, uninteresting, ineffectual manner. We must sharpen our tools and learn to use them effectively.

Scripture says, "This is the record, that God hath given to us eternal life, and this life is in his Son. He that hath the Son hath life" (1 John 5:11-12). We are dealing now with the proper use of personal testimony as an evangelistic tool. Throughout this section we will use the phrase "eternal life" as equivalent to "trusting Christ" or "becoming a Christian." If you use the name of Christ repeatedly in your testimony, you will find that it often programs your prospect so that his answer to the second diagnostic question does not truly reflect his own relationship to Christ. The word *Christian* is such a highly connotative word that using it in the testimony can also generate difficulties.

Giving a personal testimony—simply telling what eternal life has meant to you—is the first aspect of witnessing. Now, if you cannot tell someone that Christ has saved you, you are not an evangelist; you are an evangelistic field, and you need an evangelist to lead *you* to conversion.

This is not to say you must know *when* you were converted. However, you must know *if* you have been converted. Many people don't know when they became Christians. One of the great preachers of our generation, Dr. Peter Eldersveld, said he could remember clearly when he was three years old, and he knew that at that time he trusted in the blood of Jesus Christ alone for his salvation. He was well taught by his parents and came to a very early faith and could remember nothing else.

In order to witness for Christ you must have the assurance that you have eternal life and know that Christ Jesus is your Savior.

A. MOTIVES FOR RECEIVING ETERNAL LIFE

When we refer to "eternal life," we mean more than the everlasting life we will spend with God in heaven. Jesus said in John 10:10, "I am come that they might have life, and that they might have it more abundantly." And in John 17:3, He added, "This is life eternal, that they might know thee the only true God, and Jesus Christ, whom thou hast sent."

Hence, eternal life has two dimensions: the abundant life of knowing God on this earth and the everlasting life of growing to know Him even better throughout eternity in heaven.

Your testimony starts with the first dimension and points to the blessings of knowing Christ in the here and now, such as fellowship, love, forgiveness, freedom from fear, etc. It concludes with a statement that you know for sure that when you die you will go to be with God in heaven.

Let us now consider some of the blessings which may well meet the needs of the prospect and motivate him to receive eternal life.

1. Fellowship. Christ provides us with Christian fellowship and friends. Why do unsaved people attend church? The answer: friendliness. Friendliness is significant to people because they are lonely. A basic human need is friendship. When people hear that God creates a fellowship, they find this meaningful.

2. Love. God fills us with His love. Our homes in America have every luxury conceivable. However, many lack the essential ingredient of love. Strife and jealousy lurk in gadget-filled rooms, and many marriages are little better than an armed truce. People long to be loved. A testimony to the love that God brings into a life and a home may awaken your prospect to a need that has not been met for years.

3. Forgiveness. God forgives us and relieves us of our sense of guilt. A major problem people are unable to cope with is guilt. Guilt fills our psychiatric hospitals, for it fractures the human personality. It causes anxiety and depression. It creates havoc in the human heart. The greatest picture of relief from guilt is in Bunyan's allegory. As Christian kneels at the cross, the burden of guilt falls off and rolls into the empty tomb, never to be seen again. The burden of guilt is lifted at Calvary.

4. A friend in my trouble. Christ is a friend to lean upon in trouble. He imparts strength to the discouraged, the worn down, and the defeated. It has been charged that Christ is a crutch. How do you answer that? "That's fine. I'm a cripple. I need a crutch."

5. Adoption. He adopts us into His family. "God setteth the solitary in families" (Psalm 68:6). God is our Father, and we are brothers and sisters in Christ. Frequently we say to a person who has just accepted Christ, "Welcome into the family of God. I have discovered something. We are related. You and I are brothers and sisters, and we are members of the greatest family on earth: God's family."

6. New perspectives. He gives a whole new perspective on life. One of the most devastating questions you can ask anybody is "What are you living for?" Most people have no idea. When one becomes a Christian, all this is changed. We are given a clarity and perspective unknowable to the non-Christian. The enigmas of the universe, the questions that perplex people, begin to fall into place, and we begin to see the puzzle of life more clearly.

7. Freedom from fear. He delivers us from the fears of living and dying. Many people are fearful. Some will say they are not afraid of hell, but they are afraid to take the garbage out at night.

B. ESSENTIAL QUALITIES OF AN EFFECTIVE PERSONAL TESTIMONY

1. Emphasize the positive. One of the common errors in giving a testimony is to belabor the first point and minimize the third. Just the opposite should be our method. You do not help people by giving them a tedious life history. They have no particular interest in where you attended school, where your parents live, or when you moved from here to there. Rather, do as Jesus commanded the demoniac: "Go . . . and tell how great things the Lord hath done for thee." Emphasize the positive benefits.

I remember one Christian who accompanied me on an evangelistic call. In response to my request that he give a testimony, he said, "When I accepted Christ, I lost all my friends. They wouldn't have anything to do with me. Then I lost my job. You know, all the people who do worldly things (and he mentioned half a dozen things that evidently thrilled the people we were visiting) give you up when you give up these worldly practices." It was as if he had given a five-minute discourse on why one should not become a Christian! Suppose you saw a cigarette ad that showed an emaciated man, his countenance manifesting excruciating pain, and he said to you, "Smoke my brand of cigarettes. It will help you develop cancer more quickly. You can have less wind if you join us. And your hair will smell worse!" Such an ad would not convince you to buy that brand. It seems that many Christians are about as effective when they tell why a person ought to become a Christian. Emphasize the positive benefits of having eternal life.

2. Identify with your prospect. When you share what you were before you received eternal life, you either encourage people to "tune you out" or to sit up and listen carefully to what you are saying. At this point you are making an effort to identify with your prospect and have him identify with you. By "identify," I mean that you need to select truthful statements about yourself that will help prospects see themselves in you. This means that you will have to listen carefully and remember what the prospects shared earlier in the introduction. As has been said earlier, the use of personal testimony helps to preclude the objection raised when the prospect is asked questions about his spiritual life that are personal.

In the conversation concerning his secular life and church background, you have gained enough insight to determine whether your prospect is self-righteous, indifferent, a libertine, an agnostic, etc. If, for example, you discover your prospect to be a self-righteous intellectual who is caring for his elderly parents, you would make a fatal mistake by saying, "My parents did not do right by me. They did not give me any religious instruction, and their reprobate lives led me to become a wretched character. I embezzled my employer's funds and was unfaithful to my wife. Then I met Christ." Your prospect would think, "Good, you needed Him, but I don't!" And he would start watching his silverware in case you had a spiritual relapse.

How much better to say to your pharisaical philosopher: "I never gave any thought to the reason I was here in the world until one day when such and such happened. Oh, I knew there was a heaven, but I never gave much thought about how I could get there." It does no good to tell a very righteous person what a great criminal you were. Instead, tell him the aspects of your life that were similar to the life of your prospect. You thereby let him know that you were the same as he is. Then, when you tell him that you found something very vital was missing from your life, he will sense something is lacking in his life. If we give a strong statement of our certainty of eternal life and the fantastic value of that assurance, this will act as a logical stepping-stone into the first diagnostic question.

3. Do not give answers before you ask questions. As we present the Gospel, it should have certain elements of mystery. You confront the prospect with a problem in a manner that identifies him with the problem. As you let him see and feel the problem, the suspense mounts and he gets into the problem; then you solve the problem by presenting Christ in the Gospel. However, you do not want to give any answers to the questions you will ask later.

Suppose you were witnessing to John, and Barbara is your companion on the visit. Before you establish what John is trusting in for his salvation, you ask Barbara to give her testimony. She says, "The pastor came to see me and asked me why I thought I should go to heaven. I didn't know I needed to trust only in Christ, so I told him I hoped I was good enough to get in. I went to church every Sunday, helped needy people at Christmas, and never intentionally hurt anyone. But the pastor told me I could never get to heaven that way because I was a sinner and needed the cleansing blood of Jesus Christ. So I stopped trusting what I was doing and started trusting Christ's work on the cross for me."

Now you turn to John and ask, "John, what are you trusting in for eternal life?" His certain reply will be, "I am trusting in the blood of Christ." He may not have the slightest idea about why Christ's blood avails for anything, or what is involved in the act of trusting Him for salvation; he is just parroting the "right answer" he heard Barbara give in her testimony.

If the testimony is used during the "introduction of the Gospel" (see outline), speak in general terms as you tell how you received eternal life. That is, tell what your life was like before, and then say something like this: "And then I received eternal life and everything was changed." Go on to tell of the changes in your life. It will be noted that you have not told them anything about how you received eternal life or that it was a gift received by faith.

If, however, the testimony is all you have time for, you must make especially clear just how you passed from death unto life.

4. Be specific. You must not generalize or you will lose your audience. To be effective, you must be specific. You can say, "It is wonderful!" What, exactly, is wonderful? Or you may say, "I have peace." Exactly what do you mean? In what way do you have peace? Be specific—make your testimony concrete.

"It is wonderful to know when I lay my head on my pillow tonight that if I do not awaken in bed in the morning, I will awaken in paradise with God."

"I had a Christian son killed in Vietnam, yet my heart is filled with peace because I know he has eternal life. Even though he was killed by an enemy mortar, he has a home now in heaven, and one day we'll be reunited there."

People remember specifics. They forget generalities. What are some points we might make in sharing what eternal life means to us?

5. Avoid clichés. Christian jargon is meaningless to the non-Christian. Clichés jangle unbelieving ears. For example: "Receive Christ, and you'll receive a blessing." This is so common to us, but the non-Christian will cringe at the thought of receiving a blessing. What is it to receive a blessing? How does it come, by mail? Or does it fall from the sky? We must always distinguish the connotation from the denotation of a word. The denotation is what the word actually means according to Webster or a theological dictionary. For example, the word "evangelism" is undoubtedly, by derivation, one of the most beautiful words in our language. It comes from the word *evangel*; in turn, it comes from "good angel," and it is the glad tidings. Nothing could be more beautiful.

However, what does evangelism connote to some people? It stirs up images of Elmer Gantry and people on the street corners beating drums, shouting, and doing all sorts of unpleasant things. The connotations of a word are the barnacles it picks up as it sails the sea of life.

6. Use direct and indirect quotations. Quotations arouse interest.

7. Avoid giving a travelogue. Details about when and where you lived or traveled decrease interest, deal with externals, and miss the real spiritual matters you want to share.

8. Focus on God's faithfulness. Details about your sinfulness or backsliding also detract from your objective of pointing the person to God and His grace in your life.

9. Use humor constructively. If the situation becomes tense, you can relieve the tension by saying something comical. But avoid a frivolous attitude toward the Gospel.

10. Speak pictorially. "I was in bed, and the Gospel came on the clock radio. Fortunately it was out of my reach, so I couldn't just roll over and turn it off. I got out of bed, and just about the time I got to the radio . . ." Here is a situation people can visualize. If they are not seeing in their minds the thing you are talking about, they are probably seeing something personal they are thinking about, rather than listening to you.

C. ADULT CONVERSION TESTIMONY

To apply the above suggestions, you will generally find it practical and helpful to write out your testimony before you give it. The length should be about three hundred words. If you were converted at an age when you remember graphically the details before and after your conversion, you will want to include the following three essential elements in writing your own personal testimony:

1. What I was before I received eternal life
2. How I received eternal life
3. What eternal life has meant to me

Let us now consider each part of the adult conversion testimony to see how it can be made meaningful to others.

1. What I was before. Select one life concept such as loneliness, strife, guilt, fear of death, emptiness, rejection, insecurity, depression. Then include it (only one concept per testimony) in an opening statement, saying, "Before I received eternal life, my life was filled with a paralyzing fear of death."

Next, move from the general statement to a specific illustration out of your own life experiences. Give concrete details to make your illustration come alive. People remember specifics but forget generalities. For instance, you may want to say something like, "When I was in college, I was living in a small mobile home. One night a terrible storm arose with wind gusts over fifty miles an hour! The wind was so strong that the rain was blowing horizontally across the ground. Our little mobile home was rocking on its concrete-block foundation, and a bolt of lightning struck a tall oak tree right next to it. I was really frightened and sat on the edge of the sofa fearful that I was going to die."

2. How I received eternal life. At this point, you may want to say something like, "Not many months later, a friend shared with me the most wonderful news I'd ever heard—that God had provided eternal life for me and what the conditions were to receive that life. As a result, many things have changed in my life."

Notice, you did not give away the answers to the two diagnostic questions you are about to ask.

3. What eternal life has meant to me. At this point, you may want to share the life concept in reverse. If you selected fear of death as your life concept, you will now want to speak of courage in the face of death. If you chose the concept of guilt, you may now want to speak of forgiveness. The reverse of depression is hope; of emptiness, purpose; of rebellion, obedience, etc.

Then you will want to illustrate the reverse life concept with another illustration from your experience.

For instance, you may want to say, "The fear of death is now gone, and in its place is courage when facing death situations or thoughts about death. Not long after I received eternal life we were driving north on an interstate during an ice storm that put a sheet of glazed ice on the highway," etc. Go on to describe in detail your close call with death. Then conclude, "God gave me complete peace in the knowledge that if death came, it could only usher me into His heaven! What a difference it makes knowing that I have eternal life. And it's the same today. I know that if I were to die right now, I would go to be with God in heaven. May I ask you a question?"

Your testimony regarding eternal life leads naturally into the two diagnostic questions which will be discussed in the next chapter.

Now you can shape, sharpen, smooth, and perfect your personal testimony and fulfill the admonition of the apostle Peter: "Be ready always to give an answer to every man that asketh you a reason of the hope that is in you" (1 Peter 3:15). Go over your testimony, and get rid of the rough spots. Eliminate the trite sayings. Get zip and life into it, and then ask God to help you use it. In three minutes you should be able to effectively tell what you were before receiving eternal life, how you received it, and what it has meant in your life.

D. CHILDHOOD CONVERSION TESTIMONY

There are some Christians who have no recollection of when or how they became Christians. They received Christ at such an early age, they do not remember ever not being a Christian. How shall these people give a testimony?

Whether they remember it or not, we know how they became Christians. They came to understand that they were sinners in the sight of God. They came to realize that God loved them and that Christ died for their sins. They came to trust in Him for their salvation and to receive Him as Lord and Master of their lives. How do we know that is the way they became Christians? Because that is the only way anyone becomes a Christian. Whether this happens in an emotionally packed hour in an evangelistic crusade, or gradually when the person is two, three, four, or five years old, every Christian has come to understand those things and to trust in Jesus Christ.

However, the important things to emphasize are the benefits that eternal life has brought. This is especially important for the person reared in a Christian home and church whose lifestyle has not drastically changed. Internal feelings, purposes, and motives have been changed by Christ, and these things should be emphasized.

A Christian who has backslidden drastically and then returned to a closer fellowship with Christ need not include this in a testimony of this type, since the introduction of this whole new area will only serve to confuse the person to whom you are speaking.

Sometimes laymen like to use the testimony of their pastor to get into the Gospel. This can be helpful if the prospect has come to the church and heard him preach. It might be introduced with such words as, "Did you ever happen to hear how our pastor got into the ministry?"

E. "YES" TESTIMONY

The trainer's testimony should be given before presenting the Gospel. The concluding line can go something like, "And I am very certain that if I died tonight in my sleep I would awaken in heaven." Then the trainer turns to the trainees on the team and asks, "John and Mary, do you know for certain that if you died tonight you would go to heaven?" The trainees smile and say enthusiastically, "Yes!" This is what we call a "Yes" testimony.

There are two specific benefits to the "Yes" testimony: (1) It helps shy, reluctant trainees to break the sound barrier. Hence, it is especially helpful early in the training semester. (2) It reinforces the testimony of the trainer and thus increases the credibility of what the trainer has said and what will be said in presenting the Gospel.

F. ADAPT YOUR TESTIMONY TO THE PROSPECT'S NEEDS

Under normal circumstances, you should share your testimony before the diagnostic questions. But sometimes, in order to heighten the prospect's interest, you may share it—or you may want to ask another team member to share his testimony—just before you ask the commitment question.

When doing questionnaire evangelism, share it after the questions and just before your Gospel presentation.

Remember, in any case, when the prospect becomes resistant, you should always personalize your presentation of the Gospel. The best way to do that is to weave your personal experience (i.e., your personal testimony) into your presentation. People will argue doctrine till the blood runs, but they cannot argue with your personal testimony.

Most people used to reply that they were not certain that they had eternal life. This was especially true when you emphasized the word *certain* when you asked the question. Increasingly today, however, many people are saying yes, they do know they have eternal life, while further questioning reveals that they don't. Therefore, I have added the phrase "or is that something you would say you are still working on?"

Six

ASKING DIAGNOSTIC QUESTIONS

Every science has progressed to the degree that its instruments of measurement have been developed. This is true in medicine. The foundation of good medicine is sound diagnosis. Where remedies are applied without such diagnosis, we say the practitioner is a "quack."

This same truth applies in the spiritual realm. Jesus Christ often employed questions to diagnose people's needs and spiritual condition. In Matthew 9:28 He said to the two blind men who came to Him asking for mercy, "Believe ye that I am able to do this?" In John 5:6 He asked the lame man by the pool of Bethesda, "Wilt thou be made whole?" And Acts 8:30 records that on the road to Gaza, Philip launched his witness to the Ethiopian eunuch with the question, "Understandest thou what thou readest?"

Likewise, we today, unless we can accurately diagnose the person's spiritual condition, shall very likely endeavor to apply the wrong spiritual cure or apply the right cure in the wrong manner. Therefore, we have developed two diagnostic questions that are of invaluable assistance in determining a person's spiritual condition. In applying these, we should keep in mind that, whether in the realm of medicine or of the spirit, no diagnostic tool is infallible.

We want to offer people eternal life in Jesus Christ. The two diagnostic questions enable us to ascertain (1) whether or not they have what we want to offer them, and (2) what they are basing their hope of eternal life upon.

I. THE TWO QUESTIONS

A. FIRST QUESTION:

"Have you come to a place in your spiritual life where you know for certain you have eternal life, or is that something you would say you're still working on?"

This question brings the person to the point of saying, in effect, "I don't have eternal life." We always want to find out if the person already has eternal life.

Suppose you were selling an encyclopedia, and you spent two hours in a home presenting a family with the wonderful advantages of owning the *Americana*. Then you asked them what they thought of it. The father turns and says, "It's marvelous. In fact, I think it's so wonderful that I bought a set last week and it's in the next room." No encyclopedia salesman would be that stupid!

Yet many who are witnessing for Christ make this very mistake. They do not find out whether the person has eternal life already. So after presenting the Gospel, they hear these lovely words: "Oh, yes. I've always believed that."

Most people will say they are not certain they have eternal life. This is especially true if you emphasize the word "certain" when you ask the question: Have you come to the place in your spiritual life where you know for *certain* that you have eternal life and that you are going to heaven? If one says, "I know I have eternal life," you must then determine on what he is basing that hope and distinguish true assurance from presumption. The Westminster Confession of Faith points out that ". . . hypocrites, and other unregenerate men, may daily deceive themselves . . . of being in the . . . estate of salvation; which hope of theirs shall perish." Dr. McDowell Richards, president of Columbia Theological Seminary, said one day, "Assurance is having a confidence of eternal life which is rested upon the sure foundation of Jesus Christ, but presumption is presuming ourselves to have eternal life when, in fact, our confidence is based on nothing more than the flimsy foundation of our own self-righteousness."

B. 1 JOHN 5:13

After ascertaining that they do not have eternal life, you will want to pull out your New Testament and say something like . . .

"For years I felt the same way you do. I certainly didn't know I was going to heaven. In fact, I didn't know anyone knew that or even that it was knowable. And then I made a wonderful discovery. I discovered it was possible to know for certain that when I left this world, I was going to enter into heaven. That's the greatest thing I have ever learned in my life. I wouldn't trade it for all the tea in China. I discovered that the Bible was written for that very reason. It says, 'These things have I written unto you . . . that ye may know that ye have eternal life'" (1 John 5:13).

You probably noticed that I left out the center phrase of the verse which would give away the answer to the next question. Put your New Testament back into your pocket or purse. You have memorized the essential verses, so you don't have to wave your "weapon" in your friend's face while you are witnessing to him.

C. PERMISSION

Before you ask the second diagnostic question, you should get permission to proceed with the Gospel. I'm sure you would never barge into a person's home without knocking, unless you were a robber! Likewise, you should never invade the privacy of a person's life without first asking permission.

To do this we suggest you use the following sentence: "May I share with you how I discovered eternal life and how you can know it, too?"

Don't say, "Would you like for me to tell you how you can know this?" And don't proceed with the second question until you obtain their permission to do so. If they have said yes to the first question, leave off the second part of your question asking for permission: ". . . and how you can know it, too." If they seem restless or appear to have a time problem, you may want to ask if they have ten, twenty, or thirty minutes for you to share, whatever the situation seems to allow.

If they give you permission, then say, "Wonderful! But before I get into it there is a question that I think brings the whole subject into focus, and I would be interested in your opinion on this matter. (Lead right into second diagnostic question.)

D. SECOND QUESTION:

"Suppose you were to die tonight and stand before God, and He were to ask you, 'Why should I let you into My heaven?' What would you say?"

The second question enables us to discern what foundation one is trusting in for eternal life. Why do we ask, "Why should God let you into heaven?" rather than, "What must one do to be saved?"

The latter is a biblical question that has a biblical answer. One who has gone to Sunday school and has some acquaintance with the Scriptures will respond like a computer. Feed such a person the question in biblical language and he will push a mental button, the machine will whirl and hum, and the right answer will come out: "Believe on the Lord Jesus Christ, and thou shalt be saved, and thy house." This may be his sincere faith, or merely a parrot reply devoid of true understanding. You will have no way of knowing which.

In asking the question, "Why should God let you into heaven?" we feed a question that has not been programmed. There is no rote—no automatically learned—answer. Also, it is a neutral question, i.e., it does not lead the person to give a rote answer.

Some have said that that question deals with "pie in the sky by and by," and that we should deal with the here and now. We have found, however, that most questions that deal with the here and now lead to vague and uncertain answers. For example, "Are you following Christ in your life?" Response: "Well, more or less." Or "Is Jesus Christ the Lord of your life?" Response: "I guess so, but not as much as IIe should be." It is easy to see that such answers as these make it difficult to proceed in a clear fashion. We have found that the diagnostic questions selected generally get clear and unambiguous answers that facilitate the presentation of the Gospel.

From the answer given, you then know what the person is truly trusting in for eternal life. It's helpful at this point to rephrase the answer: "Let me see if I understand you. You would say to God . . ." and then repeat what he has just told you. This will help preclude his saying at the end of your presentation, "Oh, I've always believed in Jesus Christ and trusted Him alone for salvation."

E. HOW TO GET AN ANSWER

Often when you ask a person, "Why should God let you into heaven?" you will get an answer something like, "Well, I don't know." Is there some way to get an answer that will let you know in what he is trusting? Here are several methods we have found effective.

1. Change the wording. Much like a football player, you have "hit the line" and can't get through. You need to back up, gain a bit more speed, and hit it again in a different place.

Stress the significance and importance of the question. "That's really a thought-provoking question, isn't it? When I first heard it I was no theologian, but I did have enough sense to realize that it's truly a significant question. I came to realize that it's the most important question in the world. If I could not give God the right answer, I would miss heaven, and the other option isn't too pleasant to think about.

"I figured that was a question I really needed to know the answer to. I knew that Jesus had said, 'What shall it profit a man, if he shall gain the whole world, and lose his own soul?' I know you don't have a theological dissertation prepared on the subject, but, just offhand, what comes to your mind? What do you *think* you would say if He asked you, 'Why should I let you into My heaven?'"

Your prospect will find it harder to say again, "I don't know." You have discussed that this is an important question—the most important question in the world, according to your authority, Jesus Christ! Also, you have taken the edge off the situation by pointing out that you do not expect him to have a theological dissertation on the subject. Finally, you have changed the wording from, "What would you say?" to "What do you *think* you would say?"

2. Make the question general. In the event your prospect gives another "I don't know" or "It's hard to say," you still need to get an answer. You will now want to change from a personal question to a general one.

"Well, I sort of felt the same way. That's a difficult question to answer. Let me change the question and take the spotlight off of you. You've been going to church all your life. I'm sure you have gathered some idea as to what the entrance requirements for getting into heaven are. I would be interested in what you think the entrance requirements for anyone to get into heaven are."

If this elicits a suitable response, you may then add, "Now I suppose that since we have had time to look at it, these are really the things upon which you yourself are basing your hope of getting into heaven, aren't they?"

In this case you have made it more difficult to plead ignorance. You have reminded your prospect that he's been sitting in church for years. He's not going to admit: "I'm so stupid I have not learned a thing! I just sat there sleeping!" Also the question is no longer right on him—not, "What would you say?" but *"What are the entrance requirements?" (in general for anyone).* On only very rare instances will you ever have to go beyond this to get an answer to the question.

3. Tell what your answer was. However, what if he still is evasive and doesn't know? You might do this, but only as a last resort. *"Well, here's what I thought.* You have to keep the Golden Rule and live by the Ten Commandments, be a good citizen and neighbor, and not hurt anyone intentionally. Are these the ideas that have been going around in your mind?"

Here you are on the dangerous ground of putting out words for him to claim as his own. This tends to be leading. The only reason for using this approach is that by this time your prospect has given good evidence that he is not trusting Christ and probably is trusting some form of good works, but has not been able to verbalize it.

4. Agree that he doesn't know. If there is still no answer, or if again he acknowledges that he does not know what he would say, you can now nail it down with, *"Then you just really don't know how to get into heaven, do you?*

"You're sort of like the man in Jesus' story. The king came to Him and said, 'Friend, how camest thou in hither?' Do you know what He said? He said the same thing you said! He was speechless! He really didn't know what to say. Do you know what happened to him? The servants bound him and cast him into outer darkness. Now, we don't want that to happen to you, do we?

"Do you remember the *$64,000 Question* that used to be on TV? If a contestant gave the wrong answer, he would be told, 'Step down.' And you know, the same thing happened if he gave no answer. There are some situations like that in life where a wrong answer and no answer produce the same result. It's a long way to step down from God, and we don't want you to have to do that. Would you like me to share with you what the biblical answer to that question is?"

II. FOUR COMBINATIONS

It is of vital importance, not only to be able to administer diagnostic tests, but also to be able to properly interpret the results of these tests. I have been told that anyone with normal intelligence could learn to give an electrocardiogram in about an hour's time, and yet it takes years of study for a doctor to be able to interpret the results. Fortunately, it will only take the average trainee a few minutes to be able to intelligently interpret the results of these two diagnostic questions, but those are minutes that are very well spent.

There are four possible combinations of answers which may be obtained by the two diagnostic questions. These are laid out in schematized form in the accompanying illustration. The following is an interpretation of the diagnostic results of the questioning and suggested procedures for each one.

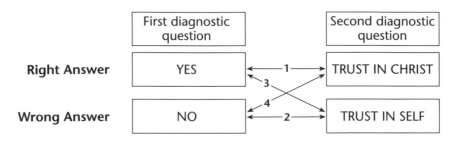

A. FIRST COMBINATION: A CORRECT ANSWER TO BOTH QUESTIONS

That is, the person declares that he knows he has eternal life and that he is trusting in Jesus Christ alone for his salvation.

1. Interpretation of diagnosis: Apparently he is a Christian! I say "apparently" because we should always remember that no diagnostic test is infallible. The person might simply be demonstrating, as happens in rare instances, that he has a head knowledge of that which he does not possess in his heart. Since we, however, are not the judge of men's hearts, we will assume he is a Christian and treat him accordingly.

2. Recommended procedure: Share with him other aspects of the life of your church, since he is apparently a candidate for membership. Ask questions concerning the areas of church life in which he is most interested, so that you can further inform him of what your church is doing in those areas. Share with him the nature of the evangelism ministry you are involved in and what the purpose of your visit is. Enlist him as a prayer partner for one person on your team. Possibly share a brief presentation of the Gospel with him or have one of your trainees do so if they have progressed far enough in their training to be able to make an effective presentation. This will challenge your prospect in the area of witnessing and may also be used to encourage him to become a part of your church and its outreach ministry. Most Christians are quite impressed with another layman who can give a well-organized and interesting presentation of the Gospel.

Whatever you do, don't ask if you can practice your E.E. presentation. Many people would be offended to have you overtly use their valuable time to practice your presentation. Instead, tell them that as visitors to your church, they are probably interested in what your church believes; then ask if you can share with them briefly what your church believes about the Gospel.

Another effective approach is to tell people you enjoy listening to other people's testimonies. Ask them to share briefly how they received eternal life. You are taking an interest in them and giving them opportunity to confess their faith. Then, ask if you can share with them how you received eternal life. If they agree, share the Gospel in a testimony format. In other words, instead of introducing each point with, "The Bible says," say, "I discovered that heaven is a free gift . . . man is a sinner . . . God is merciful," etc.

B. SECOND COMBINATION: AN INCORRECT ANSWER TO BOTH QUESTIONS

That is, the person declares that he does not know that he has eternal life and states that he is trusting in his own good works to get him into heaven.

1. Interpretation of diagnosis: Apparently he is a non-Christian. I again say "apparently" because of the small possibility that he may have misunderstood the questions and have been confused in his answers.

2. Recommended procedure: This is the stock answer of the non-Christian, and the recommended procedure is to present the Gospel, as given in detail in both the smaller and larger presentations.

C. THIRD COMBINATION: A CORRECT ANSWER TO THE FIRST QUESTION AND AN INCORRECT ANSWER TO THE SECOND

That is, he says that he knows he is going to go to heaven and that the reason that God should admit him is because he has lived a good life, followed the Golden Rule, kept the commandments, etc.

1. Interpretation of diagnosis: This is what we call "presumption"—the person presumes himself to be going to heaven without any biblical foundation for that hope. These people are somewhat analogous to the Pharisees who "trusted in themselves that they were righteous."

2. Recommended procedure: Before you can proceed with such a person as this, his illusions must be destroyed; that is, the bubble of his false hope must be popped. This may be done in the following manner:

(Witness, commenting on prospect's answer:) Have you ever considered just how good a person would have to be in order to be good enough to go to heaven? In other words, have you ever thought just what is the passing grade?

No, I'm not really sure.

Let me tell you what the Bible says. It says, "Be ye therefore perfect, even as your Father which is in heaven is perfect," and "Whosoever shall keep the whole law, and yet offend in one point, he is guilty of all." You see, the passing grade is one hundred, and God doesn't grade on the curve. He says we will give an account of every idle word, and every thought, and every deed we've ever committed, and if we fail to live up to His perfect standard, we fall short of the entrance requirements for heaven. After looking more carefully at what God's entrance requirements are, are you really certain how that interview would turn out? (This question should be asked in a somewhat light and jovial fashion so the person does not feel like he's being given the third degree.)

No, I guess when I stop to think about it, I'm really not certain how that would turn out.

Well, you know, I have some good news for you. In spite of everything I've said, it is possible to know for sure that you're going to heaven, but it's in an entirely different way. Would you like for me to share that with you?

You have thus brought the prospect to realize that his confidence was misplaced and that he is not really sure at all what would happen to him and would like to know how he could be sure. Thus, you have accomplished one of the basic objectives of the introduction, even with this most difficult of the four possible combinations of the answers.

D. FOURTH COMBINATION: A WRONG ANSWER TO THE FIRST QUESTION AND A CORRECT ANSWER TO THE SECOND

This is the person who declares that he does not know for sure he would go to heaven, but that his only hope is that he is trusting in Jesus Christ who died for his sins.

1. Interpretation of diagnosis: This is most probably a lack of assurance. However, it could be caused by the person having gained a head knowledge of the way of salvation, but lacking assurance because he has never really appropriated it unto himself. In either case we will deal with it as if it is simply a lack of assurance. If it is the latter problem, you may find the individual a few weeks later going about telling people that he just became a Christian.

2. Recommended procedure: Take the prospect to some of the assurance verses in the Scriptures, such as John 6:47 or 1 John 5:11-12. Using, for example, John 6:47, you may proceed as follows:

Would you please read this verse for me aloud? (handing him an open Bible).

"Verily, verily, I say unto you, he that believeth on me hath everlasting life."

Let's look at that together for a moment. Jesus is speaking, and He says, "Truthfully, truthfully, I say unto you, he that believeth [or trusteth] in me has everlasting life." In whom are you trusting for your hope of eternal life?

In Jesus Christ.

Then you have fulfilled the condition set forth in this verse, haven't you?

Yes, I have.

Here Christ gives us a solemn promise. He says that those who trust in Him have—not will have, shall have, may have, or might have, but *have* as a present possession—eternal life, which, of course, means heaven. Do you believe that Jesus would tell you a lie?

No, I don't believe He would.

Then do you believe that He is telling you the truth in this verse?

Yes, I do.

Do you, then, have eternal life as Christ declares?

Well, yes, He says so!

I think it would be helpful if we were to have a word of prayer and ask God to grant you the assurance that you need and would like to have.

Thank you. I'd appreciate that.

Would you pray to Christ out loud the following prayer after me? "Lord Jesus Christ (he repeats each phrase), I do trust in You for my salvation. I do believe You died for me. I do repent of my sins and desire to follow You. In Thy name, Amen." You asked God to give you the assurance of eternal life. Do you now believe His promise that you have eternal life?

Yes, I do.

And if you died in your sleep tonight, where would you wake up?

In heaven!

Praise the Lord!

This prayer is similar to a prayer of commitment, except for the tense of the verbs. You are not indicating that he is necessarily doing this for the first time now but merely that he does trust in Christ whenever that trust may have begun.

This approach may also prove useful in dealing with a person who gives two wrong answers but later, in spite of all that you have done, changes his story and declares that he has always trusted in Christ and cannot be moved from that opinion. Instead of arguing and angering him, it might be well to ask whether, since he did not know for sure that if he died he would go to heaven, he would like for you to lead in a prayer and ask God to give him that assurance. Such a prayer as this may be used to bring such a person to Christ if he really has not been trusting in Him.

E. HOW TO DEAL WITH THE WRONG ANSWER

Let me share a word of my own experience from over the years in dealing with wrong answers in the hope that you may avoid some of the mistakes I have made.

Early on, I answered quite directly: "No, that is not correct, Mr. Jones. The answer the Bible gives is quite different from your answer." The problem I ran into here should be obvious. Someone has said that the most pleasant words in the English language are "You are right," which would seem to indicate that some of the most unpleasant words are "You are wrong." These words tended to raise the hackles on my prospect's neck, and I often found myself engaged in an argument right at the outset. I won a number of arguments and lost a great many people.

Finally, I decided to try a different approach. Instead of telling them from the onset that their answer was wrong, I said that their answer was interesting but that it raised a number of questions. And then I went into the Gospel and waited until the end of the Gospel presentation to tell them that they had been wrong. However, I then discovered a new problem. Since some time had elapsed since they had given their answer, I found that many people would now try to wiggle out of their answer or else deny they had ever said it. So I found myself right back where I started.

After a good many years of struggling with this problem, I was led by the Lord to a solution, which I mentioned briefly in chapter 4. I had thought that there must be a way to tell them from the onset that they were wrong and yet make them happy to hear it. We now respond to their wrong answer something like this: "You know, Mr. Jones, when you answered that first question ('Do you know for sure you have eternal life?') I thought I had some good news for you. But after hearing your answer to this second question ('Why should God let you into heaven?'), I *know* that I have some good news for you. In fact, I would go so far as to say that you are going to hear the *greatest* news you have ever heard in your entire life! That's quite a statement, isn't it? Well, let's see if I can back it up. All my life I thought just what you said [If this is not your experience and you can't make this statement, then you can say, "Multitudes of people have thought just what you said."]—if ever I were to get to heaven I would have to earn, deserve, or merit it. And then I discovered the most wonderful thing in the world—that according to the Bible, heaven—eternal life—is an absolutely free gift! Isn't that amazing?"

This should be said with great enthusiasm and exuberance. I have found that usually it will produce an enthusiastic and open response on the part of the listener. This is due to a number of factors: (1) It is such incredibly good news; (2) it is almost universally unknown by the unregenerate person; (3) the shock effect of hearing the most unexpected news right at the beginning; (4) and very importantly, the enthusiastic and exuberant manner in which the Good News is told precludes a hostile reaction.

F. HOW TO DEAL WITH THE RIGHT ANSWER

When prospects give right answers and are apparently Christians, should you go ahead and share the Gospel? Yes, in most cases, but with some precautions.

Remember the guidelines given earlier: Don't ask if you can practice your E.E. presentation! Instead, tell them that as visitors to your church, they are probably interested in what the church believes; then offer to share with them briefly what the church believes about the Gospel. This way, you are first and foremost meeting their needs. Or you can ask them to share briefly how they received eternal life.

When you have finished, you may want to explain to them a bit about the E.E. ministry, since many people are looking for a church that is evangelistic and may even want to enlist in the training.

"A bird in the hand is worth two in the bush." It is better to share the Gospel with a Christian than to run the risk of going to two or three addresses and finding no one at home. Remember that you are in a training ministry and that it is more important to train a soul-winner than to win a soul. Remember also that those who are already Christians make good, easy, nonthreatening prospects with whom your trainees can grow by sharing the presentation.

G. BRIEF REVIEW

By this time you have come far from the front door. As the door opened you were strangers. Now your prospect knows you as one who is interested in him, his background, and his opinions. He also knows you are knowledgeable in the spiritual realm. You know a great deal about him. You know his interest in the church, his attitude toward your church, his view of himself, and most important, his eternal destiny as of this moment. If he is lost, you hope, by God's grace, that his destiny will change within the next hour or two. You are now ready to present the facts of the Gospel.

Seven

ANALYZING THE GOSPEL PRESENTATION

In the Introduction you found out what the person is trusting in for salvation. Equally important, *he* has found out. Until you helped him clarify it, he probably wasn't aware of what he was trusting in for eternal life. We begin now to tear down this inadequate foundation. Now we are about to show the "product" and show the prospect that he needs it. Remember, you put the value on your product by the way you speak about it. It will seem as valuable to your prospect as it does to you. Think about what you are saying. Talk about God's Good News in a manner befitting the greatest story ever told! The expression on your face may be far more important than the words on your lips. Start thinking about heaven before talking about it!

Beware of your attitude at this point lest you convey: "Would you like *me* (wise guy) to tell *you* (stupid) how you can get smart (like I am)?" In other words, avoid talking down to people. People who have been going to Sunday school classes and worship services know a lot of facts that form a spiritual jigsaw puzzle. Each Sunday they get another piece or two to put in the box. This week they got a sermon about the Good Samaritan. That was nice. Into the box it goes. Occasionally they shake all the pieces around, but the pieces don't seem to fall together. Christianity seems to be just a large number of pieces floating through the air—Noah, David and Goliath, the Tower of Babel, Jesus healing a blind man, and a little man up in a tree—isolated stories without much meaning and with no interrelationship. A few pieces are missing. These we supply as we present the Gospel. These key pieces enable everything else to fall into place. The things in this presentation that most people don't know are:

1. Man cannot save himself
2. God is holy and just and must punish sin
3. Christ is God
4. His death on the cross was for our sins

5. He offers heaven as a gift
6. The meaning of grace
7. The meaning of faith

These are the points we must emphasize as we go through the Gospel presentation. To verbally underscore them, you must stop and say these key points deliberately. You dare not go through the whole Gospel at the same pace and in the same tone of voice, or your host will say, "That's very interesting. It's time to go to bed. I can hardly keep my eyes open." Charles Spurgeon says that if you gently rock the cradle, you will put them to sleep, but if you give the cradle a good jerk, the babies will wake up!

I. GRACE

It seems that everyone has heard of grace. Perhaps it is the most frequently used concept in Christian circles. Tragically, however, few can tell you what grace means. The non-Christian adage, "God helps those who help themselves," is deeply embedded in the American mind. Because our ancestors dug and clawed a nation out of the wilderness, the American traditionally wants to stand on his own two feet. He feels he must carry his share of the load. All of this is commendable. However, if this spirit carries over into an understanding of grace, it can be eternally fatal.

God has revealed Himself as "the help of the helpless." As long as a person thinks he must contribute his own efforts to the work of God, he does not understand his true condition or the work of Christ. He does not realize that sin has incapacitated him so that he cannot do anything meritorious in God's sight. Neither does he know the sufficiency of Christ's sacrifice. By adding his supposed goodness to the work of our Lord, he is saying he believes Christ's work was insufficient.

Paul's teaching in Romans 11:6 is that grace and works are mutually exclusive: "If by grace, then is it no more of works: otherwise grace is no more grace. But if it be of works, then is it no more grace: otherwise work is no more work." This must be communicated to your prospect if there is to be a good profession. For salvation your prospect may be trusting wholly in Christ, wholly in self, or partially in Christ and partially in self. Many unsaved people who are related to a church fall into the latter category. However, that position is essentially the same as trusting fully in self. "Assuming that Christ has done His part sufficiently, if I am to be saved I must do my part acceptably. If, on the other hand, I am lost, it must be because I did not do enough to win God's favor." This is the logic of partial trust in Christ and partial trust in self. As one has said, "Grace is not the thread of gold decorating the garment; rather, like the ancient mercy seat, it is gold, pure gold, through and through."

A. HEAVEN IS A FREE GIFT

Making this statement just once does not deal with the point. Every religion in the world teaches that man must *earn* the favor of God by doing something. He must qualify himself. He must make himself worthy of God's gifts. In contrast, Christianity proclaims that God's favor, His blessings, and heaven itself can be had only as free gifts. You cannot obliterate the non-Christian concept of making yourself worthy of God's favor by saying the contrary statement only once. Say it numerous times in different ways! "Heaven is free!" "Eternal life is God's gift to you." "His favor is given graciously." "You do not—you cannot—earn your way to heaven." "Never can you deserve to dwell with the holy, sin-hating one." After all this, maybe he will understand—maybe he won't. Pray that God will graciously open the ears of your prospect and give him understanding.

B. IT IS NOT EARNED OR DESERVED

Here you contrast man's way with God's way. Man's way is to try to earn, to deserve, to pay for, or to work for everything. From birth he is programmed to work for everything: grades, rewards, wages, etc. With man, nothing is free. Contrariwise, God's way is grace—to receive freely what we don't deserve (Ephesians 2:8-9). Ask, "How much do you pay for the air you breathe, intelligence, physical life?" If they are all free gifts from God, how much more are eternal life and heaven.

Master and use the illustration about a friend's gift that illustrates that no amount of human effort can earn the free gift of eternal life. Use questions to focus attention, to draw the prospect into the conversation, and to heighten interest: "How good do you suppose I'd have to be to earn my way to heaven?"

Most people don't realize that man cannot save himself; therefore, this truth must be repeated and emphasized many times and in many different ways.

Transitional sentences make the presentation flow smoothly. They point back to what has been said, then point forward to what is going to be discussed next: "This can be seen more clearly when we understand what the Bible says about man."

II. MAN

A. IS A SINNER

Most people know they are sinners, even though they may not realize the seriousness of that accusation. Many times they have heard, "All have sinned." They conclude that sin is something everyone is doing; therefore, it cannot be so bad. "Oh, yes, I'm a sinner. But not so bad a sinner that I can't go to heaven by being reasonably good."

The best way to tell people they are sinners without unnecessary offense is to state the general principle: "All have sinned." Quote Romans 3:23. Define sin. Then use the three-sins-a-day illustration to reveal that though a person may appear to be in pretty good shape with only a few sins a day, by the end of a lifetime that will add up to many sins.

They don't know that because they are sinners and God's standard is perfection, they cannot qualify for heaven.

We must clear the deck. The Scripture says to tear down and to build up. We have to tear away, clear away, the old foundation on which they have built their hope of eternal life before we can build a new one.

B. CANNOT SAVE HIMSELF

In telling a man he is a sinner and cannot save himself, you simply show him that what he has told you will not work. By showing him that God's standard is perfection (Matthew 5:48) and by illustrating with reference to the omelet and the bad egg, you are showing him that a little sin will contaminate the whole life, that he has fallen short of God's standard and is therefore unacceptable to God. Hence, you convey the idea that he needs to hear more of what you are offering him.

It is good at the end of "Grace" to show that what he is trusting in is inadequate—that no one could get to heaven on that basis. You might say, "You understand now that because God's standard is perfection and none of us have come up to it, it is impossible for anyone to get to heaven by doing enough good things?"

His reply would be, "Yes, I do."

Now your prospect has reaffirmed that you not only understood him correctly and knew what he meant when he answered the question as to why God should let him into heaven, but now he sees that what he meant is an impossibility.

The reason this is a good place to do this is that you have not given him anything to substitute for it yet. After you have given him the right answer, he might say, "Oh no! I didn't mean that! I meant this—what you just said." But by the end of point one you haven't given the right answer. All you have done is taken away what he was trusting in formerly.

Occasionally one will disagree with you and say, "No, that's not what I meant." He realizes he may have shown that what he's trusting in is wrong. He may not want to admit this. Your reply in such a situation is, "Wonderful! I'm glad that I found this out now, for I thought that's what you meant. Tell me, what did you mean?" Thus you can get another commitment from him at this point. All he is going to do is point to some other part of himself—that is, to something else in himself that he is trusting in. Then you can continue with the Gospel.

III. GOD

A. IS MERCIFUL; THEREFORE, HE DOESN'T WANT TO PUNISH US

This deals, in the first place, with the good news that God is merciful. He loves us in spite of what we are because of who He is. Use 1 John 4:8 here to underscore that "God is love." You may want to add that He has loved us with an everlasting love (Jeremiah 31:3).

The nature of God is an element left out of many presentations of the Gospel. To leave it out, especially in the present day, deprives the Gospel of much of its meaning. Perhaps two hundred years ago most people had a valid conception of God. This is not true today. Ultimately, most theological heresy is caused by a misconception of the nature of God. When we fail to understand His nature, we cannot understand His Gospel. Many church people hold a Christian Science concept of God as merely love. If this is a person's view of God, he will fit all you say as you present the Gospel into that mold, and it will be meaningless to him. God is love—so what if man is a sinner? God is love—so what if Christ died? God is love—so why worry whether everyone believes in Him since everyone will be saved anyway?

A good response could be to point out that the second commandment is the one most frequently broken today: "Thou shalt not make unto thee any graven images." You may have heard the story of two servicemen who returned to base on Saturday night after a week's leave. They had lived it up wildly during the week and had done everything a serviceman could do on leave. On Sunday morning they went to chapel to find the chaplain preaching on the Ten Commandments. As they were slinking out the door after service, one was heard to say to the other, "Well, at least I ain't made no graven images lately!" But the problem with all he had done, basically, was the fact that he had started with a graven image—not made of wood or stone, but conjured up in the factory of his mind. Men create gods in their own image.

One time I was reading to a lady what God said He would do to the guilty. She said, "Oh, my God would never do that!" After much effort to persuade her otherwise, I finally said, "Madam, you are right. Your god would never do that. The problem is, your god doesn't exist except in your own mind. You have created a god in your own image, according to your own liking, and now you have fallen down and worshiped him. This is idolatry."

This is one of the most prevalent sins of our day. How often have you heard someone say, "God would never do that!" What god wouldn't do it? The God of the Bible? He says a thousand times exactly what He will do. If one says God wouldn't do these things, he is speaking of the god he has made up—a false god.

Therefore, in a time when this heresy is so prevalent, we need to stress the true nature of God—not only that He is loving and kind and merciful, but also that He is holy and cannot condone sin. He is also righteous and has promised to punish sin and visit our iniquity with stripes. It is the nature of God that makes the whole concept of Christ's person and work meaningful.

We have found that we can avoid many arguments on the justice and righteousness of God if we will first deal clearly with the great biblical truth that God is love. And after expounding on His mercy, grace, and love, we can then introduce the subject of His justice by saying that the same Bible that tells us God is merciful and loving also tells us that God . . .

B. IS JUST; THEREFORE, HE MUST PUNISH SIN

Here you deal with the bad news that sinful men must stand before a holy God at the judgment. Most people don't know this, so you may want to use one or all of the following Scriptures:

Exodus 34:7—"[He] will by no means clear the guilty."

Ezekiel 18:4—"The soul that sinneth, it shall die."

Habakkuk 1:13—"Thou art of purer eyes than to behold evil."

Romans 6:23—"The wages of sin is death."

The bank robber illustration used here (see the extended Gospel presentation in chapter 3) illustrates that if human judges are expected to sentence the guilty, how much more should we expect justice from the sovereign God.

The transitional sentence used here is: "God solved this problem in the person of Jesus Christ." The word *problem* used here does not mean some impossible-to-solve difficulty that caught God off guard, but an apparent dilemma in the mind of man that must be resolved.

IV. JESUS CHRIST

A. WHO HE IS: THE INFINITE GOD-MAN

In our society, people know many facts about Jesus of Nazareth, but many do not know that He is divine. When they hear "Jesus is the Son of God," they have some faulty understanding. Perhaps they believe that He is only different in degree from every human being. "Are we not all the sons of God?" they ask. They do not see anything unique about Jesus except that He was more successful than we in keeping God's law and He was a brilliant teacher. For others, the claim that Jesus was the Son of God means that He was more than a man, but they believe He was less than God. In other words, He was God and man mingled in one nature, so He is seen as a superhuman being but not as a fully divine being. We must underscore the truth that the babe of Bethlehem's manger was none other than the Word of creation, the infinitely mighty God who created and sustains heaven and earth and all things. By infinite, we mean limitless and measureless in His attributes.

You may want to lead into this point by asking the prospect who he understands Jesus Christ to be. The use of questions such as this will keep you from a monologue. But if the prospect is already very talkative, such questions might not be necessary.

If the prospect's comments are true but incomplete, such as, "Jesus was a great teacher," avoid telling him he's wrong. Rather, say, "Yes, and He was also the Son of God," etc. Thus you will build upon the prospect's reply with a positive response.

B. WHAT HE DID: HE DIED ON THE CROSS AND ROSE FROM THE DEAD TO PAY THE PENALTY FOR OUR SINS AND TO PURCHASE A PLACE IN HEAVEN FOR US

Nearly everyone we meet knows that Jesus died on the cross of Calvary. Relatively few are aware of the significance of that death according to the teaching of the Scriptures. The death of Christ has no meaning for a man until the concept of imputation grasps his soul as it did Luther's. One must see that his sins were laid to Christ. He must realize that Christ assumed his guilt. As Paul put it, God made Christ to be sin for us that we might be made the righteousness of God in Him. The Cross has meaning for a man when he knows that his guilt was imputed to the Son by the Father, and when he knows, further, that the Father laid upon the Son the hell that every sinner deserves. Let a man see his sin laid on Christ on the cross and then that cross has meaning for him.

A word about visual illustrations is in order here. It is very helpful if we enable the person to whom we are speaking not only to hear the Gospel but to see it, as well. This can be accomplished with illustrations, that is, the employment of concrete objects in action situations. Examples of such illustrations are the following:

1. The record book illustration. The transference of the "record book" from the hand representing self to the hand representing Christ, and the subsequent falling of the wrath of God upon that sin. This is used to illustrate what Christ has done for us.

2. The chair illustration. This illustrates the transference of our trust from what we have done (indicated by the chair in which we are then sitting) to what Christ has done for us (visualized by another chair in the room, to which we transfer our weight). This is an illustration of saving faith.

3. The motive for living a godly life. In this illustration a pen or small vase or other object from the person's table may be used to represent the gift of eternal life. This illustrates that one's efforts to do good works are done out of gratitude for the gift received rather than in an effort to obtain it. This illustration is placed at the very end of the presentation in order to fit good works into their proper place since everyone knows that good works have something to do with Christianity. It is important that we put them in their proper place, or else the person may put them in an improper place.

In using a visual illustration, it is important for the witness to fix his own eyes on the object he is using rather than looking at the person to whom he is speaking. This will call the listener's attention to the illustration and enable him to properly understand it.

4. Tetelestai. The primary meaning of the Greek word is "it is finished." But according to papyri commercial documents found in Egypt the word *tetelestai* was printed across an item that had been paid in full. Hence, it can be said that when Jesus said, "It is finished," He was also declaring that by His death He paid the penalty for our sins.

V. FAITH

The subject of faith is crucial, for this is the point of personal appropriation of eternal life. John Calvin said that the Roman Catholic Church taught him the deity of Christ, the Trinity, the Atonement; but the one thing the church did not teach him was how to appropriate the Atonement for himself. Even today there are those who know all of the doctrines of the faith, but they don't know how to get eternal life for themselves. Their problem: an inadequate or false concept of saving faith.

Theologians have rightly pointed out that there are three elements to saving faith: knowledge, assent, and trust. We may know *about* something without giving assent to it. For example, one cult teaches that Christ is incarnate today in a man in India. I know about this, but I do not assent to it. Similarly, one may have the knowledge that the Bible teaches that man is a sinner who cannot save himself without assenting to the truth of this statement. Thus, to knowledge must be added *assent* to the facts of our historic faith. However, one can know about and assent to many historical facts without *trusting* them. We know about Alexander the Great and assent to the historical record concerning his conquests. Further, we assent to the fact that he was a military genius. However, I hope no one is trusting Alexander to do anything for him! That would be rather ludicrous. Added to knowledge and assent is what Luther termed *fiducia*: trust.

A. WHAT SAVING FAITH IS NOT

Before you share what saving faith is, it is important to deal with what it is not. It is not *mere intellectual assent*. Many people believe in God's existence in much the same way as people believe in George Washington or Napoleon. The devil believes in God's existence (James 2:19), and demons believed in Christ's deity (Matthew 8:29), but simply assenting to those facts will not take them to heaven.

Furthermore, saving faith is not *mere temporal faith*. Temporal faith is trusting Christ for temporary emergencies or needs of this life, such as for sickness, financial pressures, traveling dangers, or major decisions. Such faith is good, as far as it goes, but it can save no one.

B. WHAT IT IS—TRUSTING JESUS CHRIST ALONE FOR OUR SALVATION

It is important to define saving faith clearly as trusting Christ alone for eternal life. You can effectively illustrate the meaning of saving faith with the use of an empty chair. Let that chair represent the Lord Jesus. Your prospect knows it is a chair. He believes (assents) that the chair will hold him off the floor, provide comfort to his body, and relax his weary spirit. But it's not doing any of these things for one obvious reason: He's not sitting in it. Neither is that chair of any benefit to you for the same reason. Now the chair in which you are sitting can represent all you once trusted for eternal life. Point out that this is inadequate for your needs, and when God shakes the world in the final judgment, it will drop you into hell.

By actually moving from the "chair of your own good works" to the "chair of Jesus Christ," you visually and verbally illustrate the meaning of trusting Christ alone for salvation. Just as you are no longer in the "chair of your good works" but in the "chair of Jesus Christ," so you have transferred your trust for eternal life from yourself to the Lord.

As we said above, a more subtle substitute for saving faith is trusting the Lord for temporal well-being while trusting self for eternal life. Some have difficulty making this distinction, but the distinction is necessary. It spells the difference between weal and woe eternally.

Let us consider Martin Luther. Before his conversion, he was not an agnostic skeptic or atheist. He believed in God. While in the monastery, he undoubtedly trusted God for many things. When he made the pilgrimage to Rome, did he not trust the Lord for safety, lodging and meals, and health? Certainly! Similarly, John Wesley trusted the Lord to take him safely from England to his mission post in the New World. All the while, these men were trusting themselves for a successful journey from earth to heaven! They knew about and trusted in "transportation by faith" long before they knew and trusted "justification by faith."

You can use the "chair of Jesus Christ" to illustrate the concept of trusting Him for temporal matters. As you restate that your prospect was trusting God for health, you can place glasses or a pen on the "chair of Jesus Christ." Trusting Him for travel mercies can be represented by a key ring. A billfold will indicate trust in God for financial needs. All the while, the prospect is still sitting in the "chair of his own good works." He is still trusting in himself for the eternal well-being of his soul.

Before leaving the point of faith, it is important to explain the role of good works and the motive for godly living. You may want to explain that, as the president of Princeton once said, we do not do good works to gain eternal life, we do them out of gratitude for eternal life. I think this is an excellent illustration for several reasons. First, it recapitulates the essence of the Gospel, which is good. You tell them what you're going to tell them, as well as what you have already told them. Because they know good works has to be in there somewhere, when you finally put good works in the right place, they grasp it. Second, using this illustration is good because it is visual and easy to understand. Third, it comes from a very authoritative figure. It is not just my opinion—it is that of the president of Princeton. Fourth, it is expressed in what I think is a memorable statement: "All the rest of my life was simply a P.S. to that day."

Eight

CALLING FOR COMMITMENT

The commitment is like landing an airplane and requires very careful training to be done effectively. Because it will be seen less often than the other parts of the presentation, and because of satanic pressures and distractions, it should be practiced twice as often and learned very carefully.

It is the "hinge" part of the presentation, refocusing from what the person understands about the Gospel to what you want him to do. All that precedes the commitment is aimed toward it, and all that follows is determined by the prospect's response to the commitment.

Many witnesses are afraid to ask for a commitment because they are not well prepared, or they don't know if they have brought the prospect with them in understanding the Gospel, or they fear rejection.

We should remember that it is only the Holy Spirit who can bring a person to repentance and faith, so even as we are inviting the person to accept Christ, we should be praying to the Holy Spirit to enable the prospect to do so.

If you learn the commitment section well, you will not be distracted when the phone rings, someone spills the coffee, or an unexpected person enters the room.

I. THE QUALIFYING QUESTION

"Does this make sense to you?" Many people are afraid to ask for a commitment when they finish presenting the Gospel because they do not know whether they have brought the person with them or have lost him somewhere along the way. The qualifying question, "Does this make sense to you?" will elicit a response which is either positive or negative. A positive response will be something of this sort: "Oh, yes, that is wonderful! Why didn't I hear it before?" etc. A negative response will be something like: "Well, that is very complicated. I will have to give this a lot of thought. I'm not sure. . . ."

What to do: If the response is positive, you know that the person is with you, and you are ready to ask the commitment question. If the response is uncertain, go back to the beginning and quickly review the main points of the Gospel, asking as you go, "Do you understand this point, 'Man is a sinner'?" etc. Whatever you do, don't ask, "What doesn't make sense?" because that would open a door for all kinds of extraneous discussion that will not benefit your prospect's understanding or response. Asking the qualifying question provides you with an opportunity to tailor the Gospel to the prospect's particular needs for understanding the Gospel.

II. THE COMMITMENT QUESTION

"Would you like to receive the gift of eternal life?" It is important to know exactly how you are going to ask for the commitment and even what words you are going to use. For the inexperienced, this is a tense moment, and therefore the commitment question should be thoroughly learned. This will help the novice through his anxiety. Tensions can be eased at this point by having each team member pray silently. The importance of the question may be highlighted by leading into the question with the statement, "You have just heard the greatest story ever told, about the greatest offer ever made, by the greatest person who ever lived, and this raises the greatest question you will ever have to answer. Would you like to receive the gift of eternal life?"

A. THE WORDING OF THE COMMITMENT QUESTION

By using this question, you are coming out of the Gospel at the same place you went in. That is, you began your presentation by asking the person if he would like for you to share with him how he could have eternal life. Having done that, and having ascertained that he understood, you are now asking him if he would like to receive this eternal life.

You are asking for the initial commitment at the most positive point possible. "Would you like to receive the free gift of eternal life?" This is obviously a better place to begin than saying something like, "Would you like to crucify your old nature?"

B. EXPECT A POSITIVE RESPONSE

If the person responds, "No," or "Not yet," you may be able to discover the underlying cause for delay and deal with it by asking the following nonthreatening question: "I'd be interested to know, if you were to receive the gift of eternal life today, what difficulties do you foresee you might meet?"

C. DEALING WITH A NEGATIVE RESPONSE

If the Gospel is rejected, make your exit sweet, remembering that it is the Gospel, not you, that has been rejected.

III. THE CLARIFICATION OF COMMITMENT

One danger at the point of closing is that the novice may be afraid to ask for a commitment. To overcome the hesitancy to close, we have endeavored to make it as simple and as pleasant as possible.

However, another danger at the point of closing is a premature commitment—a commitment which is not based on a thorough understanding of what is involved in accepting Christ as Savior and Lord. Therefore, at this point we recommend clarification, which would involve, essentially, the series of statements and questions found in the clarification of commitment section of the presentation. These statements and questions elaborate on the meaning of faith and will help confirm the prospect's desire for such a commitment.

He is asked if he is willing to transfer his trust from what he has been doing to Christ alone. He is asked if he is ready to receive the resurrected and living Christ. He is asked if he would like to receive Him into his life as Savior and Lord. And he is asked if he is willing to repent from what he has been doing that is not pleasing to God.

The emphasis given at this point will depend upon the attitude of the person to whom you are speaking. If he is evidently repentant and moved, perhaps even to tears (as occasionally has been the case), this need not be belabored. If, however, the person seems to be thinking that he just might get in on a good deal without its affecting his life, the aspect of repentance and the lordship of Christ should be heavily emphasized.

IV. THE PRAYER OF COMMITMENT

The gift of eternal life is received by faith. Prayer is one way of expressing that faith. The apostle Paul stated it this way: "With the heart man believeth unto righteousness; and with the mouth confession is made unto salvation. . . . For whosoever shall call upon the name of the Lord shall be saved" (Romans 10:10, 13). The prospect needs to know that you will help him express his faith in a simple prayer.

Many commitments have been lost at this point because of the way prospects were asked to pray. Adults who have been in church for many years should know how to pray, but many have never prayed audibly in their lives. They are horrified at the thought of having to pray spontaneously in front of a stranger. Therefore, in asking them to pray, I have found the following wording very helpful (note especially the pronouns):

Well, Rene, if this is really what *you* want, *we* can go to the Lord in prayer right where we are. *I* can lead *us* in prayer, and *we* will tell Him what you have told me just now—that you want Christ to come into your heart to be your Savior and Lord and that you want to repent of your sins and receive the gift of eternal life. Is this really what you want, Rene?

Yes, it is.

All right, then, let us bow our heads in prayer.

In the prayer itself, I recommend three parts that are helpful:

1. Pray for her that God would give her faith and repentance.

2. Pray with her in short phrases of the Gospel outline, allowing her to repeat after you.

3. Pray for her, that the Holy Spirit will grant her assurance. Give the Spirit of God some time to seal these things to her heart (an example of such a prayer is at the end of the longer presentation).

V. THE ASSURANCE OF SALVATION

At this point it is important to direct the new believer to the promises of God and help him take hold of them by faith. A very simple and forthright promise that we almost always use is John 6:47. After the prayer, the witness might say something like this:

Rene, that was the most important prayer you have ever prayed and the most important decision you have ever made. I would like to show you what Christ has to say about what you have just done. (Open your New Testament and let her read aloud John 6:47. After she reads it, say:)

Hold that place for a moment and let us analyze that carefully. It is Christ the Son of God, the King of the kingdom, who is speaking. He says, "Verily, verily, I say unto you, he that believeth on me hath [that is Old English for 'has'] everlasting life." We have shown that this is not merely an intellectual assent—you have had that all of your life—but it is placing your trust in Christ *alone* for your salvation. Christ is saying (paraphrased), "He that trusteth in Me alone for salvation, he that resteth upon Me for eternal life, *has* (a present possession) eternal life." Some people think that means a continued existence somewhere, somehow, but eternal life in the Bible always means "in heaven."

Now, Rene, you just told Christ in your prayer that you trust Him alone for your salvation. As best you know your heart, Rene, did you really mean that?

Yes.

Well, Rene, do you believe that Jesus Christ meant what He said in this promise you just read?

I do.

Then let me ask you this question: If you died tonight in your sleep—and you just might—where would you wake up?

In heaven.

Who said so?

Jesus Christ.

Rene, now if you were to meet God at heaven's gate and He were to ask you "Why should I let you into My heaven?" what would you say?

I'd say, I'm trusting in Jesus Christ as my Savior.

(Reaching over and shaking her hand . . .) If you really meant in your heart what you just said in that prayer, then you have the promise of Jesus Christ that your sins are forgiven; He has adopted you into His family and has given you eternal life. (The "if" clause is inserted here in order not to give the person a false assurance. We are saved by trusting in Jesus Christ, not by *saying* that we trust in Jesus Christ.) Let me welcome you, Rene, to the family of God.

Nine

DISCIPLING
NEW BELIEVERS

The great commission commands us to make disciples, not merely to get decisions. To go with the Gospel is only the beginning. To disciple another properly requires a vision of what the grace of God can do with a sinner. The apostle John said to his spiritual offspring, "I have no greater joy than to hear that my children walk in truth" (3 John 1:4). Those who are satisfied with merely proclaiming the Gospel and receiving professions are like immoral seducers. The seducer is satisfied merely to exploit and then tell of his exploits rather than entering into a meaningful marriage commitment. Do not judge the effectiveness of your evangelism and discipleship by what you see in the person you have evangelized. Measure your effectiveness by your spiritual grandchildren. If those you evangelize and disciple produce good disciples who can disciple others, then you have done your job well. A disciple is a functional, maturing, reproducing follower of Jesus Christ.

I. RESPONSIBILITY

The responsibility for discipleship is twofold: First, it is the responsibility of the individual evangelist and the team who leads the new believer to Christ; second, it is the responsibility of the local church family. I will deal with the individual evangelist's responsibility in this chapter and with the local church's in the next chapter.

The "parent" who was present at the time of "birth" is the person who should also nurture the new believer toward maturity. Until you have done everything possible to develop your disciple into a vital, reproducing member of the local church, your responsibilities are not fulfilled.

Occasionally a new believer and the spiritual parent may encounter difficulty relating to each other due to differences in age, gender, personality, schedules, etc.

When this becomes evident, the spiritual parent should take the initiative to place the new convert up for "adoption."

First, attempt to enlist another person on the witnessing team to take this responsibility. If this is not feasible, check to see if another E.E. participant, including the parent's prayer partner, is available. In any case, never leave the spiritual offspring as an orphan.

II. PREREQUISITES

To produce functional, maturing, reproducing followers of Jesus Christ, the discipler must meet a number of prerequisites.

A. EFFECTIVE EVANGELISM

It has been well said that the best follow-up begins with effective evangelism. The Gospel must be proclaimed without compromise. But persons must be respected and communicated to in a way that enables them to intelligently accept or reject the Gospel. Our Lord indicates in the parable of the sower that those who reproduce 30, 60, and 100 percent are the ones who heard the Gospel with understanding (Matthew 13:23). It is impossible to disciple or follow up properly on someone who has not been effectively evangelized. A spiritually stillborn person has no new life to develop.

B. HEART

Paul said to his spiritual children in Thessalonica, "We were gentle among you, even as a nurse cherisheth her children. So being affectionately desirous of you, we were willing to have imparted unto you, not the Gospel of God only, but also our own souls" (1 Thessalonians 2:7-8). To be a parent requires a Godlike love.

It requires a special kind of love for parents to care properly for helpless infants. When infants are hungry or thirsty or when their diapers are dirty, they cry out for attention—regardless of the time. Unless parents care for the child with a Godlike unselfish love, the child will not become what it was meant to be.

Likewise, rearing spiritual children to become mature disciples requires a special Godlike love—giving, unconditional, sleepless! Scripture says, "We love him, because he first loved us" (1 John 4:19). The more you open yourself to God's love, the more it can flow through you to those who need it.

C. PERSPECTIVE

Ask God to give you an eternal, heavenly perspective on life. Endure "as seeing him who is invisible" (Hebrews 11:27). Move toward the city "whose builder and maker is God" (Hebrews 11:10). With eternity's values in view, we are much more willing to let God's grace mold our lives and make us into models for discipling others.

D. WORK

There is more glamour and adventure in evangelism than there is in developing mature disciples. To the Colossians, Paul said, "Whom we preach, warning every man, and teaching every man in all wisdom; that we may present every man perfect in Christ Jesus: *Whereunto I also labour, striving according to his working, which worketh in me mightily*" (Colossians 1:28-29). Discipling requires expenditure of energy. It is laborious, hard work, but it is also rewarding. Paul urged, "Therefore, my beloved brethren, be ye stedfast, unmoveable, always abounding in the work of the Lord, forasmuch as ye know that your labour is not in vain in the Lord" (1 Corinthians 15:58).

E. RELATIONSHIPS

It is loving, caring people—not materials and programs—that make disciples. Non-personal media such as books and tapes are only tools. They may supplement, but they can never become a substitute for personal communication. Without relational involvement, your follow-up and discipling will be like a robot caring for an infant.

Proper relationships begin with your own relationship to the Lord. Christ has made you a new creature (2 Corinthians 5:17). You are acceptable to God the Father in Him (Ephesians 1:6). If God the Son—the righteous judge of the universe—accepts you, who can condemn you? (Romans 8:31-35). As you accept His acceptance of you in Christ, you are free to grow.

As you walk with Christ, you should be a model of dedication for those you are seeking to disciple. This is not empty egotism but the authentic demonstration of redeemed humanity. There is what Luther called an alien dignity that God gives to His people. Paul, writing to the Thessalonians, said, "Not because we have not power, but to make ourselves an ensample unto you to follow us" (2 Thessalonians 3:9). To the Philippians he said, "Brethren, be followers together of me" (Philippians 3:17). To the Corinthians he declared, "Be ye followers of me, even as I also am of Christ" (1 Corinthians 11:1). Whether you like it or not, you are going to multiply "after your kind." Therefore be sure you are the kind that should be multiplied.

III. PROCEDURE

It is not enough to do a job right. The right job must be done in the right way. Let me share with you now the procedure we find most effective.

A. ASSURANCE SCRIPTURE

Immediately following the new believer's prayer to receive Christ as Savior, you, the evangelist, must help him understand what the Bible says concerning assurance of salvation. The Scripture I use for this is John 6:47: "Verily, verily, I say unto you, he that believeth on me hath everlasting life." John said that the Scriptures were written so that we could know we have eternal life (1 John 5:13). You cannot guarantee assurance to each new believer—it is the believer's responsibility to make his own calling and election sure (2 Peter 1:10). Nevertheless, you must make certain the believer understands the promise of assurance as the Word of God presents it.

B. PARTNERS IN GROWING

You should take the booklet *Partners in Growing* and say to the new believer, "This is for you." You are about to ask him to sign a decision card he will keep.

Ask him to read the inside cover of the booklet: "My Spiritual Birth Certificate." Ask, "Is this the decision you have made?" Write your name and phone number on the certificate first, then ask the new believer to sign the card, also.

The pages in the booklet that follow give printed guidance for the new believer. The key sentences are printed in bold type to provide help for the evangelist and lighten his learning load. Read aloud the bold type reviewing the main points of the Gospel. Continuing with the bold type, emphasize the . . .

C. FIVE MEANS OF GROWTH

It is important to help new Christians understand that God wants them to grow and has provided the means for that spiritual growth:

1. Bible. Reading in the booklet 1 Peter 2:2, stress the importance of the Bible. Give him a Gospel of John. Challenge him to read one chapter a day from John. Tell him that as he reads, he may encounter something he doesn't understand. Suggest that he put a question mark in the margin. At this point offer to come back for a seven-day callback to answer those questions. By making your appointment at this time, the new believer understands that your motive for returning is to further his understanding and growth.

2. Prayer. Continue reading the bold type about prayer. Explain that prayer is simply conversing with God; therefore, simple language from the heart expressing our love to God, our gratefulness to Him for eternal life, and asking Him about various needs that may arise in our daily life is appropriate.

3. Worship. As you read about worship, offer to meet him for a worship service next Lord's Day. Ask if he needs a ride or would prefer to meet you at the main entrance of the church. If he is already attending a Bible-teaching church, encourage him to continue to worship there faithfully.

4. Fellowship. Stress the importance of fellowship. Someone once suggested that fellowship is "two or more fellows on the same ship." Emphasize every Christian's need for spending time with fellow believers for mutual encouragement, growth, and strength. You may also want to invite him for dinner after worshiping together on Sunday.

5. Witness. Finally, read the bold type stressing the importance of new believers confessing their faith to others through witnessing. Ask, "Who will be the first person you will want to tell about this decision?" and then, "Is that person a Christian?" You may be able to aid him in presenting the Gospel to friends or family.

At the back of the booklet, you will find John 3:16 and an opportunity to personalize that great promise from Christ. There is also a simple Bible study based on the Gospel of John in the booklet.

As you part, ask for any prayer requests and be sure to pray for them with the team later in the car or back at the church.

D. WHAT YOU CAN DO

1. Pray. Intelligent procedure begins and ends with prayer. Paul said, "Night and day praying exceedingly that we might see your face, and might perfect that which is lacking in your faith" (1 Thessalonians 3:10). "We pray always for you, that our God would count you worthy of this calling, and fulfil all the good pleasure of his goodness, and the work of faith with power" (2 Thessalonians 1:11).

By prayer you may pursue every person with whom you have opportunity to share the Gospel. God will move in response to your petitions and work through the circumstances that surround them.

2. Correspond. Intelligent procedure also utilizes written correspondence. Most of the New Testament epistles are follow-up letters. Correspondence can be used to reinforce personal contact or to maintain contact with individuals who are too far away to disciple personally.

3. Telephone. People who can be discipled into the local church should be called by one of the team members within twenty-four hours. This should be brief and friendly. Remember to smile whenever you talk on the phone. This makes your tone of voice more pleasant.

If the phone call is to someone who has made a profession of faith, indicate that you are glad you had the opportunity to meet him, you are looking forward to seeing him at church on Sunday, you hope he will enjoy the Bible study group at church, and you are looking forward to getting better acquainted next week when you visit again.

If the phone call is to someone who did not make a profession of faith but is still open, tell him how much you enjoyed getting a chance to meet him and that you are looking forward to seeing him at church on Sunday. Say that you hope he will enjoy "The Truth and the Life" class and that you are looking forward to seeing him again and will answer any questions he has after reading the Gospel of John.

If your team contacted a person who was already a Christian but not active in a local church, when you phone tell him you were glad to meet him, you are looking forward to seeing him at church on Sunday, you are sure he will enjoy the adult class in the School for Christian Living (use whatever name you have for the particular class rather than just "adult Sunday school"), and you are looking forward to getting better acquainted with him in the weeks to come.

Saturday afternoon or evening is a good time to make a second phone contact with those who can be discipled into the life of your local church. A call should be made by a team member who has not written or phoned before. It is probably best if the team member who is going to sit with him is the one who phones on Saturday. Briefly, pleasantly tell him you are looking forward to seeing him at church on Sunday and confirm the time and place you are to meet.

4. Loan cassette tapes. Cassette recordings can be a valuable way of ministering to spiritual needs. But remember that nonpersonal media, such as cassette tapes, must supplement personal, face-to-face ministering.

One advantage of cassette tapes over printed material is that voice inflection emphasizes things in a way that cannot be done in printed matter.

Quality cassette recordings can sometimes enable you to be more effective in follow-up than you might be otherwise. If you can effectively evangelize but are not a very good teacher, you can use materials recorded by good teachers. Then you can discuss the material, and both you and the tape listener will learn.

The best tapes for follow-up are not recordings of public presentations. A person speaking to a group gears his presentation to the group. When one person listens to a tape, for maximum impact the presentation should be geared to him as an individual.

If you can afford it, begin your own tape ministry. When you lend a tape and mention that it is your personal tape, people are more likely to listen to it. However, if you cannot afford to develop your own tape ministry, urge your church to develop a lending library. For follow-up, it is essential to have a number of tape players available for lending. Of course, if you lend tapes and players belonging to the church, you should assume responsibility to return them so others may use them.

When a new Christian listens to a good, taped Bible teaching within twenty-four hours of his profession of faith, he will get off to a good, healthy start. He will be more likely to continue growing and become a vital part of the local church. Many people who will not complete written studies will listen to tapes. Sometimes tapes have an impact on other members of the household also.

Listening to the tape in private helps prepare for involvement in a small group later. Wisely selected, properly prepared tapes can be effectively used in get-acquainted coffees or home Bible-study groups.

This Is the Life is a series of taped messages prepared for new believers. It contains six thirty-minute presentations on the following topics:

- Knowing You Are Going to Heaven
- Staying Right with God
- Getting into the Bible
- Practicing the Art of Prayer
- Continuing in Fellowship
- Transforming the World

Cassette tapes are also very useful with responsive non-Christians. If the person has a question, lend him a tape that deals in depth with that question. This can be an effective means of maintaining contact and witness. Offer to loan the tape with the understanding that you want to discuss it after it has been listened to.

Sometimes the person will listen with more attention to a tape than he will to you. People cannot interrupt and argue with the tape; therefore, they tend to listen with more attention.

Be sure you listen to any tape you give away before you share it with someone else.

These tapes can be left at the time of the profession or within twenty-four hours. In some cases, they can be loaned out during the seven-day callback. Delivering the tapes within twenty-four hours after a profession of faith also gives opportunity for brief face-to-face personal contact, so you can affirm what has happened in the person's life the day before.

IV. SEVEN-DAY CALLBACK

The first week of a new believer's life is extremely important. What happens then usually has a great effect on future development. But the work has just begun. Your responsibilities are not fulfilled until you have done everything possible to develop your disciple into a vital, reproducing member of the local church.

The normal time to make your seven-day callback visit is during your regular E.E. visitation time and with the same team members. A checklist of procedures is printed for your convenience and should be read en route to the visit so the team knows exactly how to participate. I suggest the following steps:

A. INTRODUCTION

1. Reintroduce team
2. How has your week been?
3. Church—last Sunday

B. PERSONAL TESTIMONY

A team member shares his New Christian testimony.

C. TWO QUESTIONS

1. God's "Why?"
2. Assurance

D. GROWTH

Ask if he's used the means for growth.
  1. Bible
     • Daily reading (underline, question marks)
     • Promise memorized
     • Tapes listened to
     • Bible group ("Starter Series")
  2. Prayer
     • *Partners in Praying*[1]
     • Enlist person as your prayer partner
  3. Worship—next Sunday
  4. Fellowship—Sunday dinner

[1] *Partners in Praying* is a special booklet available through Evangelism Explosion that explains the E.E. prayer partner ministry.

5. Witness—family and friends (Acts 16:31)
6. Satan (1 John 4:4)

E. PARTING PRAYER

V. THE LOCAL CHURCH FAMILY

Remember that by spiritual birth, new believers become members of a family. They have new brothers and sisters who will need to extend to them the love, care, and fellowship so essential to their growth, health, and assimilation into the family.

In the next chapter we will discuss how the church as a family can aid in the discipling process and contribute vitally to the new believer's growth and health.

Ten

FOLDING INTO THE CHURCH

Discipling of the new believer begins with the individual evangelist and his team. They are the "spiritual parents" who were present at the time of "birth" and are responsible for initiating the discipling of their younger brother or sister in Christ.

But the discipling process continues as the evangelism team introduces the new believer to the local church. I said it before, and I need to say it again: Your responsibilities as a spiritual parent are not fulfilled until you have done everything possible to develop your disciple into a vital, reproducing member of a local church.

The church is a family—the forever family of God! It is composed of the young and the old, the mature and the not-so-mature. A healthy local church is where discipleship continues. New Christians are not orphans to be institutionalized, nor do they join the "Christian country club." They are born into the family of God. The local church is the microcosm of that universal family, so it is in the context of the local church—God's forever family—that the new believer will find the environment he needs to continue growing and serving the Lord. But what kind of church environment will best enhance the new disciple's spiritual life and growth?

I. A HEALTHY ENVIRONMENT

A newborn baby, to enjoy healthy development, needs the warmth, love, and security of his parents' arms; the nurture of his mother's milk; opportunity to exercise his limbs, eyes, ears, and vocal chords; warm room temperature; fresh air; and regular bathing.

A young plant needs good soil, water, sunlight, fertilizer, cultivation, favorable temperature, and loving care. Likewise, a new Christian, to thrive and develop into a mature disciple, has some basic "environmental" requirements.

A. A HEALTHY BODY

In 1 Corinthians 12:27 the church is called the "body of Christ." The entire twelfth chapter describes what a healthy body should be like. Its members will reflect spirituality (vv. 1-3), diversity (vv. 4-11), unity (vv. 12-13), necessity of each member's involvement (vv. 14-24), charity (vv. 25-26), and ministry (vv. 27-28). To be healthy, a local church must also be a place where the Word is properly proclaimed (2 Timothy 4:2), and where baptism (Acts 2:38), the Lord's Supper (1 Corinthians 11:23-26), and biblical church discipline are administered (Matthew 18:15-18; Galatians 6:1).

B. MOTIVATED BY LOVE

An environment of love is absolutely crucial in order for new believers to grow. I don't think it's accidental that the chapter in 1 Corinthians describing a healthy body is followed by one on love! When new believers start attending your church, it's important that you share with them your church's Statement of *Faith*. But what kind of Statement of *Love* do they find? Do they say of your church what was said of the early church, "Behold how they love each other"? Do they feel truly loved by their new brothers and sisters in God's forever family? This certainly is a goal worthy of aspiration. You are to be motivated by love in all that you do. As you are motivated by love, you best reflect the God who is love. Thus motivated, you will seek to discover the gifts the Spirit bestows within His Body. Then you will use those gifts within the local body where he has placed you to edify one another and to build up new believers in their newfound faith. Speaking of the Holy Spirit, let me add that a healthy environment will be marked by a . . .

C. BALANCE OF THE WORD AND SPIRIT

Genuine discipleship requires acceptance of Scripture as God's Word and reliance upon the Holy Spirit to enable you to be all you were meant to be. You will never be more filled with the Spirit (Ephesians 5:18-19) than you are filled with God's Word (Colossians 3:16).

Do not seek to be saturated with Scripture and ignore the Spirit of love. You will become an argumentative pharisee, harsh and abrasive. On the other hand, don't totally concentrate on the Spirit of love without the objective truth of God's Word. You will become an emotional, unstable, ignorant fanatic. God wants you to walk in obedience. He wants you to give as much of yourself as you can to as much of Christ as you know, on a daily basis.

D. PROPER PRIORITIES

This balance of the Word and the Spirit will enable you to have proper priorities. Proper priorities will enable you to use your time effectively and become what God intended you to be and do what He wants you to do. In general, priorities are the important things God wants us to do, in contrast to the urgent things pressing upon us to be done. In John 17, Jesus prayed to the Father for His followers, to whom He was about to say farewell and who would become the pillars of His church. In His prayer, Jesus gives His church His order of priorities for all time.

1. God. "That they might know thee the only true God, and Jesus Christ, whom thou hast sent" (John 17:3). Jesus also said, "Thou shalt love the Lord thy God with all thy heart, and with all thy soul, and with all thy mind" (Matthew 22:37) and "Seek ye first the kingdom of God, and his righteousness" (Matthew 6:33).

2. God's people. "I have manifested thy name unto the men which thou gavest me out of the world" (John 17:6). When you are in proper relationship with God, it will show itself by your being in proper relation with His people. This means visible identification with them. Worship in the celebrating assembly. Participate in group Bible studies. There you discover your gifts and use them. You find a soul friend and grow together toward maturity. You partake of the vital life in small cell groups, and your life is transformed.

3. God's world: "As thou hast sent me into the world, even so have I also sent them into the world" (John 17:18). God leaves us here for the purpose of bearing witness to the world. God wants us to change the world, to bring His love into the lives of others and His truth into the whole of life. Our relationship to God and His people will be perfect in heaven. We were eligible to enter heaven the moment we trusted Christ. Therefore, we must still be here to be channels through which He can reach those in the world who are yet to believe.

E. GODLY LEADERSHIP

A healthy environment is one where there is a core of people committed to God's priorities, evidencing a balance between the Word and the Spirit, expressing genuine love for each other and for new believers, and following godly leaders. A true leader is one who influences followers to achieve a purpose. And one of the principal ways a church leader influences followers—be they new believers or mature—is by godly example. The recognized leaders of the local church must be models of discipleship, so that those who are less mature will see the truth of God's Word in their lives and more easily duplicate their dedication.

II. GROUP INVOLVEMENT

New believers desperately need group involvement! They cannot live or grow in a vacuum. They cannot become true disciples apart from vital relationships with fellow believers in a local church. Someone has said that it's inconceivable that anyone would want to spend eternity with God's people in heaven if he doesn't enjoy being with them for a brief time here on earth. New believers need loving, caring, edifying relationships with God's people—both with individuals and in groups.

Part of a congregation's responsibility of folding new believers into the church is providing such opportunities for individual and group involvement. I said it before, but it's so important that I need to repeat it here. It is people—loving, caring people—that make disciples, not printed materials, taped messages, or effective methods and procedures. So what are some group involvements a church can provide for new believers?

A. GET-ACQUAINTED COFFEE

The get-acquainted coffee is an informal social situation to allow new Christians to become acquainted with each other and with older Christians. Also, responsive seeking people who have not professed faith should be invited. This gives them opportunity to see more of the implications of the Christian faith. It may be all that is necessary to bring them to trust Christ. A get-acquainted coffee should have both a leader and a host who will hold the coffee in his home. The leader should be a mature Christian with experience in working in small groups.

The format is very flexible and spontaneous, but there are specific things that should be accomplished. The leader should set a very friendly atmosphere. Serving coffee and light refreshments helps people relax. The leader should steer the conversation so that Christians can share a word of personal testimony. For many new Christians, this gives an opportunity to express their faith for the first time in a small group. Prayerfully choose your host or hostess and leader. Work with only one group at a time, and do not add more groups until the need is obvious.

B. SUNDAY MORNING WORSHIP

During your immediate follow-up conversation, one team member should offer to transport the person to church or meet him at a particular place so they can sit together. Usually it is overpowering for all three team members to sit with the new person in the morning worship. But it is important for one team member, and possibly his family, to sit with the new person.

During the worship service, help make the worship more meaningful to him. He may not bring a Bible, so share yours with him. He may not be familiar with the hymnbook. He may be embarrassed by ignorance of the worship. The more formal your worship is, the more important it is for you to sit with him and help him. After the service, introduce him to other church members. Help him develop as many personal relationships with Christians as possible.

C. BASICS CLASSES FOR NEW BELIEVERS

New believers need to be informed very quickly on three basic things:

1. How to properly feed on the Word of God
2. How to keep their lives clean before God
3. How to properly relate to the family of God

With an effective evangelism ministry you may have professions of faith almost every week. Therefore, it is wise to have these topics taught individually or in self-contained classes. You may want to offer this basics class during your Sunday school hour. Each class should stand alone, without need of any prerequisites. Then a new believer may enter the class the Sunday following his profession of faith regardless of which topic is being taught that week. E.E. offers a new study book entitled *Partners in Discipleship,* which covers these topics and other basic subjects for new believers. The study book can be used for one-on-one discipleship or group study.

When the new believer has finished this basics class, the next step is a "This Is the Life" class. I have prepared tapes and a book for this class which can be ordered from the E.E. International office. The subjects covered are assurance/cleansing, Bible, prayer, worship, fellowship, and witnessing. The content of both classes is such that a new believer can enter at any point.

Do not call the class by any name that indicates it is for "new believers." Very few will attend if this is done. Instead, call it the "Christian Adventure Class" or "Discovery Class" or "New Beginnings Class" or something of that nature.

After completing these classes offering spiritual "milk," the new believer can pretty well fit into most other Sunday school classes or Bible study groups. However, new believers should not indiscriminately be placed into classes. If possible, new Christians should be placed in classes that are taught sequentially so that their understanding can develop and they can handle heavier concepts. That brings us to . . .

D. SCHOOL FOR CHRISTIAN LIVING

The school for Christian living, or, as many churches call it, Sunday school, is a very important part of the church life. It provides not only an opportunity for more personalized education in the Word of God and Christian living but also gives opportunity for dividing into small subcongregations. New Christians should be encouraged to attend adult classes after they have finished their basics classes. Participants in the Evangelism Explosion ministry should be regular attenders at a weekly class. It is impossible for anyone to know everything about the infinite God in one lifetime. So regular study is necessary.

E. HOME BIBLE STUDY GROUPS

Early Christians often met in homes to study the Word of God. Home Bible study groups provide opportunity for Christians to experience the vital love of the family of God. Individual Christians can talk over the Word and discover their gifts and abilities. Such groups also give opportunity for Christians to use their individual gifts in the body.

Small groups are always important, but whenever the church grows beyond one hundred regular attenders, they become even more important. The average person can remember the names and faces of forty to sixty people he associates with on a regular basis. Therefore, if he is in a group of between 100 and 120 people, he will feel that he knows every other one and will still not feel lost in the crowd. However, when the number is larger, he will lose his identity unless he is part of a smaller subgroup. Home Bible studies provide opportunity for local assemblies to have subcongregations without the great expense of elaborate buildings. They also add a warmth and unstructured accountability into the lifestyle of believers. A large church without small subgroups with properly trained leadership will lack strength for service and will become impersonal.

When Bible study groups are formed, they should agree that they will later divide to multiply the number of groups. If this is not done, they may become closed cliques and defeat their vital function in the local church.

Bible study leaders should be trained in an apprentice relationship with a good, home Bible-study leader. Those with the gift of teaching should disciple others to teach.

There should be close communication between the leaders of the home Bible-study groups and the church staff. Caution must be exercised not to allow people with doctrinal differences to infiltrate the group and do damage to it and, eventually, to the whole church.

F. SUPPORT GROUPS

Whenever one has an eager new believer who is open to attending a Bible study support group, the trainer should suggest one for a six-week period. A support group features sharing, caring, counsel, prayer, and a Bible study on the basics of the faith, usually lasting one and a half to two hours. Suggest that the group meet in the new believer's home. This provides a comfortable, familiar setting into which his unsaved friends and relatives may readily come. A sponsoring couple who are members of the local church should also attend. This, then, provides a bridge into the church.

Often, at the end of six weeks, several friends and relatives have been saved, so the study can be moved and the process repeated. One church in Minneapolis, through a combination of E.E. calls and support groups, had a chain of more than fifty conversions. Nearly 50 percent of those converts identified with the church.

At a later point some of these groups may become "growth groups" into which still more church members can be added. Not more than 50 percent of the group should be church members, though, because too many Christians in the group will discourage new Christians from asking questions and sharing.

New believers will usually attend a support group for a number of weeks before identifying with the church. In the meantime, they can be fed and their hesitancy to enter the church can be overcome.

G. FELLOWSHIP MEALS

Christians in the early church often broke bread together. This was a social time for them to get better acquainted with each other. This is still a good way for Christians to share one another's lives.

In some large churches the pastoral staff arranges for all the membership to entertain each other once a quarter. They are careful to see that new friendships are established this way rather than merely continuing old ones.

Getting new Christians and older Christians around a table can be an effective manner of blending them together. When you lead someone to Christ, invite him to your home for dinner. Also invite another member of the church who has been a Christian for some time. Try to select the individual on the basis of his interest and age so that there will be something in common with the new Christian. Explain to the church member that you have someone else coming to dinner who has started attending church. Do not go into a lot of detail about his profession of faith.

Ask the church member if he is willing to help you. Indicate that you would like for him to invite the new Christian to his home for dinner at a later date, if the two of them appear to be compatible. Also ask the church member to invite another church member when he invites the new Christian to his home. The church member in each case should be asked to do the same thing you have done. This can cause a chain reaction that will beautifully blend the old and new members in your church.

Non-Christians who have heard the Gospel and have not yet trusted need to be involved socially with believers. Invite them to dinner. Watch your friendships grow—and watch them come to Christ!

III. OTHER BASIC "FOLDING" MINISTRIES

A. STAFF/MINISTER/OFFICER CONTACT

A full-time staff person, minister, or church officer contacts those who have made professions of faith or who were already Christians and have no active relationship with a local church. This should be done after the seven-day callback to be sure that time is being used to the best advantage.

The purpose of this call is to demonstrate interest in the person and to encourage him to become an active member in the church. This contact can be face-to-face or over the telephone.

B. PRAYER

Effective prayer and effective evangelism cannot be separated. When the team returns to the church after the contact, they should have a time of prayer together. Each member of the team should briefly pray. Express gratitude to God for the great things He has done. Needs of the Gospel presenters to be more effective in sharing in the future should be brought to the Lord. Intercede for the person contacted and those related to him.

Trainers must be models in prayer as much as they are models in presenting the Gospel. It is wrong to assume that all Christians know how to pray properly. Many Christians have difficulty praying aloud in the presence of other people. Trainers must be sensitive to this and seek to help any trainee having difficulty. If you are a trainee who has difficulty praying aloud with someone else, you should tell your trainer.

Paul reminds us that no one is completely adequate in the matter of prayer. He says,

"The Spirit also helpeth our infirmities: for we know not what we should pray for as we ought: but the Spirit itself maketh intercession for us with groanings which cannot be uttered" (Romans 8:26). Jesus promised, "If two of you shall agree on earth as touching any thing that they shall ask, it shall be done for them of my Father which is in heaven" (Matthew 18:19). Ask your trainer to claim this promise with you and apply it to praying aloud with others.

C. REPORTS

Written reports are absolutely necessary! To maintain an effective ministry, I suggest the following reports:

1. Initial contact result report. Completing a brief report on each initial contact will help you crystallize the experience and more permanently impress it in your mind. Then you will retain the things that will help you be effective in sharing the Gospel with others and ministering in the future to the person contacted. Turning this written report in to the evangelism office makes it possible for staff and other persons in the church to assist in the total discipling process. Special report forms can be created for this purpose. Forms are also available through E.E. International.

2. Public report boards. First, you should fill in on your report board details about your witnessing during the training ministry itself. As each team returns to the church, they should indicate the results of their contact on the public report board. (See Appendix C for suggested board layout.) This enables the report-session leader to get an overview of the calling activities. He can call on people who indicate exciting results or particular problems to share with the group. Also, this enables the report-session leader to know which teams are still out. Prayer can be offered in the group for those who have not yet returned. During the first few weeks of the training semester, the trainer should put the report on the board. Trainees should closely observe and then alternate weekly putting the report on the board. The trainer should check the report to see that it is accurate.

Next, you should fill in on your report board details regarding witnessing as a way of life. It is usually best to maintain a second board for witnessing in the daily life. This should give each participant an opportunity to record each attempted sharing of the Gospel. By having two boards (one for witnessing in the ministry and a second for witnessing in the daily life outside the ministry), emphasis is placed on the ministry as a means to an end rather than an end in itself. Be sure the report board for witnessing in the daily life includes opportunity for every attempted sharing of the Gospel, not merely professions.

3. Public-report session. The public-report session keeps vitality in the evangelism discipleship training ministry. After on-the-job training, the teams return to the church for refreshments and for sharing. Morning groups may bring their lunch to the report session, while evening teams might have light refreshments and coffee. The threefold purpose of the public-report session is:

a. Inspiration. You might be on a team that spends two hours driving around looking for someone at home and, finding no one, returns rather discouraged. This may happen to your team a number of weeks in succession. If you never hear reports from those who have had glorious visits, you might conclude that you would be better off to stay at home. However, in the public-report session you learn that while some had the same experience as you, others presented the Gospel and had professions. You get an overall picture and sense that you are part of a mighty work that God is doing in your city. This inspires you to continue.

b. Instruction. Problems you encounter can be discussed and solutions shared. Specific objections raised by those contacted can be considered and answers discovered. In this way the instruction is very relevant to the actual situations. Everyone learns in the school of real life, and the training does not degenerate into abstract theology.

c. Intercession. As victories are reported, praise God in prayer. As professions are reported, seal them with intercessory prayer. Teams that are late returning need to be upheld by intercession, also.

4. How to make the reports count. Proper procedure in the public-report session will enable you to gain a lot of inspiration and instruction in a little time.

Prepare for the public-report time by closely observing what happens in the contact. During the contact analysis, determine what is to be shared and who will be the spokesman. Concentrate on what will be of value to all participants. Report on (1) follow-up calls, (2) professions of faith, (3) new insights gained in effective witnessing, and (4) problems encountered for which solutions are needed.

Each report should be about two minutes in length. Do not waste time telling what did not happen. Prayer can be offered briefly after each report or in one period at the end of the report time. Do not use people's last names in public. Word might get back to them that they were talked about in the group.

Do not make negative comments about people contacted by the team. We are to look at others through the eyes of Christ. Therefore, snide comments about people being fat or skinny or ugly, etc., are totally out of place in a public-report session. Do not make light of sharing the Gospel. While it is obvious that God has a sense of humor, humor must be used with taste and discretion in public-report sessions.

Trainers should make the public reports the first few weeks. Then trainees may alternate as they are able. Sometimes it helps new trainees to make the report if the trainer stands with them. New trainees should not be forced to speak before a group if this is very disturbing to them.

The public-report session should begin and end at the designated time. It should not begin until teams return with positive things to share. It should end at the designated reasonable time so that participants are willing to stay for the last report. Those who return late can share their reports the following week. At Coral Ridge, report time for the morning group is from 11:30 to 12:00. For the evening groups, it is from 9:30 to 10:00.

D. CORRESPONDENCE

Remember that most of the New Testament Epistles were follow-up letters to new believers in the various first century churches. Some of them were also pastoral letters. Hence, a healthy church discipling-ministry will use this age-old means of communicating with its disciples to reinforce spiritual decisions and to strengthen personal relationships.

1. Notes to initial contacts. A note from one team member to the person or persons contacted is a good thing. It should be written the same day the contact is made. It will strengthen the personal relationships and reinforce spiritual decisions. Notes should be written to any person contacted who can be discipled into your church. These should be legibly handwritten.

2. Notes to new Christians. Express thanks for their hospitality. Mention that you and the others on the team (team members should be mentioned by name) are looking forward to seeing them in church on Sunday. Be sure to mention the time of the service they indicated they would attend. Indicate that you are looking forward to seeing them again next week (when you return for the seven-day callback). Welcome them to the family of God, and tell them you are available to be of help any time you are needed.

Sample Note to a New Christian

Dear Chris:

Welcome to the forever family of God at First Community Church. Thanks for your hospitality to George, Mary, and me. We are looking forward to seeing you at the 11:00 service on Sunday. I am sure you will also enjoy the "Discovery Bible Group" at 9:15 Sunday morning.

I hope you are finding your Bible reading as exciting and helpful as I am. Remember to underline the things that stand out to you and put question marks by those things you want to talk about when we get together next Wednesday morning at 10:15. Chris, please remember that we are available anytime you might need us. Once again, welcome to the forever family of God at First Community Church.

Your friend,

Jim

3. Notes to those who make no profession. Again, express thanks for their hospitality. Invite them to return to your church, and encourage them to read the materials you left with them. Let them know that you are available to visit with them again in the future.

Sample Note to a Person Who Made No Profession

Dear Chris,

After leaving your home Wednesday morning, George, Mary, and I were talking about how much we enjoyed getting to know you. You are a very interesting person. We look forward to getting better acquainted in the weeks ahead.

I am sure you will find "The Truth and the Life" group next Sunday morning at 9:15 very interesting. We will be looking for you there and at the 11:00 service.

As you read the Gospel of John, be sure to put question marks by those things you want clarified when we get together next Wednesday morning at 10:15.

Remember that George, Mary, and I are available if we can be of any help to you. Your friend,

Jim

4. Notes to those who are already Christians. Thank them for their hospitality. Invite them to return again. Suggest possibilities for involvement. Ask about their availability, and express your desire to see them again.

Sample Note to One Who Is Already a Christian

Dear Chris,

Welcome to the forever family of God at First Community Church. George and Mary commented to me after we left your house about how much they appreciated the opportunity to get acquainted with you. It's always good to meet another member of God's forever family.

I am sure you will find the couples' class next Sunday morning at 9:15 as exciting as I have found it to be. After the group is over, maybe we can worship together in the 11:00 service.

In the weeks ahead, George, Mary, and I are looking forward to getting better acquainted with you and your family.

Please remember that we are available if you ever need us for anything. Your friend in Christ,

Jim

5. Church mailing list. The church office should add to the church mailing list those with a potential for future discipling into the local congregation. This includes those who make professions of faith, Christians not actively related to another church, and people who do not make professions but are not hostile to the Gospel.

They should receive any regular informational mailings about activities in the church life. Occasional mailings for special programs help to build attendance and good relations. Mailings concerning financial stewardship should never be sent to individuals who are not members of the church. There should be a systematic purging process so that names are not left on the list for unlimited, extensive periods of time.

6. Pastor's follow-up letter. After the visitation team has made contact, the pastor should write a follow-up letter to those who show a potential for discipling into the local church.

When the pastor writes to a person who has made a profession of faith, his letter should be friendly but general. There should be no mention of the profession of faith with the visitation team. It is not uncommon for intimate and personal things to be shared with visitation teams. Professing one's faith is a very personal and intimate thing.

If someone who was not on the team, even the pastor, indicates that he knows about the profession of faith, the person contacted may think that other confidential things were shared as well. This can jeopardize future relations. The convert should be urged to use the services of the church and encouraged in Bible reading. The pastor may also indicate that the members of the church are looking forward to visiting again.

E. MEMBERSHIP

1. Personal invitation to church membership class. As periodic new-member classes are conducted, the team members should personally encourage all those who have made professions of faith and are not actively related to other churches to attend the new-member class. Of course, attending the class does not obligate the person to join the church. It does give him information so he can determine God's will in the matter.

Those with whom you have shared the Gospel who did not make a profession of faith but are open to the Gospel may be invited to the new-member class, also. One of their problems may be that they misunderstand what it means to be a member of the church. By attending the classes, many of their questions may be answered. Also, it should be emphasized that no one should join the church until he has had a personal interview with a staff member or officer of the church in which he indicates that he personally trusts Christ.

2. Pastor's invitation letter to new-member class. One week before the new-member class begins, the pastor writes a friendly letter to all possible candidates for church membership. He collects these names from the initial contact result report and from the callback follow-up report. All those who made professions, Christians not active in other churches, and those making no professions who are not hostile should receive a letter.

Usually it is wise to circulate the list of names of people who will receive the letter among the trainers in the E.E. ministry before the letter is mailed. Sometimes they will add names to the list or indicate names that should be removed from the list.

3. Staff/officer phone invitation to new-member class. Allowing time for the pastor's invitation letter to the new-member class to be received, a staff person or church officer should follow up with a phone call. After getting the right person on the phone, opening comments may go something like this:

> Pastor Kennedy asked me to give you a call. He wrote you a letter recently inviting you to the new-member class. He wanted me to be sure the letter had been received and to answer any questions you might have about attending the new-member class.

There is a significant increase in the number of people attending the new-member class when this telephone procedure is used. Sometimes all it takes is a few words to encourage and to resolve an uncertainty in the mind. Other times you may have to ask the pastor himself to call at another time. Some people will be absolutely closed to membership in your church, and this is also helpful information to have. Usually

Friday and Saturday evenings and Sunday afternoons before the new-member class begins are the best times to try to make telephone contact.

4. Membership application. Membership applications should be personally given by the team member closest to the potential new member, or they can be mailed by the church to those who indicate interest. All persons who make professions and Christians not active in other churches should be urged to complete the application and attend the classes.

The application should be completed before the new-member class begins and brought to class to be handed in during the first class session. The membership application should ask for basic information about the person: where he lives, his family, his work, his church background, his general interests or areas of ability for service in the church, and how he will be uniting with the church. This varies in different churches. Coral Ridge Church receives new members by profession of faith, reaffirmation of faith, and transfer of letter.

Do not use forms that go into great detail before people commit themselves to the local congregation. This basic information will help the church family properly minister to the new members. If your church has a covenant or set of vows, these should be printed on the membership application.

5. Membership classes. Those who are interested in membership are invited to, and encouraged to attend, membership classes conducted by the pastor. At Coral Ridge we hold such classes for one hour each week for four weeks following the Sunday evening service. Other churches may find that other times are better. These classes are not absolutely compulsory, but we do stress their helpfulness in familiarizing the individual with the church, its beliefs, and its activities. The subject matter is:

Session 1. Doctrine—What all Christian churches believe in common.

Session 2. Doctrine—What our church believes. During this class we give everyone a three-by-five-inch index card with the two diagnostic questions on it. We ask participants to take an inventory of their spiritual life. Each person is asked to place his name on the card so it can be attached to the membership application, and then a presentation of the Gospel is made. While that presentation is in progress, the cards are sorted into three stacks: right answers, wrong answers, and fuzzy answers. At the conclusion of the presentation, the pastor reads some of the correct answers and asks the new-member group to indicate whether the person writing that answer trusts in Christ or himself. Of course, the group responds, "He is trusting in Christ." After a few correct answers, the pastor will read a wrong answer and ask the group to indicate in whom the person is trusting. No names are given publicly with the answers, so no one is embarrassed. However, there is a great impact when a card is read and an entire group says the answer indicates that the person is trusting in himself for eternal life.

Session 3. Baptism, the Lord's Supper, and church government.

Session 4. Basic Christian duties. This is covered in conjunction with the vows of membership. Scripture reading; prayer; church attendance; stewardship of time, talents, and possessions; and witnessing are dealt with in detail.

Plenty of time is allowed for answering questions, but we don't bog down in the meeting. We make personal appointments as we see the need, or deal with touchy points in the new-member interview. Due to our evangelism outreach, we expect to have people from varied backgrounds. The classes outlined are of great help in clarifying any confusing issues for them. Of course, you will have to tailor the content of these classes to your own church's position.

6. Staff/officer new-member interview. Prior to or during the four-week period of the membership classes, a staff person or officer meets with each person who has filled out an application for membership. Sometimes this is done in the prospective new member's home. Other times it may be done by appointment at the church. When the number of new members grows, it is usually best for this to be done by appointment at the church. This makes the most efficient use of the interviewer's time and provides an atmosphere with less distraction.

The interview is a must! The purpose is twofold: for the staff person or pastor to get acquainted and, more important, to determine where the potential new member is spiritually. The interview takes much the same form as the seven-day callback mentioned in chapter 9. It needs to be stressed again that this interview is a must! It is done before any new member is received. We believe the careful, private investigation of an individual's spiritual understanding of his faith by the pastor is the most important step you can take in building a spiritual church. Usually at least one hour is necessary for this interview.

During this time, the interviewer should see if the potential new member has any questions that have been generated by attending the classes. Then the assurance questions and God's *why* are discussed. If the spiritual inventory card has been used and followed with the presentation of the Gospel to the group, the interviewer may have a wrong answer on the card but find that the person has now come to trust Christ.

If he has not trusted Christ, the Gospel must be presented. If the Gospel is rejected, the person should not be received into church membership.

If he is trusting Christ, you will want to discuss the method of uniting. At Coral Ridge we receive members on profession of faith, transfer of letter, and reaffirmation of faith. Those who are trusting Christ and are active members of other churches are received by transfer. Individuals who have trusted Christ in the past but have not been actively involved in a church recently unite by reaffirmation of faith. Persons who have only recently trusted Christ are received on profession of faith.

During the new-member interview it is important to discuss the need for balance in spiritual intake and output. One of the significant problems in the church today is that many new members do not change roles when they unite with the church. Until a person trusts Christ and unites with the church, he is an object for ministry. When he unites with the church, he becomes a channel for ministry to others. In order to make this change in role, it is important to discuss those things that will enable the new member to both give and receive.

7. New member public recognition/baptism. The keynote for this event is to make it meaningful. We follow this procedure:

a. The new-member group meets with a staff person before the Sunday morning service. The individuals have been carefully catalogued by method of uniting prior to this time so that proper acknowledgment may be made when they are introduced to the congregation. They are given reserved seats in a prominent place in the sanctuary.

b. Each individual is introduced during the service. As their names are called, they stand. When the group is formed, the pastor asks the questions related to their membership vows. After their very audible, positive response, he welcomes the new members to the church family.

c. Each new member is given an attractively designed name badge to wear to all church functions. This helps us to be able to distinguish members from nonmembers and is a great assistance to developing body life among the members.

d. Following the service, new members file out first and form a receiving line. Others may extend to them the right hand of fellowship as they leave the sanctuary.

e. Following the Sunday evening service a reception is held in honor of the new members. Every effort is made to warmly welcome them and to make this a day they will never forget.

8. Baptism should be scheduled in conjunction with receiving new members. Though Christians may differ as to the meaning of baptism, one thing most evangelicals agree on is that water baptism is a visible sign of vital relationship to the local congregation. Since the great commission commands us to baptize, we must seek to vitally relate to the church all those who receive Christ as a result of sharing the Gospel with them.

Note: You may find a great source of responsive prospects in the relatives and friends of new members. Urge new members to personally invite their relatives and friends to the service of public recognition and/or baptism. Then your visitation teams can make contact and evangelize. Some churches provide attractively printed invitations to new members for this purpose.

9. New-member sponsors. After new members have been received into the church, their names may be assigned to mature members who agree to be their sponsors for a period of three months. Assignments are made by a committee of people who are well acquainted with the congregation. Tentative assignments should be made as soon as membership is applied for. All assignments should be checked by the minister before being finalized. Letters of final assignment should be mailed as soon as the members are officially received. A copy of the application for membership can be given to the sponsor to acquaint him with his new member.

A system of records showing who is sponsoring whom is important. It is also important that sponsors be supervised by an officer of the church or a staff person. During the three-month period they serve, they should meet with their staff-sponsor at least twice to share the results of their sponsoring activities. A checklist enclosed in the sponsor assignment letter should be turned in by each sponsor on each new member. The letter and checklist outlining a sponsor's responsibilities to new members and their families (see examples on the next page) are sent to each sponsor.

SIDE 1

Comments:	SPONSOR CHECKLIST

NEW MEMBER

Name _____

Address_____

Phone No. _____

SIDE 2

Check the following items as you do them. This list is to be turned in at the first Sponsors Meeting.

☐ 1. Pray for them daily by name.

☐ 2. Welcome them personally as new members.

☐ 3. Call on them in their homes. Be observant and note any interesting features about their home which will help you to know them better. Notice books and magazines, and any hobby indications.

☐ 4. Find out which morning service they are attending. Greet them at the church and introduce them to others. You may want to come to church together or sit together for the next few Sundays. When the member misses a service you should telephone—not as a truancy officer, but to inquire whether there is illness and to express regret that you did not see each other.

☐ 5. Invite them to attend the evening service with you.

☐ 6. Try to get the new member into church organizations and activities, perhaps arranging to go together or prodding an organization if it is negligent in its recruiting. Your relationship to the new member will help bridge the gap between joining the church and enlistment into its total ministry.

☐ 7. Give him an invitation to your home and/or arrange for social occasions at the homes of other church members.

☐ 8. Discover and try to use the new member's talents in the ministry of the church.

☐ 9. Give such guidance in Christian living as can be tactfully offered, i.e., suggestions for family and personal devotions.

☐ 10. Watch for any sign of failure to get a good start and try to correct it—calling on others to help as needed and notifying the pastors immediately if there are problems or difficulties you cannot handle.

COMMUNITY CHURCH

494 Main Street
ANYTOWN, USA

JOHN JONES
MINISTER

Dear John Doe:

You have been selected to be a sponsor for one of our new members.

The first 90 days in the lives of new members are most critical! It is important that they be made to feel that they are a part of the church family and that they find their place of service in the ministry of the church.

As a sponsor you will be expected to do the things listed on the enclosed New Member Sponsor Checklist.

On Sunday, February 8, at 5:30 P.M., we would like for you to meet with all the other sponsors of new members in the church Fellowship Hall. At that time you will be able to share the problems and the joys you have encountered. Also at this meeting you will be asked to turn in your "Sponsor Checklist" indicating what you have done with your new member.

I am enclosing a copy of a letter which was recently sent to each new member.

This is a silent service. The new member does not know that you are his sponsor. However, if he should ask you if you were assigned to him, tell him we do this with all new members so that they may quickly and meaningfully become a part of the church family.

If for some reason you are not able to serve as a sponsor of the person here named, notify me immediately.

Let me underscore again the importance of your relationship to the new member. Call me for any assistance I can provide.

Sincerely in Christ,

Minister of Visitation

10. New-member class socials. As soon as possible after the official reception of new members, there should be a class get-together. This provides an opportunity for new members to become acquainted with each other in a way that is not possible during the periods of instruction. The new members may share in a potluck dinner, or the church may provide a buffet or a coffee and dessert. Workers related to various church activities present the new members with specific program opportunities. After a time of getting acquainted, when each person states his name, where he is from, and his occupation and family status, there is a time of spiritual sharing. Individuals, at random, tell how they came to know Christ and the results.

The meeting is closed with a time of prayer and with the word that there will be a similar gathering three months hence, at which time each new member will be asked (1) How is the church meeting your needs? and (2) How are you fitting into the ministry of the church?

A second get-together is scheduled for three months after the new member has been received. This is started with coffee and dessert. Then each new member is asked to put on paper his answers to the two questions announced at the first social. This is followed by discussion of the two questions.

11. Undershepherd program/parish plan. Anytime a church grows to more than 100–120 members, it needs to be subdivided. The larger the church, the more important this subcongregation structure is. The Sunday school, choir, and E.E. fellowship provide some opportunity for subgrouping by age and interests. As the church grows, the need for pastoral attention increases. Therefore, some program is needed that groups members of the church and provides them with a mature Christian leader so that they may be properly shepherded. It has been said, "If shepherds would beget shepherds, then sheep would beget sheep." The key to any successful undershepherd or parish program is the training of leaders. The pastor needs to disciple lay pastors so they can shepherd the flock. Many plans are available for this type of program. Select one that meets your needs, but be sure you train the leaders!

As new members unite with the church, they should be assigned to specific officer discipling groups. They should be told who their undershepherd or parish leader is and what his responsibilities are toward them and the church.

F. SPIRITUAL BIRTHDAY CARD

The spiritual birthday card can be an easy way to reinforce a new Christian. Standard Christian birthday cards can be used with a brief handwritten note. Team members may send the cards to those they lead to Christ on the anniversary of the first, sixth, and twelfth month of their new life in Christ.

G. FOLLOW-UP BIBLE STUDIES BY EVANGELISM EXPLOSION

E.E. International offers four helpful tools for discipling new believers. I would suggest you look closely at each of the following options to decide which would best fit your church's ministry to new believers.

1. *First Steps.* This booklet offers five lessons based on the Gospel of John and is designed to be used immediately after a person's profession of faith. It reviews the basics of salvation and aims to strengthen the new believer's assurance.
2. *Partners in Discipleship.* This booklet can be used following *First Steps.* It deals with eight more basic topics essential for a new believer's continued understanding and growth. This tool can be used for one-on-one discipleship or in a class situation.
3. *Plant a Seed* series. Five Bible-study booklets acquaint new believers with the means of Christian growth: Bible, Prayer, Worship, Fellowship, and Witnessing. A *Leader's Guide* is provided with the series.
4. *Beginning Again.* This is the most recent booklet I have written for new believers and is what we use at Coral Ridge Church. It includes: (1) a review of the Gospel presentation, (2) first steps for new believers, (3) a Gospel of John, (4) fulfilled prophecies, and (5) guidance on how to choose a home church.

H. OTHER BIBLE STUDIES

When you are not able to personally follow up a new believer, correspondence Bible studies can be very helpful.

The Living in Christ series produced by Grason Publishers has been widely used in conjunction with the Billy Graham Crusades. Also, many churches have found them helpful in their local follow-up programs. This series consists of four booklets: *Knowing Christ, Growing in Christ, Obeying Christ,* and *Sharing Christ.*

Project Philip of the World Home Bible League is being used by more and more churches. For information write: World Home Bible League, Project Philip Division, P.O. Box 11, South Holland, IL 60473.

I. CHURCH GROUPS

People in local congregations have a way of gravitating together according to mutual interests. This may be a particular ability, age, or sex grouping. Balanced involvement is what is important. If a person is overcommitted to many groups, he may simply drop out of them all. If he is not involved in any group, he will not feel he belongs. It is important that members in the various groups actively enlist new people. Otherwise they may come in the front door, bounce off one group after another and then bounce out the back door, never to return again.

The following is a list of some groups that may exist in your church.

Choir
Women of the church—circles
Men of the church
Midweek school of the Bible
Sunday school teacher training

Special weekday Bible classes
Bible memory groups
Boy Scouts or Christian Service Brigade
Girl Scouts or Pioneer Girls
Youth activities

J. SPIRITUAL ADOPTION

Occasionally a new Christian and his spiritual parent may have personality differences that make the discipling process difficult. On some occasions the age difference between the spiritual parent and the new Christian works against this, also. If the new Christian is of the opposite sex and approximately the same age, problems may develop. When these factors are present, the spiritual parent should take the initiative to place his new Christian for adoption. First you should attempt to have another person on your witnessing team take this responsibility. If this is not feasible, check with other teams to see who might help. In any case, do not leave your spiritual offspring without anyone to guide him.

K. EVANGELISM EXPLOSION TRAINEE

Most people in the E.E. ministry should at least attempt to become a trainer. Not all have the gift of evangelism, but all do have the responsibility to witness. Ninety percent of those who are now effective trainers in E.E. ministries around the world once felt they could never do this. Personally, I doubt that one percent of E.E. participants are gifted evangelists. But most witnesses find that as they continue to be part of the E.E. training fellowship, they produce more fruit and keep their witnessing skills sharp.

Many churches require Evangelism Explosion training for every potential leader. At Coral Ridge Church we have observed that choir members, Sunday school teachers, and leaders in any position are much more effective in ministry when, through our E.E. training, they are equipped to verbally share the Gospel.

L. TEACHER TRAINING

For a church to be healthy, it must have both evangelism and education. Not many are called to be teachers, says James, so E.E. participants with the gift of teaching should be encouraged to use it. Some will be teachers in the E.E. ministry itself. Others will be teachers in various aspects of the life of the church. After teachers have learned to share the Gospel, they will be able to evangelize the people God brings to their classes. Also they will channel their students into the Evangelism Explosion ministry, which equips for friendship, evangelism, discipleship and healthy church growth.

M. LEADERSHIP TRAINING

Jesus trained His first leaders with an on-the-job training course in personal evangelism: "Follow me, and I will make you fishers of men" (Matthew 4:19). I don't believe we can improve on his method. In 2 Timothy 2:2, Paul told Timothy to select leaders who were both faithful and able. In Ephesians 4:11-12, he reminded the church that pastors should equip their people for ministry. One of the shortcomings of the church today is that it places people in positions of leadership without properly training them. But commitment is not a substitute for competence. The two must go hand in hand. Leaders must be trained!

These are just some ideas for use in folding new believers into the church. You will certainly come up with others, and we would like to know about them. Write to us at E.E. International, P.O. Box 23820, Fort Lauderdale, Florida 33307.

Eleven

ENLISTING
AND
ENLARGING

If you want your friendship, evangelism, and discipleship ministry to continue to grow and your church to experience healthy growth, you will need to have periodic times for enlisting new trainees. They may come from your church leaders, prayer partners, church members, and new converts. You will also include reenlistment of both new and veteran trainers. Without such regular periodic enlistment, the witnessing ministry will certainly diminish and may die. We will consider this in four aspects.

1. Enlistment principles
2. Enlistment procedures
3. Enlistment qualifications
4. Enlistment presentations

I. ENLISTMENT PRINCIPLES

Some basic principles should be kept in mind as you consider your role in the next training semester and enlist people into your E.E. ministry.

A. WE EXIST TO GLORIFY GOD

"Man's chief end is to glorify God and to enjoy Him forever." This is the underlying theme of the Bible. Paul exclaimed, "For of him, and through him, and to him, are all things: to whom be glory for ever" (Romans 11:36).

Scriptures teach that we must consciously seek to glorify God through our lives in several ways. First, we should willingly seek the work of the Spirit of God through His Word to change us from "glory to glory" (2 Corinthians 3:18). Then, as Paul prayed, we should accept one another and "with one mind and one mouth glorify God, even the Father of our Lord Jesus Christ" (Romans 15:6). Furthermore, God is glorified in

His church as individual believers employ their God-given gifts to "minister the same one to another, as good stewards of the manifold grace of God" (1 Peter 4:10). Another way to glorify Him is through good works: Jesus said, "Let your light so shine before men, that they may see your good works, and glorify your Father, which is in heaven" (Matthew 5:16). Then, too, we are to glorify God in our bodies (1 Corinthians 6:20). In fact, Paul tells us, "Whether therefore ye eat, or drink, or whatsoever ye do, do all to the glory of God" (1 Corinthians 10:31). But how can we *best* glorify God?

B. THE WAY WE BEST GLORIFY GOD

The way we best glorify God is by abundant, responsible reproduction of disciples. When we get to heaven, we will still be able to glorify God in all of the above ways: unity, good works, eating and drinking, etc. However, there is one thing we will not be able to do in heaven that we can do in this present world—produce disciples!

Jesus desires that we glorify Him in this way: "Herein is my Father glorified, that ye bear much fruit; so shall ye be my disciples. . . . Ye have not chosen me, but I have chosen you, and ordained you, that ye should go and bring forth fruit, and that your fruit should remain: that whatsoever ye shall ask of the Father in my name, he may give it you" (John 15:8, 16). This undoubtedly refers to two types of fruit: the fruit of the Spirit and the fruit of witnessing. The fruit of the Spirit shows itself in Christian character—love, joy, peace, patience, kindness, goodness, faithfulness, gentleness, and self-control (Galatians 5:22-23). Such fruitfulness comes as a result of abiding in Christ—that is, maintaining an intimate relationship with Jesus without which He says we can do nothing (John 15:4).

Jesus also desires that we be properly pruned, healthy branches in right relation to the vine (Himself) and that we produce abundant, visible fruit—disciples. Thus Jesus commissions us, "Go ye therefore, and teach [make disciples of] all nations" (Matthew 28:19). Through our witness, we are not merely to obtain decisions, we are to obtain disciples—visible fruit that "remains" (John 15:16).

But what is a disciple? Jesus makes it very clear in Luke 14:26-33 that discipleship is demanding. Throughout the Scriptures the word "disciple" implies that the person not only accepts the views of the teacher, but that he also practices them. The disciple of Christ today may be described as a learning follower, one who believes Christ's teachings, rests upon His sacrifice, imbibes His Spirit, follows in His footsteps, and obeys His commission to make other disciples. The question then arises, "How can we best do this?"

C. THE WAY WE REPRODUCE MOST EFFECTIVELY

We can reproduce disciples most responsibly and abundantly when we are in a witnessing fellowship of a *local church* where experienced teachers and trainers help the less experienced with classes and on-the-job training.

In a fellowship of Christ's church, the potential multiplication of reproducers is greatly increased. The souls of men are more valuable than anything else in this world. Jesus asks, "What is a man profited, if he shall gain the whole world, and lose his own soul?" (Matthew 16:26). Being used of God to channel His grace to individual souls is the most important thing for us in this world. However, winning one soul is like picking an apple. Training a soul winner is like planting an apple tree, cultivating it, and harvesting from it bushels of choice apples for years and years. It is possible to win souls and not to train soul winners. However, it is not possible to train soul winners without winning souls in the process.

Classes led by experienced, able teachers provide opportunity for in-depth understanding of the truth of the Gospel and the best means of communicating it. However, classes alone do not tend to produce soul winners. Usually a student enters a class aware of his ignorance. After attending class for a while he discovers that there is a greater gap in his knowledge than suspected. Add to this the seriousness of soul winning—the realization that the Gospel can make the difference between heaven and hell for eternity—and the witness may choke up. His mouth will remain closed. He may become a "theoretical expert," knowing more and more about less and less until he knows everything about nothing! But he seldom becomes a soul winner through classes alone. He needs on-the-job training in a local church.

On-the-job training with a qualified trainer provides the experience necessary to break the "sound barrier"—to open the mouth and actually verbalize the Gospel. Experience in real situations removes fear. It inspires one to begin using the simple Gospel and depending on the power of God for results. It short-circuits the fears that classes alone cannot dispel. For this reason Christ "ordained twelve, that they should be with him, and that he might send them forth to preach" (Mark 3:14).

The local church is God's primary base for evangelistic activity in this world. It is the visible family of God. Having children outside a family situation is a violation of God's order. It can mar and scar a child's total health. The church is the bride of Christ (Ephesians 5:23-32). As the bride the church is joined "to him who is raised from the dead, that we should bring forth fruit unto God" (Romans 7:4). The great commission is not obeyed simply by discipling and teaching. We are also commanded to baptize "in the name of the Father, and of the Son, and of the Holy Ghost [Spirit]" (Matthew 28:19). Baptism of adult converts is a public identification with the visible family of God. Reproduction is not responsible unless we also do everything in our power to meaningfully relate the new believer to the visible family of God.

In the family of God, new disciples should find love, protection, and increasing knowledge of the truth. They should be strengthened and encouraged by their older brothers and sisters in the family of God. As they mature, they should learn to accept responsibility for those who enter the family of God after them.

D. SPIRITUAL MULTIPLICATION WAS EVIDENT IN THE EARLY CHURCH

The application of the discipleship principles I've been setting forth had a very dramatic effect on the growth of the apostolic church. Virgil Gerber describes it in these words:

The New Testament gives us a thorough, well-documented report on the origins of growth of first century churches. Sometimes it is easier to spiritualize such a report than to document the conclusions with hard statistics. But the New Testament report is carefully documented with precise numerical figures:

The First Church in Jerusalem began in an upper room with a small band of 12 disciples.

On the Day of Pentecost 3,000 were baptized, instructed in the Word, and *added* to the Jerusalem community. With careful detail Dr. Luke records the growth pattern from the Day of Pentecost to the imprisonment and questioning of the early disciples. The membership of the Jerusalem Church now stands at 5,000.

In Acts 5:14 the emphasis is upon the fact that multitudes of men and women were added. In Acts 6:1 and 7 the number of disciples was *multiplied*. From this point on, both the book of Acts and the New Testament Epistles underscore the multiplication of churches, as well as church members. New congregations were planted in every pagan center in the then-known world in less than four decades.

In Acts 9:31 church multiplication is not in terms of a single church, i.e., the First Church of Jerusalem, but in the collective sense of geographical multiplication of believers in all Judea, Galilee, and Samaria. It focuses on the transition from the mother church to emerging congregations in other places. Again in Acts 16:5 there is the change from church (singular) to churches (plural). Churches were planted. Churches increased in number daily. The Great Commission cannot be divorced from visible, structured, organized churches. In order to function and fulfill the Great Commission, there has to be some kind of structure.

In Acts 21:20 Paul uses the word "myriads" in his report. A myriad is a measurement of 10,000. So the apostle reports tens of thousands of Jews alone who turned to Christ and became identified with local churches.[1]

There was an evangelism explosion! Too often today the number of Christians in the church subtract or, at best, add. From Gerber's observations, it may appear that we have another option in spiritual mathematics—to multiply. If God enabled the number of Christians to multiply in the first-century church, why can He not do the same today? Why not ask God to help your church to experience true healthy growth numerically, spiritually, and organizationally? Ask Him to show you how your church's congregation can grow in quality and multiply in quantity.

E. NOT EVERYONE IS WITNESSING AND MAKING DISCIPLES

To multiply like the early church, the whole church needs to be a witnessing fellowship. Ideally, it should be, but it is not. Practically, there are basic reasons why we can't expect *everyone* to be so involved.

1. The church is a mixed multitude. The church in this world is always a mixed multitude of believers and unbelievers. In the parable of the wheat and the tares, Jesus indicated that this condition would continue to the end of time. In the world to come, at the judgment, the distinction will be made. It is interesting that Jesus draws a contrast between wheat and darnel. The darnel looked exactly like wheat through all

[1] Virgil Gerber, *God's Way to Keep a Church Going and Growing* (Regal Books, 1973), 16–17.

stages of growth until the time of harvest. Then it had no "fruit." Perhaps there is the implication here that those who do not bear fruit are not true believers.

2. There are varying levels of maturity. Another reason we can't expect everyone to be witnessing and making disciples is because not everyone in the church is at the same level of maturity and commitment. Thus, it is vital to have within the church a group of men and women committed to God, to the all-important task of world evangelization, to each other, and to the church.

A witnessing fellowship develops moral and spiritual strength. It encourages each individual and provides opportunity for united expression of the life produced by the Gospel. Scripture encourages such fellowship. "Iron sharpeneth iron; so a man sharpeneth the countenance of his friend" (Proverbs 27:17). "Two are better than one; because they have a good reward for their labour. For if they fall, the one will lift up his fellow: but woe to him that is alone when he falleth; for he hath not another to help him up" (Ecclesiastes 4:9-10). "If two of you shall agree on earth as touching any thing that they shall ask, it shall be done for them of my Father which is in heaven. For where two or three are gathered together in my name, there am I in the midst of them" (Matthew 18:19-20).

F. YOU WILL INVARIABLY MULTIPLY OTHERS LIKE YOURSELF

If you are a functionally mature, responsible, reproducing Christian, you will produce others like yourself. To a great extent the spiritual quality of life in those who were multiplied through your ministry will depend upon the spiritual quality of your life.

The quantity of multiplication is determined by your passion for spiritual reproduction. Jesus said, "Ye have not chosen me, but I have chosen you, and ordained you, that ye should go and bring forth fruit, and that your fruit should remain" (John 15:16). "Herein is my Father glorified, that ye bear much fruit; so shall ye be my disciples" (John 15:8). The apostle Paul believed that God was "able to do exceeding abundantly above all that we ask or think, according to the power that worketh in us" (Ephesians 3:20).

Whether you are in the fellowship of Evangelism Explosion or not, these principles remain true. You are constantly producing missionaries or mission fields, strong saints or crippled Christians, a pitiful few or an abundant harvest.

Enlistment is best accomplished by personal, prayerful, private contact between people who are in the witnessing ministry and those who are not.

II. ENLISTMENT PROCEDURES

A. SHOULD ENLISTMENT BE DONE PUBLICLY?

It might appear that it would be better to have the pastor publicly enlist people from the pulpit on Sunday, but that is not the case, for several significant reasons.

1. You might scare the "fish." Some of the people to be called on during the week would be present in the congregation. If the pastor pressures the congregation to get into the witnessing ministry so they can go out and win poor lost souls, the "poor lost souls" are going to be on their guard when a team knocks at their door.

2. People's ego defenses are armed. When Christians are urged publicly from the pulpit to enter the witnessing ministry, they arm their ego defense mechanisms. You would think they would feel guilty not being a part of the witnessing ministry, but in most cases that is not true. They remember rumors they heard about visitation teams: Someone who was visited said he would never, never come back to the church because the team treated him like a heathen. So the silent saints remain in their pews on Sunday. They sit in their homes on the nights the teams go out and say to themselves, "I am serving God better here watching my television than those fanatics who are out driving people away from Christ and our church."

3. Laypeople may not identify with the pastor. Let me illustrate it this way. Suppose you were in a large group gathered to hear a very famous and distinguished four-star general lecture on "The Principles of War." The printed program informs you that the general graduated from West Point with highest honors. He completed post-graduate work at the War College in Washington, D.C. When he stands to speak, he is the perfect picture of the model soldier. His words flood forth with an overwhelming eloquence. For twenty minutes you listen in awed silence to his masterful oratory. You are astonished at the breadth and depth of the man's knowledge and his command of the English language. It is obvious that he has thoroughly mastered the principles of war and knows very well how to communicate them to large crowds.

In concluding his speech, the general says, "Now I want you to be a soldier like me. Of course, you will not be able to attend West Point or the War College, but I will give you a twelve-week course that will expose you to everything I have learned in my twelve years of higher education. If you are not a yellow craven coward, you will enlist today."

The wheels of your mind begin to turn. You think, "I wish I were like that general, but I am not. He has an exceptionally alert mind and a natural ability to speak. He has had so much formal education. He is one in a million and I am just one of a million common people.

"I don't want to be a coward, but what he is talking about is dangerous. I am not like him so I cannot do it. Besides, I am sure that many others here are much more qualified than I, and they surely will respond. Anyway, somebody has to stay home. We can't all be heroes."

On the other hand, suppose you are sitting in your living room one pleasant afternoon. The doorbell rings. When you respond you are greeted by the smiling face of an old friend you have not seen for a number of years. You invite him into your living room so that you may reminisce over old times and catch up on what's been going on since you were last together. Your friend tells you that he has been in the army for the past three years. Enthusiastically, he relates one adventure after another. Then he says, "I know I'm not a general, but the general couldn't fight the war without me and many others like me. I know what I do is dangerous, but I'm fighting for what is right and it has given meaning to my life. You and I are very much alike. Wouldn't you like to enlist with me and see your life really count for something?"

Once again, the gears in your mind are in motion. Your thoughts say, "My life sure hasn't had the meaning or excitement that his has. We are a lot alike. If he can do it, I think I can, too."

Who is the best recruiter? In the army of Jesus Christ the experienced lay evangelist can be a much more effective recruiter than the "professional general in the pulpit." The ongoing work of evangelism depends on the laymen enlisting and assisting in the training of other lay evangelists. The apostle Paul told Timothy, "Thou therefore, my son, be strong in the grace that is in Christ Jesus. And the things that thou hast heard of me among many witnesses, the same commit thou to faithful men, who shall be able to teach others also. Thou therefore endure hardness, as a good soldier of Jesus Christ. No man that warreth entangleth himself with the affairs of this life; that he may please him who hath chosen him to be a soldier" (2 Timothy 2:1-4).

You are in touch on a regular basis with soldiers in the army of Jesus Christ who are "absent without official leave (AWOL)." Pray that God will enable you to be His instrument to make them good soldiers of Jesus Christ who can fight the forces of evil by verbally sharing His Gospel with the lost.

B. ENLIST PRIVATELY, PERSONALLY, AND PRAYERFULLY

1. Everyone enlists. Everyone in the witnessing ministry is responsible for enlistment of new trainees. That includes the leaders and every trainer, junior trainer, and trainee in the ministry.

Though many people at the end of their first training semester are ready to become trainers, some are not. They may think, "If I am not going to be a trainer next time, then I shouldn't try to enlist anybody." If you are in that particular situation, let me remind you that you have contact with some people nobody else has contact with. You should encourage them to come into the witnessing ministry even if you are not going to be their trainer. Don't feel that you are exempt from the enlistment effort because you don't feel you are going to be a trainer. Serve as a scout. Help others who will be trainers to enlist people you know.

2. Everyone should train someone else. If you are now a trainee or junior trainer, you should purpose to be a trainer. Possibly you are thinking that you don't have sufficient experience in sharing the Gospel yet. Maybe you have not had another person profess faith in response to your presentation of the Gospel, so you don't think you should try to be a trainer. That is not the case. If you are able to pass the end of the course checkup and are willing to invest your life in two trainees, in most cases you can begin to function as a trainer. You will learn more as a trainer than you will ever learn as a trainee, or even a junior trainer. You can increase the number of people brought to Christ by being a trainer and enlisting others in the witnessing force in the next training semester.

3. Commit to be a trainer. Sometimes people let their participation in the next training semester depend on whether or not they enlist trainees. If you will commit yourself to God to be a trainer, with or without trainees, this will cause you to be more zealous in getting trainees. Then when you talk with potential trainees, you will communicate more of the urgency of being in the ministry.

4. Seasoned trainers are the best recruiters. They are usually more able to enlist trainees than people who are becoming trainers for the first time. First-time trainers are sometimes nervous and uncertain about their ability to function as trainers. This uncertainty may cause hesitancy in seeking trainees and may even cause people to be hesitant about working with the trainer as his first trainees. Therefore, seasoned trainers should seek to enlist trainees not only for themselves but also for those they have trained who are becoming trainers for the first time.

5. Some trainers are better enlisters than others. If you happen to be in this group, work with others who are less able to get trainees. If you know others in ministry who are good recruiters, encourage them to work with you to help you get trainees.

6. In enlisting, the most important thing to do is to pray. The Scripture says, "Pray ye therefore the Lord of the harvest, that he will send forth labourers into his harvest" (Matthew 9:38). Ask God to lead you to people in the congregation who need to be in the witnessing ministry, whether they become your trainee or not, then pray for God to touch their hearts and draw them in.

III. ENLISTMENT QUALIFICATIONS

Paul set forth some of the qualities you should look for in a trainee. "And the things that thou hast heard of me among many witnesses, the same commit thou to faithful men, who shall be able to teach others also" (2 Timothy 2:2).

A. FAITHFUL

"Faithful" in very practical terms means he has faith in Christ as his Savior, is an active member of your local church, and is generally supportive of the church's work. He should not hold major doctrines contrary to your church. If he does and brings them up in the calling situation, it will certainly distract from presenting the Gospel and can create serious problems. "Faithful" also means that the person has faith in Jesus Christ alone for eternal life. But you don't want to assume this without asking the enlistee the two diagnostic questions. Occasionally, someone will enlist for E.E. who has not yet trusted Christ for salvation. By asking the two diagnostic questions during the first lesson, we often have the opportunity to lead such persons to Christ.

B. ABLE

When you look for "ability," look for a person who is somewhat like you. Don't necessarily look for a person who is a super salesman with a public-relations background. Sometimes these people depend more on their natural abilities than on the Holy Spirit. The basic abilities to look for are availability and a willingness to learn. In many cases these will be quiet, meek, humble, shy individuals. If you do get someone who is a super salesman, make sure he understands that his abilities must be yielded to the Lord and sanctified by Him. Otherwise, he will fail.

Don't automatically eliminate people who are different from you. Your trainees can be older or younger than you, more or less educated, of a different race or cultural background.

C. TEACHABLE

Many people enlisting in E.E. already have some experience in witnessing and may come with preconceived ideas about evangelism. Others may have prejudices that need to be overcome. Hence, it is important that all who enlist ask God to give them a teachable heart and an open mind to learn new approaches to sharing the Gospel.

D. SPECIAL CONSIDERATIONS

1. Youth. God often uses young people to reach their peers for Christ. To effectively do this, youth, like adults, need to be equipped. E.E. offers clinics to train youth pastors and leaders, as well as materials adapted for youth. While young people can train their peers, do not enlist teenagers with the thought that they will be able to function as trainers of adults. Very few adults would be willing to be trained by a teenager. If there is an adult on the team and a call is made on adults, it will be very awkward for the teenager to take the lead and function as a trainer. If the team is composed of all teenagers, they will usually find it difficult to present the Gospel to adults in a home situation, as the adults may try to dominate the conversation or patronize the young people. When teenagers are trained, it is best that they function as trainers of other teenagers.

2. Married couples. If possible, a husband and wife should be enlisted for the same training period, for several reasons. Sometimes, when one is in the witnessing ministry and the other is not, a spiritual gulf can grow between them. It can be difficult to share what is not being experienced by both. However, there are times when both are not able to be in the same training course due to pregnancy, small children, work schedules, etc. One cautionary note: If a wife enters the training and her husband is hostile toward it, she will have difficulty completing the training.

However, even when a couple is enlisted at the same time, it is not wise for the husband and wife to be trainees on the same team or to try to train each other. Normally one is more dominant than the other. This can cause problems. The dominant one will learn the Gospel, the other will remain dependent. When married couples start calling together, they hesitate to divide after they get trained. This short-circuits the multiplication. If there are exceptions, have a clear understanding in advance.

Take your visitation team along to enlist a couple. Explain to the couple that it is best to have them on separate teams. Indicate that they can be with one of your team members. If there is hesitation, ask if there is someone else in the training ministry they would like to be with and notify that person.

3. Women. Try to enlist both men and women. Women usually are more sensitive and gentle as they deal with others. Men usually are more direct and forceful. Having both men and women on the team will lend a balance that increases the capacity for communication. It will also make it much more convenient for calling in a home where only one man or woman is home.

Women serving as trainers should not feel they are going contrary to the Bible and usurping authority over a man. They are simply being an example of how to share their faith. Peter, on the Day of Pentecost, declared, "But this is that which was spoken by the prophet Joel; 'And it shall come to pass in the last days, saith God, I will pour out of my Spirit upon all flesh: and your sons and your daughters shall prophesy, and your young men shall see visions, and your old men shall dream dreams: and on my servants and on my handmaidens I will pour out in those days of my Spirit; and they shall prophesy'" (Acts 2:16-18). The first person to whom the resurrected Christ appeared was a woman. He specifically instructed her to go and tell His brethren. She was the first witness of the Resurrection and proclaimed it first to the apostles (John 20:11-18).

4. Members of other churches. Generally, enlistment of a member from another church should be discouraged. Do not bring a layman from another church without his pastor or at least a letter of approval from his pastor. If a layman is from a church where the Gospel is not preached, he will grow dissatisfied with his own situation and will either create disharmony within his church or leave it. Then you will get the reputation of being a "church splitter" or "sheep stealer."

If it is an evangelical church and the pastor says to the layman, "I'd like for you to go and learn, and come back and start the ministry at our church," there may still be problems. The layman will get excited and enthusiastic. Then he will wonder why his pastor does not participate. A layman without his pastor or pastor's approval can create more problems than benefits.

When the pastor desires to enlist in the E.E. training of your church, he must be interviewed by the minister in charge of the training. He must commit himself to going through the entire training, both the classes and the calling. He will assume the role of a layman in your church and be assigned to a trainer. He must also enroll in the first possible certified-leadership clinic he can attend. This will provide the training he needs to certify laypeople in his church's E.E. ministry.

Usually, not more than 15 percent of a total training ministry can be made up of people who are not members of the host church. More than 15 percent would undercut the training base. It would put people in the ministry who will not be there to train others next semester. This would eventuate in a case of "suicide" for the witnessing training.

A financial charge must be worked out for each person coming from another congregation. This pays for the materials and is an expression of genuine interest that encourages follow-through on the commitment.

Pastors and laypeople discipled in a local, church-certified E.E. ministry before attending a leadership clinic receive much more benefit from the clinic experience.

IV. ENLISTMENT PRESENTATION

By now you have discovered that having a well-learned presentation of the Gospel makes it much easier to be an effective evangelist. This also applies when you enlist trainees. With a good enlistment presentation you will be much more effective in obtaining good trainees who, in turn, will become good trainers.

Proper recruitment requires that potential trainees be reasonably informed about the Evangelism Explosion Discipleship Training Ministry. The better informed they are, the less likely it is that they will drop out.

Once you have prayed and considered various individuals, according to the criteria we have suggested, make plans to go to your contacts and challenge them personally to become trainees. Share a brief word of testimony concerning what the E.E. training has meant to you. Use the booklet *Partners in Equipping* to assist you. This booklet sets forth the importance of personal evangelism and the uniqueness of the E.E. ministry. If your potential recruits do not want to give you an answer during your meeting, make a seven-day callback appointment, asking them to read the booklet and ask God what He wants them to do. Be sure to contact them again for their decision.

For enlistment, we recommend the following steps:

1. Pray—Ask God to show you potential recruits.
2. Consider—Sort through the criteria for potential disciples.
3. Contact—Set up a time to get together with your contact.
4. Testify—Share what E.E. has meant to you.
5. Invite—Challenge the person to join with you in E.E.
6. Inform—Leave *Partners in Equipping* for further understanding.
7. Follow-up—Contact the person again later for a decision.

Seasoned E.E. participants work hard at recruiting new trainees, just as hard as they do when witnessing or training soul winners. Since it is important to train as many people as possible to share their faith with others, regular enlisting by every E.E. participant is absolutely essential for an effective, growing E.E. ministry. Be on the alert at all times for opportunities to challenge others—pastors, church leaders, laypeople, and youth—to join the E.E. training. This is the way your E.E. ministry will grow, because enlisting leads to enlarging!

Twelve

HANDLING
OBJECTIONS

When you present the Gospel, the arch foe will have his workmen doing their best to block your presentation. Fears and doubts will arise in your heart, and your prospect will raise objections. Earlier we discussed how we handle our fears. In this chapter we will discuss what we do when an objection is raised.

Remember that your primary task is to witness. Millions of people have trusted Christ without ever raising one difficult question. Furthermore, don't think that everyone is going to raise tough questions.

It is important to know the source of objections to your presentation of the Gospel. Some objections are sincere questions. The one raising the question is genuinely searching for the truth, and when given logical and biblical answers, will move toward placing his trust in Christ.

Other objections, however, are smoke screens behind which are those who, in their heart of hearts, are not truly searching for God's truth. Rather, as Christ said, they "loved darkness rather than light, because their deeds were evil. For every one that doeth evil hateth the light, neither cometh to the light, lest his deeds should be reproved" (John 3:19-20). Such objections are often a device of the devil to prevent the presentation of the Gospel. Paul said, "The god of this world hath blinded the minds of them which believe not, lest the light of the glorious Gospel of Christ, who is the image of God, should shine unto them" (2 Corinthians 4:4).

Should you be offended if a person raises a question? Definitely not! Rather, when someone raises an objection to the Gospel, you need to be ready to respond with the right attitude. Peter suggested, "Be ready always to give an answer to every man that asketh you a reason of the hope that is in you with meekness and fear" (1 Peter 3:15).

I. Basic Attitudes in Handling Objections

A. AVOID ARGUMENT

Our natural tendency is either to meet an objection head-on and beat it down or to run. This tendency must be overcome for the sake of your prospect's eternal welfare. Negatively, we say: never argue.

Often it has been said that the only way to win an argument is to avoid it, and the best way to avoid it is to preclude it. That is, anticipate it and lead your prospect to agree with the Scriptures before he can raise the objection. Any skillful debater can easily win a point in an argument, but by doing so you can arouse hostilities in the prospect that will cause you to lose your "fish."

B. SHOW A POSITIVE ATTITUDE

On the positive side, you may meet every objection with: "I'm glad you said that!" You ought to be glad your prospect has enough freedom to express his inner feelings to you. As you deal with his objections, you clear away the props which have deluded him into a presumptuous sense of security. You are glad when he shows he is listening and assimilating what you are presenting.

C. USE SINCERE COMPLIMENTS

If the person to whom you are speaking begins to become hostile or irritated, a sincere compliment can be very effective in reducing tensions. The following is an example: "You know, John, you are an intelligent person and are obviously well-read, and it's a real pleasure to discuss these things with someone as interested in spiritual matters as you are." Such a comment will end many arguments before they get started.

II. Basic Methods of Handling Objections

A. PRAY

The first and most important step to remember when you encounter someone with an objection is to pray and ask God for His help. Send a "Sky Telegram" heavenward. When the god of this world attacks, you need to go over his head to the all-wise God who is over all.

Paul reminds us, "We wrestle not against flesh and blood, but against principalities, against powers, against the rulers of the darkness of this world, against spiritual wickedness in high places. . . . Praying always with all prayer and supplication in the Spirit . . . for me, that utterance may be given unto me, that I may open my mouth boldly, to make known the mystery of the Gospel" (Ephesians 6:12, 18-19). "Continue in prayer, and watch in the same with thanksgiving; withal praying also for us, that God would open unto us a door of utterance, to speak the mystery of Christ" (Colossians 4:2-3).

Regardless of the form of the objection, recognize it as a device of Satan to prevent your proclaiming the Gospel. Recognize, further, that you are not calling on your prospect in order to defeat him in a debate. By precluding objections and by dealing with those that arise in a matter-of-fact manner, you can succeed in presenting your prospect with enough information to make a decision.

B. PRECLUDE OBJECTIONS

This means answering objections before they are raised. It helps eliminate a negative spirit that could result in the presentation's degenerating into an argument.

The introduction portion of the E.E. outline precludes the objection "That's too personal," by having you take the time to get to know the person and build a rapport with him. It precludes someone's saying, "I don't like people shoving religion down my throat," by your asking for and obtaining the person's permission before proceeding to share the Gospel. By kindly repeating the person's answer to the second question—God's "Why?"—and confirming that you heard right, you preclude his stating at the point of commitment, "I have always believed that." By listening and showing a genuine interest in him, and by sharing your personal testimony, you preclude his saying, "I'm not interested."

The Gospel portion of the presentation also precludes objections. When I first started sharing the Gospel, I set forth God's justice before His mercy, and many people objected by insisting, "My God isn't like that! He's loving and merciful!" So I began precluding that objection by reversing the order; that is, I first set forth His mercy and love. Then I told them that the same Bible that tells us He is merciful and loving also tells us He is just and righteous and must deal with sin. Since taking that approach, I have seldom had anyone raise this objection.

C. POSTPONE

If an objection is raised, you must decide whether it is essential to answer it before you can continue, or whether this objection is extraneous to the Gospel and can be dealt with later, or not at all.

For example, if you ask him if he knows that he is going to heaven, and he replies that he does not believe in heaven, you obviously cannot continue without dealing with his objection. On the other hand, if he raises the question of the heathen in Africa, this is a matter that can be put off in the following way: "That's an interesting question, and I would love to discuss it with you. If you don't mind, would you hold it in abeyance until we finish what we're talking about, and if you will bring it up then, we can take a look at it together."

In this way you do not have to spend a lot of time answering extraneous objections; you also discourage his bringing up other nonessential matters. Since you have left to him the responsibility of bringing it up again, you need not answer the objection at all unless, of course, he brings it up.

D. PROMPTLY ANSWER

If his objection deals with an essential aspect of the Gospel and you would not be able to continue without responding to it, then answer it as quickly as possible and return to your presentation.

The E.E. outline is meant to be your servant, not your master. Therefore, you need not be a slave to the outline. You may show wisdom if you take up the objection "out of place." Often, what is out of place in the printed presentation can be "in place" in the living situation.

Most often, however, your prospect will introduce matters you have not planned to talk about. Suppose you are in the middle of the story of John Wesley's conversion and your prospect says, "I don't see why there have to be so many divisions in the church. Wesley started the Methodist Church, which broke off from the Anglicans. And you're not a Methodist. Why can't you all get together?"

Don't panic. Obviously this matter is extraneous. Neither a discussion of church history and denominational origins, nor a discourse on the ecumenical movement would be of any value at this point. It is also obvious that you have lost your prospect's interest. Now you need to do two things. First, you need to get back on track, and then you need to recapitulate so that your prospect can pick up your train of thought, which he has lost. One approach might be:

"I'm glad you asked that, for I can see it is something that would hinder your understanding of just what saving faith really is. I don't want to mislead you as to what the key is that opens heaven's door. Now we've seen that neither intellectual assent nor temporal faith will open that door. You must trust the living Lord to do something for you. Just as Wesley had a certain kind of faith, he recognized that it was not saving faith. He wrote in his journal . . ." (continue presentation).

In this manner, you turn the conversation away from the extraneous matter and refresh his memory concerning what you were talking about before his mind wandered from your point. Pascal, the famous French mathematician, philosopher, and theologian stated an important principle I have tried to apply in my life. He said, "In essentials, unity; in nonessentials, liberty; and in all things, charity, or love."

Return the conversation to the presentation at the point where you left it. "I suppose just because we're human we will always have differences of opinion. It's interesting, though, that I can quote the founders of other denominations in presenting the Gospel to you. The mainstream of the Christian church has been united for 2,000 years on the matters we've been discussing, such as man's sinfulness, God's holiness, and Christ's deity. We don't want nonessentials to cause you to reach heaven's door without the right key to open it, do we? For years Wesley thought he had the key to heaven. But it wasn't until after he worshiped in Aldersgate Street Chapel that he could write . . ."

E. PROMISE TO RESEARCH AND RETURN

Many Christians are very concerned that their witness will be completely ineffective if the person asks them any question they cannot answer. This, of course, is not true.

If the witness does not know the answer to a question, he can simply say: "That's a very interesting question, and I would like to know the answer to it myself. If you really want to know, I'll find out and get back to you with the answer. In the meantime, let's get back to the point we were discussing. . . ."

At this point, it is important for the Christian to realize exactly what he is and is not called to be. He is not called to be the judge or the jury to pass sentence upon the person he is visiting. He is not called to be the prosecuting attorney or even the defense lawyer. God is the judge and jury, Satan is the prosecuting attorney, and the Lord Jesus Christ is the advocate. He is not even called upon to be an expert witness. A minister would qualify as such, but not a layperson. He is called simply to be a witness. That means that he has seen or experienced something about which he has firsthand knowledge, and his character demonstrates that these experiences are credible or believable.

If a person witnessed a shooting on a street corner, the fact that he knew little about guns, their manufacture, caliber, velocity, or range would in no way impair his testimony that he saw someone shoot and kill another person. If, however, a ballistics expert who would qualify as a technical witness demonstrated the same ignorance about the caliber, range, and muzzle velocity of the weapon, he would not only ruin his testimony, he would probably lose his job. You remember the man in the Scriptures who was born blind and was healed by Christ. The Pharisees tried to make him into an expert witness. He refused by saying, "I know not: one thing I know, that, whereas I was blind, now I see" (John 9:25).

III. Answers to Common Objections

A. I DON'T BELIEVE THE BIBLE

Often, as you begin presenting the Gospel, your prospect will say, "I don't believe the Bible. You'll have to convince me some other way than referring to the Scriptures." Many laymen are devastated by this objection, and their attempt at presenting the Gospel fizzles. This need not be the case. Such an objection can be the springboard into the Gospel itself. The apostle Paul, as he preached in the Greek cities, appealed to the Scriptures even though the people listening to him did not believe in the Scriptures. He did not try to convince his audience of the veracity and authority of the Scriptures. Rather, he proclaimed them, and the Holy Spirit worked and used the proclamation to save some who then came to believe the Bible to be true. In witnessing, our primary function is proclamation, not defense.

1. The judo technique. This is actually a rather easy objection to deal with. When it comes at the beginning of a presentation of the Gospel, I would suggest that a person not use the approach of a boxer who would meet the blow head-on and try to overwhelm his opponent with counterpunches, but rather that he use the technique of the judo expert, wherein the force of his opponent's blow is used to throw him.

The individual who uses this objection is usually a person who has had at least some college education and exposure to some course on the Bible, biblical criticism, or something of this sort. And there is usually an accompanying intellectual pride that says something like this: "I used to believe those fairy tales when I was in kindergarten, but now I am an educated man and am far above believing such things." It is this intellectual pride that can be used to turn this objection into an opportunity for presenting the Gospel, somewhat as in the following illustration:

"You don't believe the Bible, John? That's very interesting, and it certainly is your privilege not to believe it, and I would fight for that right on your part. However, if the Bible is true, then obviously you must accept the consequences. But I would like to ask you a question. The main message of the Bible, which has been unquestionably the most important literary work in human history, is how a person may have eternal life. So what I would like to know is, what do you understand that the Bible teaches about how a person may have eternal life and go to heaven?"

He may reply that he does not believe in eternal life, to which you may respond, "I'm not asking you what you believe, but I am asking you what you understand. It would be a rather unintellectual approach to reject the world's most important book without understanding even its main message, would it not? What do you understand that the Bible teaches as to how a person may have eternal life? What is your understanding about what the Bible teaches on this subject?"

In about 98 percent of the cases, the response will be that it is by keeping the Ten Commandments or following the Golden Rule or imitating the example of Christ, etc. You may then respond, "That is just what I was afraid of, John. You have rejected the Bible without even understanding its main message, for your answer is not only incorrect, it is diametrically opposite to what the Bible teaches. Now, don't you think that the more intellectual approach would be to let me share with you what the Scriptures teach on this subject, and then you can make an intelligent decision whether to reject or accept it?"

Now the tables have been completely turned. Instead of being superior to the Scriptures and above even listening to them, he now finds himself ignorant of even their basic message, and he must decide whether to listen to the message of the Scriptures or be found to be not only ignorant but also an obscurantist who desires to remain in his ignorance. This is the last thing in the world his intellectual pride will allow him to be; therefore, he will almost invariably give you permission to tell him the Gospel. At this point you pray mightily that the Holy Spirit will take the Gospel, which is the power of God unto salvation, and use it to quicken him from the deadness of his sins.

2. Apologetic method. If this objection is raised somewhere else in the presentation, your answer will have to be quite different. We have found that the apologetic method of presenting the classical evidences of Christianity can be helpful at this point.

One of the most important classical evidences for the inspiration of the Scriptures is prophecy. The Bible says, "Despise not prophesyings. Prove all things; hold fast that which is good" (1 Thessalonians 5:20-21). How do we know that the prophets of the Bible have been sent by God and speak for him?

God presents us with that same question: How will you know that a prophet is sent from me? (Deuteronomy 18:22). The answer is that if the things the prophet foretells do not actually come to pass, then we know that the prophet is not from God. The gift of prophecy is one of the methods the Bible uses to authenticate itself as the Word of God.

Some people would again not appreciate the significance of this because they do not realize that this also is something strikingly absent from all other religious writings. For example, the writings of Buddha are totally lacking in any sort of specific predictive prophecy about the things of the future. In the writings of Confucius, there is absolutely nothing of any predictive prophecy. In the case of the Koran, the scriptures of the Muslims, we find only the prophecy of Mohammed that he would return to Mecca—a self-fulfilling prophecy, which he himself, of course, fulfilled. This is quite different from the prophecy of Christ, who said that He would rise from the dead. And that is just one of several thousands of prophecies that occur in the Scriptures and which are of the most *specific, concrete, and definite* nature.[1]

If the person says, "The Bible is just a book written by men," you might answer him something like this:

"Imagine that you had the ability to predict the future and you predicted to an expectant mother eight things about her unborn baby: its sex, date of birth, name, weight at birth, college, occupation, manner of death, and age at death. The chances of all eight of your predictions being fulfilled is 1 in 10 to the 17th power—10 with 17 zeros!"

Someone suggested a way to illustrate the chances of all eight predictions being fulfilled as follows: Cover the state of Texas two feet deep with silver dollars. Mark an X on one of the silver dollars, and stir them all up. Blindfold a person and send him across the state as far as he wishes to go. Instruct him to pick up one of the silver dollars. The chances of his getting the coin marked X would be 1 in 10 to the 17th power.

Now read to him eight of the Old Testament prophecies concerning Jesus Christ without telling him what you are reading. Then ask him, "About whom have I been reading?" and he will probably respond, as one man did to me, by saying, "You have been reading about the lineage, birth, ministry, suffering, death, and resurrection of Christ."

To which I responded, "That is correct, but all of the verses I read to you are found in the Old Testament, which was completed almost four hundred years before Christ was born, and no skeptic or atheist alive claims that even one of the verses that I read was written after the birth of Jesus. If the Bible were just a book written by men, then how did the writers know these things?"

[1]D. James Kennedy, *Truths That Transform* (Old Tappan, N.J.: Fleming H. Revell Co., 1974), 138.

You might want to tell him further that there aren't just eight prophecies about Christ in the Old Testament, but at least 333. The chances of all of those being fulfilled in the person of Christ is mind-boggling! The following are a few of the key Old Testament prophecies concerning Christ, and their New Testament fulfillment. You might want to copy eight of the prophecies on small pieces of paper and insert them into your New Testament so that they will be handy for use as described above.

OLD TESTAMENT PROPHECY	NEW TESTAMENT FULFILLMENT
SEED OF THE WOMAN **Genesis 3:15—4004** B.C. And I will put enmity between thee and the woman, and between thy seed and her SEED: it shall bruise thy head, and thou shalt bruise his heel.	**Galatians 4:4—5** B.C. But when the fulness of the time was come, God sent forth his Son, made of a woman, made under the law. **1 John 3:8—5** B.C. For this purpose the Son of God was manifested, that he might destroy the works of the devil.
THROUGH ABRAHAM **Genesis 22:18—1872** B.C. And in thy SEED shall ALL THE NATIONS of the earth be blessed; because thou hast obeyed my voice.	**John 11: 51, 52—A.D. 30.** And this spake he not of himself: but being high priest that year, he prophesied that Jesus should die for that nation; And NOT FOR THAT NATION ONLY, but that also he should gather together in one the children of God that were scattered abroad.
MOCKED **Psalm 22:7, 8.** All they that see me laugh me to scorn: they shoot out the lip, they shake the head, saying, He trusted on the Lord that he would deliver him, let him deliver him: seeing he delighted in him.	**Matthew 27:39-44—A.D. 30.** They that passed by reviled him, wagging their heads. . . . Likewise also the chief priests mocking him, with the scribes and elders, said, . . . he trusted in God; let him deliver him.
GALL AND VINEGAR GIVEN HIM TO DRINK **Psalm 69:21.** They gave me also GALL for my meat; and in my thirst they gave me VINEGAR to drink.	**Matthew 27:34—A.D. 30.** They gave him VINEGAR to drink mingled with GALL.
INTENSITY OF HIS SUFFERING **Psalm 22:14, 15.** I am poured out like water, and all my bones are out of joint: my heart is like wax; it is melted in the midst of my bowels. My strength is dried up like a potsherd; and my tongue cleaveth to my jaws; and thou hast brought me into the dust of death.	**Luke 22:42, 44—A.D. 30.** Father, if thou be willing, remove this cup from me . . . And being in an agony he prayed more earnestly: and his sweat was as it were great drops of blood falling down to the ground.
HIS SUFFERING BEING FOR OTHERS **Isaiah 53:4-6, 12—712** B.C. Surely he hath borne *our* griefs and carried *our* sorrows . . . He was wounded for *our* transgressions, he was bruised for *our* iniquities. . . . The Lord hath laid on him the iniquity of *us all*.	**Matthew 20:28—A.D. 30.** The Son of man came . . . to give his life a ransom for *many*.
PRECEDED BY JOHN THE BAPTIST **Malachi 3:1—397** B.C. Behold, I will send my messenger, and he shall prepare the way.	**Luke 1:17—6** B.C. He shall go before him . . . to make ready a people prepared for the Lord.
HIS MINISTRY COMMENCING IN GALILEE **Isaiah 9: 1, 2—740** B.C. In GALILEE of the nations. The people that walked in darkness have seen a great light: they that dwell in the land of the shadow of death, upon them hath the light shined.	**Matthew 4:12, 16, 23—A.D. 26.** Jesus . . . departed into GALILEE . . . The people which sat in darkness saw great light; and to them which sat in the region and shadow of death light is sprung up. . . . And Jesus went about all GALILEE, teaching in their synagogues.

OLD TESTAMENT PROPHECY

NEW TESTAMENT FULFILLMENT

ENTERING PUBLICLY INTO JERUSALEM
Zechariah 9:9—487 B.C. Rejoice greatly, O daughter of Zion; shout, O daughter of Jerusalem: behold, thy King cometh unto thee: . . . having salvation.

Matthew 21:5—A.D. 30. Tell ye the daughter of Zion, Behold, thy King cometh unto thee.

WORKING MIRACLES
Isaiah 35:5, 6—713 B.C. Then the eyes of the blind shall be opened, and the ears of the deaf shall be unstopped. Then shall the lame man leap as an hart, and the tongue of the dumb sing. . . .

Matthew 11:4-6—A.D. 28. Jesus answered and said . . . The blind receive their sight, and the lame walk, the lepers are cleansed, and the deaf hear, the dead are raised up, and the poor have the Gospel preached to them.

REJECTED BY HIS BRETHREN
Psalm 69:8. I am become a stranger unto my brethren, and an alien unto my mother's children.
Isaiah 63:3—698 B.C. I have trodden the winepress alone.

John 1:11—A.D. 26. He came unto his own, and his own received him not.
John 7:3, 5—A.D. 29. His brethren therefore said unto him, Depart hence . . . For neither did his brethren believe in him.

JEWS AND GENTILES COMBINE AGAINST HIM
Psalm 2:1, 2. Why do the heathen rage, and the people imagine a vain thing? The kings of the earth set themselves, and the rulers take counsel together, against the Lord, and against his anointed.

Acts 4:27—A.D. 30. For of a truth against thy holy child Jesus, whom thou hast anointed, both Herod, and Pontius Pilate, with the Gentiles, and the people of Israel, were gathered together.

BETRAYED BY A FRIEND
Psalm 41:9. Yea, mine own familiar friend, in whom I trusted, which did eat of my bread, hath lifted up his heel against me.

John 13:18-21—A.D. 30. I speak not of you all . . . but that the scriptures may be fulfilled. He that eateth bread with me hath lifted up his heel against me. . . . Verily, verily, I say unto you, that one of you shall betray me.

SOLD FOR THIRTY PIECES OF SILVER
Zechariah 11:12—487 B.C. If ye think good, give me my price . . . so they weighed for my price THIRTY pieces of silver.

Matthew 26:15—A.D. 30. What will ye give me, and I will deliver him unto you? And they covenanted with him for THIRTY pieces of silver.

HIS PRICE GIVEN FOR THE POTTER'S FIELD
Zechariah 11:13—487 B.C. Cast it unto the potter: a goodly price that I was prised at of them. And I took the thirty pieces of silver, and cast them to the POTTER in the house of the Lord.

Matthew 27:3, 7—A.D. 30. Judas . . . brought again the thirty pieces of silver to the chief priests and elders . . . and [they] bought with them the POTTERS field to bury strangers in.

SPIT UPON AND SCOURGED
Isaiah 50:6—712 B.C. I gave my back to the smiters, and my cheeks to them that plucked off the hair: I hid not my face from shame and SPITTING.

Mark 14:65—A.D. 30. And some began to SPIT on him, and to cover his face, and to buffet him.
John 19:1—A.D. 30. Pilate . . . took Jesus, and scourged him.

NAILED TO THE CROSS
Psalm 22:16. They pierced my hands and my feet.

John 19:18—A.D. 30. They crucified him.
John 20:25—A.D. 30. . . . in his hand the print of the nails.

FORSAKEN BY GOD
Psalm 22:1. My God, my God, why hast thou FORSAKEN me?

Matthew 27:46—A.D. 30. Jesus cried . . . My God, my God, why hast thou FORSAKEN me?

PATIENCE AND SILENCE UNDER SUFFERING
Isaiah 53:7—710 B.C. Yet he opened not his mouth . . . As a sheep before her shearers is dumb, so he openeth not his mouth.

Matthew 26:63—A.D. 30. Jesus held his peace.
Matthew 27:12—A.D. 30. When he was accused of the chief priests and elders, he answered nothing. . . .

OLD TESTAMENT PROPHECY	NEW TESTAMENT FULFILLMENT

HIS GARMENTS PARTED AND LOTS CAST FOR HIS VESTURE
Psalm 22:18. They part my GARMENTS among them, and cast lots upon my vesture.

Matthew 27:35—A.D. 30. And they crucified him, and parted his GARMENTS, casting lots: that it might be fulfilled which was spoken by the prophet.

NUMBERED WITH THE TRANSGRESSORS
Isaiah 53:12—712 B.C.. He was numbered with the TRANSGRESSORS.

Mark 15:27, 28—A.D. 30. And with him they crucify two thieves. . . . And the scripture was fulfilled, which saith, And he was numbered with the TRANSGRESSORS.

INTERCESSION FOR HIS MURDERERS
Isaiah 53:12—712 B.C.. And made intercession for the transgressors.

Luke 23:34—A.D. 30. Then said Jesus, Father, forgive them; for they know not what they do.

HIS DEATH
Isaiah 53:12—712 B.C. He hath poured out his soul unto death.

Matthew 27:50—A.D. 30. Jesus . . . yielded up the ghost.

NOT A BONE OF HIM BROKEN
Exodus 12:46—1491 B.C.. Neither shall ye break a BONE thereof.
Psalm 34:20. He keepeth all his bones: not one of them is broken.

John 19:33, 36—A.D. 30. When they came to Jesus, and saw that he was dead already, they brake not his legs. For these things were done, that the scripture should be fulfilled, A BONE of him shall not be broken.

PIERCED
Zechariah 12:10—487 B.C. They shall look upon me whom they have PIERCED

John 19:34, 37—A.D. 30. One of the soldiers with a spear PIERCED his side. . . . And again another scripture saith, They shall look on him whom they pierced.

BURIED WITH THE RICH
Isaiah 53:9—712 B.C. He made his grave . . . with the RICH in his death.

Matthew 27:57-60—A.D. 30. There came a RICH man . . . named Joseph, who . . . went to Pilate, and begged the body of Jesus . . . and laid it in his own new tomb.

HIS RESURRECTION
Psalm 16:10. Neither wilt thou suffer thine Holy One to see corruption.

Luke 24:6, 31, 34—A.D. 30. He is not here, but is risen. . . . And their eyes were opened, and they knew him; and he vanished out of their sight. . . . The Lord is risen indeed.

HIS ASCENSION
Psalm 68:18. Thou hast ascended on high. Thou hast led captivity captive: thou hast received gifts for men: yea, for the rebellious also, that the Lord God might dwell among them.

Luke 24:51—A.D. 30. While he blessed them, he was parted from them, and carried up into heaven.

SITTING ON THE RIGHT HAND OF GOD
Psalm 110:1. The Lord said unto my Lord, SIT thou at my right hand.

Hebrews 1:3—A.D. 30. When he had . . . purged our sins, SAT down on the right hand of the Majesty on high.

THE CONVERSION OF THE GENTILES TO HIM.
Isaiah 11:10—713 B.C. There shall be a root of Jesse, . . . to it shall the Gentiles seek: and his rest shall be glorious.
Isaiah 42:1—712 B.C. Behold my servant. . . . He shall bring forth judgment to the GENTILES.

Acts 10:45—A.D. 34. And they of the circumcision which believed were astonished, as many as came with Peter, because that on the Gentiles also was poured out the gift of the Holy Ghost.

Modern prophets. There are more than two thousand specific prophecies in the Bible that have already been fulfilled. This is particularly astounding when we recall that there are no such prophecies in the scriptures of any other religion and when we consider some of the modern efforts to duplicate this feat. Probably the most notable of modern so-called prophets is Jeane Dixon. We are often told of the prophecies she has made that have come to pass, but we are not often told about her mistakes. Take the decade of the fifties, for example. In that decade she prophesied who each of the presidential candidates of each of the major political parties would be. And she prophesied the winner of each of three presidential elections: in 1952, in 1956, and in 1960. How well did she do? She missed every winner of every presidential election, and she missed every candidate in every party for each of these elections.

Several years ago *National Enquirer* magazine listed sixty-one prophecies by the ten leading seers in the world, reporting events that were supposed to transpire in the last six months of that year. Compared to the prophecies of Scripture, it should be relatively easy to predict those things which lie so close at hand. How well did they do? Believe it or not, they missed all sixty-one prophecies! Some of their remarkable forecasts were that Pope Paul would retire in that year and the Roman Catholic Church would be taken over by a committee of laymen; that George Foreman would retain his heavyweight crown in his bout with Muhammad Ali in Africa; and that Ted Kennedy would get his campaign for president into high gear. The only difference between the prophecies of these modern prophets and those of the Bible is that our modern seers were unfailingly wrong, and the biblical prophets were unfailingly right. A significant difference, to say the least.

Biblical prophecies. These biblical prophecies deal with almost every nation and scores of cities with which Israel had some dealings. It cannot be said that these prophecies were written after the events, for many of the events took place hundreds or even thousands of years after the prophecies were made; nor can it be said that they are vague and obscure, because they are highly specific in their details; nor can it be said that they are merely lucky guesses, because there are more than two thousand of them that have infallibly come to pass; nor can it be said that these were things which were likely to take place, because they were indeed extremely unlikely events. It would repay the individual who wants to be a good witness for Christ and who wants to be able to defend his belief in the Scriptures to familiarize himself with some of the details of several of these prophecies. I am including here some of the prophecies about two countries. They are quite different and they are astounding to relate. I have taken these from my book *Truths That Transform,*[2] where a great many other such prophecies are also described for the student who would like to do further research in this area.

Babylonia.[3] Consider the magnificent kingdom of Babylonia. Babylon was probably the greatest city ever built. Here was the magnificent temple of Belus, and here were the world-famous Hanging Gardens.

[2]D. James Kennedy, *Truths That Transform* (Old Tappan, New Jersey: Fleming H. Revell Co., 1974), 138.
[3]Condensed from D. James Kennedy, *Truths That Transform* (Old Tappan, New Jersey: Fleming H. Revell Co., 1974), 146–153.

She drew her stores from no foreign country. She invented an alphabet; worked out problems of arithmetic; invented implements for measuring time; conceived the plan of building enormous structures with the poorest of all materials—clay; discovered the art of polishing, boring, and engraving gems; studied successfully the motions of the heavenly bodies; conceived of grammar as a science; elaborated a system of law; saw the value of exact chronology. In almost every branch of science, she made a beginning. Much of the art and learning of Greece came from Babylon. But of this majestic kingdom, this Babylon the Golden, God said, "Babylon, the glory of kingdoms, the beauty of the Chaldees' excellency, shall be as when God overthrew Sodom and Gomorrah" (Isaiah 13:19). This is but one of over one hundred specific prophecies that were made concerning Babylon alone. The specificity of these prophecies is so great that they cannot possibly be said to be obscure as are the Delphic Oracles. Nor can they be said to have been written after the event, because many of the details of the prophecy were not fulfilled until centuries after the Septuagint translation of the Hebrew Old Testament into Greek in 150 B.C. It is not possible to give a later date for these prophecies. Nor can it be said that they have not been fulfilled, for any schoolboy with a good encyclopedia can ascertain that they have been minutely fulfilled. In these prophecies concerning the future of great cities and kingdoms, God has stamped his imprimatur on the Scriptures, confirming them as divine revelations in such bold letters that "he may run that readeth it" (Habakkuk 2:2). Nor can it be said that they are simply lucky guesses, for there are thousands of such prophecies in the Scriptures which have been minutely fulfilled. Nor yet can it be said that they concern events which were likely to take place. Indeed, many of the events were totally without precedence in the history of the world and were so incredible and unbelievable in their very nature, that even though history has fully confirmed them to be true, we still stagger at the audacity of the prophets who made such bold statements.

Walls destroyed. Consider the great walls of Babylon. Herodotus tells us that these walls had towers that extended above the two-hundred-foot walls to a height of three hundred feet. The walls were one hundred eighty-seven feet thick at the base and were fourteen miles square, according to one ancient authority. The triple walls of Babylon were the mightiest walls ever built around any city. Concerning these walls, God says, in Jeremiah 51:58, "The broad walls of Babylon shall be utterly broken." Also, "And they shall not take of thee a stone for a corner, nor a stone for foundations; but thou shalt be desolate for ever" (Jeremiah 51:26). Consider these astounding facts: (1) The wall is to be broken down; (2) it is to be broken down completely; (3) it is to be broken down permanently. It cannot possibly be said that these prophecies did not come to pass. Even the skeptics attest to their fulfillment. "Where are the walls of Babylon?" asks Constantin Volney in his *Ruins.* Major Keppel said in his *Narrative* that in common with other travelers, he totally failed in discovering any trace of the city walls.

Nor can anyone say that the prophecy was made after the event, for the walls were not suddenly destroyed. The city was taken by stealth by the Medes and Persians, and the destruction of her walls was a slow process that took centuries. The walls were still in existence in the time of Alexander the Great. They still jutted into the sky at the time of Christ. In the fourth century A.D., some remains of the walls were still there, a stark reminder that the prophecy had not yet been completely fulfilled. Then the most astounding event took place. Julian the Apostate, emperor of Rome, who determined to rid the Roman Empire of Christianity and reestablish paganism, was doing all in his power to destroy the belief in the Scriptures. However, God had said that even "the wrath of man shall praise [him]" (Psalm 76:10). While engaged in a war with the Persians near the remains of Babylon (although he had no idea of the prophecy that he was fulfilling), Julian completely destroyed the remains of the walls of Babylon lest it afford any protection in the future for the Persian army. And thus the prophecy was brought to fulfillment by one of the greatest antagonists of Scripture of all time.

One cannot say it was inevitable that the walls would be destroyed. The Great Wall of China is not nearly as large or as strong, and yet, though it is older, it still stands today. The walls of Jerusalem and many other ancient cities, though destroyed many times, have been rebuilt in part and still remain to this day. I have personally walked atop the great walls of Jerusalem that God said would be destroyed, but He also said that they would be built again in troublous times. In the case of the Babylonian walls and the Jerusalem wall, exactly what God said has come to pass (Jeremiah 39:8; Daniel 9:25; Micah 7:11; Isaiah 33:20).

When Babylon was the mistress of the world, containing within its mighty walls one hundred ninety-six square miles of the most magnificently developed city of all time, with beautiful parks, lakes, aqueducts, and hanging gardens, the prophet Jeremiah made this astounding prophecy: "Because of the wrath of the Lord it shall not be inhabited, but it shall be wholly desolate" (Jeremiah 50:13). Even more astonishing is the further prophecy of Jeremiah: "And it shall be no more inhabited for ever; neither shall it be dwelt in from generation to generation" (Jeremiah 50:39). This was an astonishing prophecy, for it was virtually without precedent. Many ancient cities in the Near East had been destroyed, but always they had been built again on the ruins of the previous cities. There is evidence of sometimes twenty or thirty cities being built on the very same site. Babylon was most excellently situated on the Euphrates. It had fine possibilities for commerce. It was militarily almost invincible. Its fields were so fertile that Herodotus, having visited there, was afraid to describe what he saw lest he be thought insane.

Have these astonishing prophecies been fulfilled? Babylon was described as the tenantless and desolate metropolis (*Mignan's Travels*, 234), a barren desert in which the ruins were nearly the only indication that it had been inhabited. Regarding Babylon, Isaiah said, "nor dwelt in from generation to generation" (Isaiah 13:20). In the sixteenth century, there was not a house to be seen at Babylon (*Ray's Collection of Travels*, Rawolf, 174). In the nineteenth century, it was still desolate and tenantless (Mignan, 284). In the twentieth century, ruins are all that remain of the once magnificent city where King Belshazzar saw the handwriting on the wall (John Elder, *Prophets and Diggers,* 106). "It shall never be inhabited," prophesied Isaiah (Isaiah 13:20). Ruins composed, like those of Babylon, of heaps of rubbish impregnated with niter cannot be cultivated (*Rich's Memoirs,* 16). The decomposing materials of a Babylonian structure doom the earth on which they perish to a lasting sterility (*Sir R. K. Porter's Travels,* vol. 2, 391). Thus God guaranteed the fulfillment of His prophecies. "Thou [Babylon] shalt be desolate for ever. . . . Babylon shall become heaps, a dwellingplace for dragons, an astonishment, and an hissing, without an inhabitant" (Jeremiah 51:26, 37).

No tents. There are other amazingly specific details in this prophecy. Consider this detail: "Neither shall the Arabian pitch tent there" (Isaiah 13:20). Has this come true? Captain Mignan said that he saw the sun sink behind the Mujelibah and obeyed with infinite regret the summons of his guides who were completely armed. He could not persuade them to remain longer. Due to apprehension of evil spirits, it is impossible to eradicate this idea from the minds of these people (*Mignan's Travels,* 2, 198, 201). Continues Isaiah: "Neither shall the shepherds make their fold there" (Isaiah 13:20). All the people of the country assert that it is extremely dangerous to approach this mound after nightfall on account of the multitude of evil spirits by which it is haunted. By this superstitious belief they are prevented from pitching a tent by night or making a fold (*Rich's Memoirs,* 27).

Waves in the wilderness. Consider these two specific, but apparently contradictory, prophecies. "The sea is come up upon Babylon: she is covered with the multitude of the waves thereof" (Jeremiah 51:42). And, "her cities are a desolation, a dry land, and a wilderness" (Jeremiah 51:43). Now note the amazing fulfillment: For the space of two months throughout the year, the ruins of Babylon are inundated by the annual overflowing of the Euphrates so as to render many parts of them inaccessible by converting the valleys into morasses (*Rich's Memoirs,* 13). After the subsiding of the waters, even the low heaps become again sunburnt ruins, and the sight of Babylon, like that of the other cities of Chaldea, is a dry waste, a parched and burning plain (*Buckingham's Travels,* vol. 2, 302–305).

In spite of the unimaginable fertility of the plains around Babylon, God had said, "Cut off the sower from Babylon, and him that handleth the sickle in the time of harvest" (Jeremiah 50:16). On this part of the plain both where traces of buildings were left and where none had stood, all seemed equally naked of vegetation (*Porter's Travels,* vol. 2, 392). "And Babylon shall become heaps" (Jeremiah 51:37). And again, "Cast her up as heaps, and destroy her utterly: let nothing of her be left" (Jeremiah 50:26). Babylon has become a vast succession of mounds, a great mass of ruined heaps. Vast heaps constitute all that now remains of ancient Babylon (*Keppel's Narrative,* vol. 1, 196).

These prophecies are presented here as examples of the more than one hundred specific prophecies relating to the city of Babylon. The wrath of the Lord was poured out upon Babylon. God said, "The Lord . . . will do his pleasure on Babylon . . . for every purpose of the Lord shall be performed against Babylon. And I will bring upon that land all my words which I have pronounced against it, even all that is written in this book" (Isaiah 48:14; Jeremiah 51:29; 25:13). Let us close this discussion of Babylon with the words of one who looked with his own eyes upon the fulfillment of these prophecies. "I cannot portray," says Captain Mignan, "the overpowering sensation of reverential awe that possessed my mind while contemplating the extent and magnitude of ruin and devastation on every side" (*Mignan's Travels,* 117).

Rebuild Babylon. Thus God threw down the gauntlet to all unbelievers. Do you want to disprove the Scriptures? It is very easy! Simply rebuild Babylon! God said it shall never be inhabited, it shall never be rebuilt, but it would always remain a desolation. There was a man who set out to rebuild it. I should tell you about him. He had all of the wealth of the whole world at his command. His name was Alexander the Great. After conquering the world, he decided to have a trade route by sea from Babylon to Egypt, and he decided to make Babylon the central headquarters for his worldwide empire. He issued six hundred thousand rations to his soldiers to rebuild the city of Babylon. Alexander the Great, the ruler of the world, said, "Rebuild Babylon!" and God struck him dead! He was immediately taken with a fever, and within a few days he was dead. The ruins of Babylon still stand in mute testimony. "I, the Lord, have spoken it! It shall never be inhabited again!" (Jeremiah 50:39, paraphrased).

Egypt—basest of the kingdoms. Compare these prophecies of destruction with what the Bible says about Egypt. God said that Nineveh, Assyria, and Babylonia would be completely destroyed and would not be rebuilt. What if He had said that about Egypt? Ah, how the skeptics would laugh. But He didn't. "They shall be there a base kingdom. It shall be the basest of the kingdoms; neither shall it exalt itself any more above the nations: for I will diminish them, that they shall no more rule over the nations" (Ezekiel 29:14-15). "The pride of her power shall come down. . . . And they shall be desolate in the midst of the countries that are desolate, and her cities shall be in the midst of the cities that are wasted" (Ezekiel 30:6-7). "And I will make the land of Egypt desolate" (Ezekiel 29:12). "And the country shall be destitute of that whereof it was full" (Ezekiel 32:15). "And I will . . . sell the land into the hand of the wicked: and I will make the land waste, and all that is therein, by the hand of strangers: I the Lord have spoken it" (Ezekiel 30:12). "And there shall be no more a prince of the land of Egypt" (Ezekiel 30:13).

Let us note that the fate of Egypt is not, as in the case of Nineveh and Babylon, to be utter extinction, but rather, "they shall be there." Egypt was to continue to exist as a nation, but "a base kingdom." "The basest of kingdoms" (Ezekiel 29:15). It is to be diminished and emptied of that whereof it was full. Have these prophecies been fulfilled? After the defeat of Antony, Augustus found such great wealth in Egypt that he paid out of it all the arrears of his army and all the debts he had incurred during the war. Still he feared that the wealth of Egypt would present to him a rival. For six hundred more years, Alexandria continued to be the first city in the Roman Empire in rank, commerce, and prosperity. A hundred years later, the Muslim hordes attacked Egypt and conquered it. They were overwhelmed by the sight of the city's magnificence and wealth. Future invaders were equally astonished at the wealth of Egypt, until the nation was reduced to a state of abject poverty, finally being brought to the place of international bankruptcy, which brought about the Anglo-French dominion of Egypt.

No prince. One of the most astonishing parts of the prophecy is the statement, "There shall be no more a prince of the land of Egypt" (Ezekiel 30:13). This prophecy is particularly striking when we note that for approximately two thousand years before the prophecy was made, Egypt had Egyptian princes sitting upon its throne 98 percent of the time. It seemed as if this would continue forever. But God declares that there shall no more be a prince of the land of Egypt. What a startling declaration! There has been ample time for the testing of the prophecy, for there continued to be a prince on the throne of Egypt until the last several decades when a democratic form of government was accepted. But were any of these princes Egyptians? Let us have that question answered by the pens of skeptics and infidels. Constantin Volney said: "deprived two thousand three hundred years ago of her natural proprietors, Egypt has seen her fertile fields successively prey to the Persians, the Macedonians, the Romans, the Greeks, the Arabs, the Georgians, and at length the race of Tartars, distinguished by the name of Ottoman Turks, the Mamelukes soon usurped the power and elected a leader" (*Volney's Travels,* vol. 1; 74, 103, 110, 193). After Volney's time, Muhammad 'Ali established the princedom again in Egypt but he was not an Egyptian. Rather, he was born at Kavala, a small seaport on the frontier of Thrace and Macedonia. His father was an Albanian aga. After this, Egypt was ruled by the French and the English. The skeptic Edward Gibbon confirms this testimony when he states: "A more unjust and absurd constitution cannot be devised than that which condemns the natives of a country to perpetual servitude under the arbitrary dominion of strangers and slaves" (Gibbon, *The Decline and Fall of the Roman Empire,* chapter 59).

Today, Egypt, which has, for over two millennia, suffered under the despotic hand of strangers, has been reduced to one of the basest of nations. My guide to the Holy Land a few years ago said that he had been to Egypt thirty or forty times, but he was never going back again because it was so foul, so vile smelling, so poverty ridden that he couldn't stand another trip. His stomach couldn't take the cities of Egypt anymore. "I will make thee the basest of nations" (Ezekiel 29:14-15, paraphrased).

These are but a few of the thousands of prophecies found in Scripture that are found in no other religious writings of the world. They are clear evidence that the Scripture has been written by the hand of God.

How firm a foundation, ye saints of the Lord,
Is laid for your faith in His excellent Word!
What more can He say than to you He hath said?

"I am God, and there is none like me, declaring the end from the beginning, and from ancient times the things that are not yet done" (Isaiah 46:9-10). "Hereby ye will know the prophet is come from me because he will tell the future" (see Deuteronomy 18:22)—as the Bible and no other book, unfailingly and infallibly, does. The Scriptures are the Word of God. "Sanctify them through thy truth," said Christ, "thy word is truth" (John 17:17).

B. I DON'T BELIEVE IN THE EXISTENCE OF GOD

Some of the material dealing with this particular objection and a few of the other objections that follow is taken from the book *Answering the Tough Ones*.[4]

When a person asks how he can be sure there is a God, begin by asking him what kind of evidence he would need to believe God exists. The average person when asked this will reply, "I would have to see Him."

To this statement you might reply, "Do you believe in the existence of air, intelligence, life, love? Have you ever seen them? Is it reasonable to use two different standards of proof—one for God and another for everything else we know exists, yet cannot see?" Then suggest another approach—three evidences that have helped you believe in the existence of God.

1. **The law of cause and effect.** This is the kind of reasoning we use every day. Wherever there is an effect, we naturally and correctly assume there is a cause that produced the effect. We believe in the existence of air, intelligence, life, and love, not because we see them, but because we see their effects. We see dust blowing, leaves rustling and assume the presence of air and wind. Likewise, I believe in God, not because I see Him, but because I see in the universe all around me effects that logically point me to a great invisible cause whom I believe is God.

2. **The evidence of design.** We look at our watch and know that it didn't spontaneously self-assemble or evolve in slow stages from nothing. The watch's beautiful design suggests to us a watchmaker. Likewise, looking at the wonders of the universe and world around us, we see everywhere order, beauty, and design. We logically conclude that as a beautifully designed watch points to a watchmaker, so an elegantly designed world points to the existence of a worldmaker, a designer I call God.

3. **The presence of personality.** We look at the famous painting Mona Lisa and see evidence of personality and logically conclude that the painting could not be the result of an impersonal cause. Because a cause must always be greater than its effect and because the painting evidences personality, so the cause has to have personality; in fact, it has to be a person. Likewise we look at a beautiful, orderly world full of people evidencing personality, we reason logically that the great cause or designer we spoke of earlier must have personality—in fact, must be a person that I call God. (This third evidence is important because a cause or force will not hold us accountable, but a person can and will!)

[4]David A. DeWitt, *Answering the Tough Ones* (Grand Rapids, Michigan: Relational Concepts, Inc., 1993).

C. MY GOD ISN'T LIKE THAT

Another frequent objection is raised at the point of God's holiness and justice. "God isn't like that! He would never punish anyone." We need to realize that the biblical teaching of the just God who "will by no means clear the guilty" is unpopular even in many so-called Christian circles today. To deal effectively with this or any other open denial of biblical truth, you must appeal to authority. No help comes from saying, "I think you're wrong!" The matters under discussion are beyond what you think or what your prospect thinks. Assuming he is a rational being of sound intelligence, what he thinks could be as valid as what you think. An external authority must be called upon to settle the matter.

1. Rationalism. You could proceed by saying, "I'm glad you said that, because you have raised a very important question. It is what is known as the epistemological question. Epistemology is that branch of philosophy that deals with the questions: How do we know? How do we know what God is like, or how do we know what He will do? How can we come to know the truth about God? There are two ways.

"One way is called *rationalism.* We simply sit down, like Rodin's *The Thinker,* and meditate about God and reach some conclusions about what He is like. The problem with this method is that we do not have sufficient data to form valid conclusions about God. This approach of rationalism has led mankind down some strange and bizarre religious paths.

"We can say, 'I think God is all love and will send no one to hell,' or, 'I think God is a demon and will send everyone to hell.' Someone else may sit and think about God and conclude, 'I believe God is the sum total of human experience.'

"We could, in a similar way, reason about the color of eyes that people on Mars may have. You think they're all red eyed. I might conclude they have polka-dot eyes. Your opinion is as good as mine because we have no data on which to base our conclusions. However, if somebody goes to Mars and returns and tells us that they have red-, white-, and blue-striped eyes, then we have good reason for placing our confidence in this person who has been there. His conclusion is based upon facts."

2. Revelation. "There is another way in which we can come to the knowledge of God. He has come from where He is to where we are, and He has condescended to give us knowledge of Himself, His purposes, and His will for us. This method is known as *revelation.* For reasons I'll not go into now, the Christian church has held that God did reveal Himself through the Scriptures and preeminently in His Son. So now the question is not what either of us thinks; rather, the question is, 'What has God said in the Bible and through His Son Jesus Christ?'"

D. ARE THE HEATHEN LOST?

Another extraneous matter that is commonly introduced is the question of the heathen. If your prospect becomes uncomfortable as you talk about the heathen in his living room, he will likely try to start you talking about the heathen in India, Africa, or New Guinea. Needless to say, such a tactic should never divert the evangelist from his objective. The woman at the well tried to change the subject when Jesus got close to her personal needs. He brought her back quickly by saying, in effect, "What we are doing here now is of much greater urgency than settling a theological debate." This is Pandora's Box. We dare not open it or we may never be able to share the Gospel.

In handling this matter, you need to focus your concern on the individual you are witnessing to. "Bob," you might say, "that's a good question, but I believe we can safely leave the heathen in Africa in the hands of a God who is infinitely just and infinitely merciful. Tonight I want *you* to know for certain that *you* have eternal life. The Bible says you can know that you have eternal life, and you have told me that you aren't sure what would happen if you died tonight. Let's confine our discussion to what God has said about you and your eternal welfare. Perhaps later we can see all He has said about those who never hear the Gospel."

I have found that this almost always satisfies the person who raises this objection and precludes a very difficult theological discussion which is going to be very unsatisfying to the unregenerate mind.

If, however, after making a profession he still raises the question of the heathen, you might want to answer it in the following way, perhaps drawing for him the following diagram to help him in his understanding. The problem revolves around the question: "Would God send the heathen to hell simply for not believing in a Christ they never heard of?"

The answer to the question *stated in this form* is no. This is not to say that they will not go to hell, but it is to say that this is not the reason. Too often the person asking the question assumes that the heathen living in primitive lands are innocent. They may be ignorant of Christ, but they are not innocent, for the Bible teaches that "all have sinned, and come short of the glory of God. . . . There is none righteous, no, not one" (Romans 3:23, 10). And "the wrath of God is revealed from heaven against all ungodliness and unrighteousness of men, who hold the truth in unrighteousness" (Romans 1:18).

They are indeed lost and on their way to eternal perdition, which, of course, is a basic motive for the entire Christian missionary enterprise. The *argumentum ad absurdum* (argument to absurdity) is applicable here. If everyone who did not hear of Christ went to heaven, then I have a far more effective plan for world evangelization than any heretofore devised. Simply close all the churches, fire all the ministers, burn all the Bibles and all other religious literature, and in a few generations no one will have heard of Christ, and everyone will go to heaven! Obviously, this is absurd.

Instead of moving into the future, the same argument can be used about the past. And if we go back to the day before Christ died, practically no one had heard of Him, and therefore everyone was on his way to heaven. Therefore, Jesus came into the world and succeeded in getting a great many millions of people lost. This, too, is an absurdity. Christ did not come to condemn, but to save those who were already condemned. Men are condemned for only one thing—their sins. To hear of Christ and to reject Him is indeed the most heinous sin a man can commit, but it is, nevertheless, only one of thousands of sins which he has committed.

The fallacy of the argument rests in this: No one is truly ignorant of God or of God's will for his life. The Scripture declares that God has mercifully revealed Himself to all men in at least one of the following three ways (see accompanying illustration):

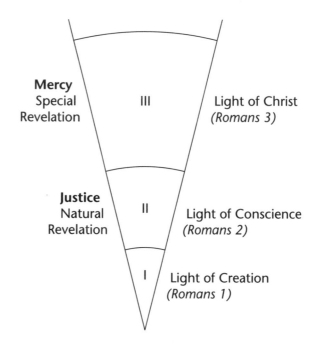

All men receive either justice or mercy. If they receive Christ they receive mercy. If not, they receive justice. Justice means that men get precisely what they deserve in light of what they have done, based on what they know. God will be unjust with no one.

Mercy
Special
Revelation

III   Light of Christ
        (Romans 3)

Justice
Natural
Revelation

II   Light of Conscience
        (Romans 2)

I   Light of Creation
        (Romans 1)

All men receive either justice or mercy. If they receive Christ, they receive mercy. If not, they receive justice. Justice means that men get precisely what they deserve in light of what they have done based on what they know. God will be unjust with no one.

1. The light of creation. God has revealed himself to all mankind in the light of His creation. The psalmist said, "The heavens declare the glory of God; and the firmament sheweth his handywork. Day unto day uttereth speech, and night unto night sheweth knowledge. There is no speech nor language, where their voice is not heard" (Psalm 19:1-3). The apostle Paul said, "Because that which may be known of God is manifest in them; for God hath shewed it unto them. For the invisible things of him from the creation of the world are clearly seen, being understood by the things that are made, even his eternal power and Godhead; so that they are without excuse" (Romans 1:19-20). Thus, we see that the creation of the cosmos bears eloquent testimony to the existence of a Creator, as can be seen by the fact that everywhere, even among the most primitive of tribes, there is found a belief in a god. The only exception to this is in modern times where, by sophisticated and ungodly evolutionary arguments, men have been taught to pervert the truth and their eyes are blinded to the obvious. "They suppress the truth in unrighteousness."

2. The light of conscience. God has placed within each one of us a moral monitor that continually passes judgment upon the rightness or wrongness of our deeds, words, and thoughts. The apostle Paul describes this thusly: "Which shew the work of the law written in their hearts, their conscience also bearing witness, and their thoughts the mean while accusing or else excusing one another; in the day when God shall judge the secrets of men by Jesus Christ according to my Gospel" (Romans 2:15-16).

By repeatedly ignoring the still, small voice of conscience, a man's heart may be hardened in sin and his conscience seared as with a hot iron, but he is nevertheless guilty for each of these acts of sin that brought him into that condition.

That man has such a conscience and is not altogether devoid of a sense of right and wrong, and thus cannot plead ignorance at the Judgment, is witnessed by two obvious facts:

a. Everywhere, throughout the world, men condemn one another for doing wrong and thus remove any possibility of saying at the Judgment, "I did not know it was wrong." The apostle Paul speaks eloquently of this: "Therefore thou art inexcusable, O man, whosoever thou art that judgest: for wherein thou judgest another, thou condemnest thyself; for thou that judgest doest the same things. But we are sure that the judgment of God is according to truth against them which commit such things. And thinkest thou this, O man, that judgest them which do such things, and doest the same, that thou shalt escape the judgment of God?" (Romans 2:1-3).

b. Everywhere, men commit sins under the cover of darkness. They may not be so hardened as to commit cannibalism at lunch, but they steal chickens at night.

3. The light of Christ. As I said earlier, there is another way in which we can come to the knowledge of God. He has come from where He is to where we are, and He has condescended to give us knowledge of Himself, His purposes, and His will for us. The Christian church has held that God did reveal Himself preeminently in His Son. So now the question is not what either of us thinks; rather, the question is, "What has God said in the Bible and through His Son, Jesus Christ?"

4. Those who seek will find God. God has obligated himself when anyone responds positively to what little information about God they possess to give them the rest of the information they need for salvation. In Acts 8:26-31, an Ethiopian eunuch sought to know more about God, and God sent Philip to give him the rest of the information needed. In Acts 10:1-6, a Gentile named Cornelius exhibited a heart after God, and God sent Peter to tell him what he needed to know to be saved. Missionaries report many similar instances today.

5. Old Testament people were saved on the same basis as those in the New Testament. When someone asks how people in the Old Testament were saved without hearing about Christ, we reply that they, too, needed to acknowledge their sin. They recognized their need for a Savior by offering a substitute sacrifice which pointed to a future Messiah. They looked forward in faith to the Savior, while we look back in faith to the same Savior who died on the cross to pay the penalty for our sins and rose from the grave to provide a place in heaven for us.

6. God will not hold accountable those with no capacity to seek him. People unable to consciously choose Christ, like babies or those born with brain damage, will not be held accountable for not trusting Christ. Revelation 5:9 states that there will be people from every language group in heaven. Certainly many of those will be those who died not having the capacity to believe or reject Christ.

7. God holds Christians responsible to proclaim the Gospel in all the world. Christ ordains that those who have not heard must hear, and that the Gospel be proclaimed in every land, nation, tribe, and tongue—to every living person. If the church took this mandate seriously, we wouldn't have to deal with the question of the heathen being lost because they have not heard. Furthermore, as I said earlier, if those who have never heard the Gospel are not lost because they have never heard about Christ, it would be better that we never proclaim the Good News. That's because when we do proclaim it, there are always some who reject Christ and are lost, so the Gospel really becomes bad news. Hence, we should burn all the Bibles, close all the churches, and bring all of our missionaries home. No, the heathen of the world are lost. You and I have a responsibility to bring them the Good News of Jesus Christ.

E. I DON'T BELIEVE IN HEAVEN

This is an objection you might receive as soon as you ask the first diagnostic question. I would suggest that you respond somewhat as follows:

"I assume, then, that you don't believe in the Bible, for the Bible obviously teaches that there is a heaven. It is, of course, your privilege not to believe in the Bible, but I would like to ask you a question." At this point you would use the "judo approach" answer to the objection, "I don't believe in the Bible." Thus you are using that answer as a funnel into which several objections can be poured.

F. I DON'T BELIEVE IN THE RESURRECTION OF CHRIST

The resurrection of Christ is the best-established fact of antiquity. I have never met a person who has read so much as one book on the evidences for the resurrection of Christ who did not believe it. I have met many people who did not believe it, but they have never examined the evidence. A nineteen-year-old young man once said to me, "Well, it's just your opinion. There's no evidence to support it." How foolish is that statement, and yet it represents the opinion of many people. The Christian faith is the only evidential and historical religion in the world. The Bible never calls us to blind faith, but it calls us to faith in evidence. Blind faith is faith without evidence. The Bible calls us to believe in "many infallible proofs." Are these proofs able to stand up to the light of criticism?

Dr. Simon Greenleaf was more qualified to examine such evidence than any man who ever lived. He was the royal professor of law at Harvard University and was declared by the chief justice of the Supreme Court of the United States to be the greatest authority on legal evidences who ever lived. He was the highest authority on evidence that could be quoted in any English-speaking courtroom in the world. After writing voluminously on the laws of legal evidences, he decided to turn the searchlight of his knowledge of evidence and his ability to sift the true from the false toward the evidence for the resurrection of Christ.

He minutely examined each thread of evidence concerning the resurrection of Christ and concluded that in any unbiased courtroom in the world, if the evidence for the resurrection of Christ were presented, it would be adjudged to be an absolute historical fact. This was the opinion of the greatest authority on evidence that the world has ever known—Dr. Simon Greenleaf of Harvard.

G. I DON'T BELIEVE IN LIFE AFTER DEATH

The fundamental reasons for our believing in life after death are the resurrection of Jesus Christ from the dead (as set forth above) and the unambiguous declarations of Scripture that man has been made for eternity and will live forever, either in heaven or in hell.

In addition to those two biblical reasons for belief in life after death, you might suggest five additional extrabiblical evidences. Not all of them are of equal weight, but when taken together like threads, they can form an exceedingly strong cord.

1. An analogy from nature. The ancient philosopher Plato explored the question of immortality primarily from the vantage point of analogies found in nature. He examined the drama of germination found in a dying seed and noticed that for the seed to bring forth a living plant, a beautiful blossom, and a delicious fruit, it first had to go through the process of disintegrating and dying. Likewise, he concluded that the human body must ultimately decay and die before it will emerge in another world and another life. It is interesting that Plato lived four centuries before Christ and the apostle Paul, yet he enunciated the same evidence of life after death to which Christ and Paul pointed in John 12:24 and 1 Corinthians 15:35-36.

2. The necessity for justice. Another philosopher, Immanuel Kant, approached the question of life beyond the grave from a different perspective. He observed that all humans have some concern for right and wrong, some sense of moral duty. Then he asked what would be necessary for that innate sense of duty to make sense. He answered his own question by reasoning that for that sense of duty to be meaningful, there must be justice, for why do right if justice doesn't prevail? Kant noticed, however, that justice does not always prevail in the world. Too often those who seek to do good suffer, and those who are wicked prosper. His practical reasoning continued by concluding that since justice does not prevail in this life, there must be another time and place where it will. In other words, he reasoned that justice demands life beyond the grave. This sounds very much like what the Bible describes in Hebrews 9:27.

But then Kant carried his logic further to reason that for justice to truly prevail, there must be a perfect judge who must know all things and have all the evidence; he must have all power to ensure that the verdict for reward or punishment is properly carried out. Thus, for Kant, practical ethics requires life after death and a judge whose description sounds very much like the God of Christianity described in the Bible.

3. The first law of thermodynamics. The first law of thermodynamics, set forth by Albert Einstein, states that energy and matter cannot be created or destroyed. They may be transformed from one form into the other, but they can't be destroyed. This was conclusively demonstrated with the dropping of the atom bomb at Hiroshima! One scientist stated that no single atom in creation can go out of existence; it can only change form. We cannot burn up anything; we simply change it from a solid to a gaseous state. By changing its temperature, we can change water from a liquid to a gas (steam) or a solid (ice).

If man—body, mind, and soul—at death ceases to exist, he, the most precious of all God's creatures, will be the only thing in the universe that does. Again, the Bible, in 1 Corinthians 15:49-51, describes for us how the Christian's body will, in fact, change its form.

4. The last words of dying people. In the library there are books quoting the words of people who stood at the threshold between life and death and testified of seeing a bit of both worlds on either side of the door. The noted infidel Edward Gibbon on his deathbed cried out, "All is dark!" And another infidel named Adams, passing from this world, was heard to cry, "Demons are in this room and are about to pull me down!"

In contrast, Augustus Toplady, author of the hymn "Rock of Ages," cried out, "All is light, light, light!" And Everett, for twenty-five minutes before he was gone said, "Glory, glory, glory!" Thousands of people have been granted some preview of that which was to come, the world into which they were passing.

5. The recollections of resuscitated people. Many scientists have been quite skeptical about the possibility of life beyond the grave. However, it is worthy of note that recently several scientists have caused a stir in the scientific world by announcing that the conclusions of their investigations have led them to believe that life goes on beyond the grave. These conclusions have been reached from careful interviews with hundreds of people who have been pronounced clinically dead and have later been revived and have told of the experiences they had in the interval. I have personally talked with people who have experienced in this world a foretaste of either heaven or hell. Since there is no consensus either in medicine or in law as to just when death takes place, these experiences leave some questions to be answered. But they do provide interesting modern testimony to the fact that people live on beyond death, either in joy or in torment.

I have found these testimonies to have a very sobering effect upon some skeptical individuals. The following information, therefore, may be used with discretion in answering the objection, "I don't believe in life after death":

"The evidence is now conclusive: There *is* life after death." This is not the statement of an overenthusiastic preacher or of some recondite theologian in his ivory tower, but the somber pronouncement of a scientist—made to a large group of other scientists. The statement: "The evidence is now conclusive: There *is* life after death." The speaker: Dr. Elizabeth Kubler-Ross, psychiatrist. The occasion: a national conference on death, dying, and beyond, in which a thousand scholars, medical experts, and professionals in the care of the dying participated.

Dr. Kubler-Ross was apparently not a Christian, nor even a particularly religious person, but that was her sober conclusion from the examination of hundreds upon hundreds of cases of terminally ill patients. In her testimony she declares that she has carefully scrutinized the statements of hundreds of people who have had the experience of being pronounced clinically dead (legally dead), but have been resuscitated and have told of what happened during that interval. You have said in the past, "Oh, well, when somebody goes there and comes back, then I will listen." Well, friend, start listening, because someone has been there and has been back—not merely someone, but four or five hundred different someones. Their statements have been carefully analyzed and compiled by scientists—by not only Dr. Kubler-Ross—but others, as well, including Dr. Raymond Moody of the University of Virginia. By the way, where did this national conference take place, and where was this startling declaration made? The University of California at Berkeley! Right out of the center of the counterculture comes new proof of life beyond death. Dr. Kubler-Ross says that hundreds of cases of individuals who have died and have had out-of-body experiences have been scientifically verified. "We've just been afraid to admit it," she said.

Would you like to know what happens when you die—what the experience of dying is like? Five hundred people have testified to that experience, and the amazing thing is the unanimity of their testimonies. They have been collected from a wide variety of people, from all sorts of backgrounds, by a number of different scientific investigators. Dr. Moody of the University of Virginia sums up all of his findings in this way: "There is a buzz or a ring at the moment of death, followed by rapid progression through an enclosure, or tunnel, toward light. [*I am the light of the world.*] There is surprise at being outside the body. Next comes a panoramic review of one's life." And note this: People who were paraplegics, who had been paralyzed for years, had legs they could move; they had a body, albeit a spiritual body, with legs they could move and limbs they could use. And astounding as it is to report, those who had been blind for many years finally had eyes through which they could see. In fact, in every case they reported on, the people who came into the resuscitation room—people who were blind—reported on who was there, what they did, and what they said.

They all reported floating up out of their body and looking down on all of the people in the resuscitation room, and described accurately the details of what they had seen. These were not just a few, but over five hundred separate cases taken from all over the world. And then, note this: Every one of these people reported seeing, usually at a distance, a person whom they described as a religious "figure." This was even true for atheists. The Bible says that there is one with whom we have to deal, and that one is Jesus Christ! Even atheists will have to appear before Him. There is no escape! Many were quite irritated at being brought back into their limited, and often crippled, physical bodies.

Dr. Kubler-Ross said, in conclusion, to her colleagues, "We now have factual support, replicated again and again, in hundreds of cases by different people. For me, there's no longer a shadow of a doubt. I used to say, 'I believe in life after death.' Now *I know.*" One thousand medical professionals and scholars stood to give this psychiatrist a standing ovation when she concluded.

H. WHAT ABOUT REINCARNATION?

This is a question which is more often raised today with the increasing interest in oriental religions. I would respond as follows: "The Bible says, 'It is appointed unto men once to die, but after this the judgment' (Hebrews 9:27). Thus, the Bible teaches that man dies only once, and after this there comes the Judgment. And the Scriptures make it very plain that after the Judgment there comes either heaven or hell. I wonder if you understand why people believe in reincarnation?

"It is, of course, a belief of Hinduism and Buddhism, but not of Christianity. It is an incorrect conclusion drawn from two correct understandings. These people realize, first, that to dwell with God one must be perfect and, second, that man is sinful. Therefore, they postulate a series of thousands of reincarnations during which time man gradually becomes better and better until he arrives at perfection.

"This same basic idea is seen in the concept of purgatory—that man must be made perfect before he can enter paradise. In this case, however, it is not by reincarnation, but through a stay in some fiery place of purgation. A common garden variety of this concept, held by many Americans is, 'I'm not good enough now to live with God, but if I just work a little harder, I'm sure that one day I will arrive—by loving my neighbor and doing the best I can.'

"All three of these views ignore the atonement of Jesus Christ and His perfect righteousness. By His death He once and for all takes away all of our sin, and by His perfect obedience in this life He clothes us with His righteousness so that we are instantly made perfect to stand in the presence of God through the righteousness of Christ alone."

I. HELL ISN'T REAL

In dealing with the denial of the reality of hell, sometimes we find it helpful to say, "You know, it is a fact of psychology that we deny most passionately those things we fear most desperately. I wonder if the reason you don't believe in hell is that deep down in your soul you fear that if there is such a place you might go there." Often the reply is, "I guess you're right!"

You must go on then and assure your prospect, "I don't want you to believe in hell so that you can live your life in mortal terror of going there. You can know for sure that you're not going to hell. That's what the Gospel is all about. I believe in hell, but

I know that I'm not going there because of God's promise. This is much better than saying, 'I know I'm not going to hell because I don't think there is such a place.'"

J. WE HAVE OUR HELL RIGHT HERE ON EARTH

This is an objection which is not infrequently heard. A recommended response is the following:

"You know, you're right! At least in part. That's just what the Bible says. We do have an 'earnest' of our inheritance right here in this world. I'm sure you know what an 'earnest' is. Earnest money paid down on a house is a pledge that more is to come. The word is even more interesting in Greek. The Greek term translated 'earnest' is *arabòne*. It was used in Greek for a swatch of material. For instance, a woman who was planning to recover her couch would bring home a swatch to hold up to the wall and curtains and chairs. Of course, the swatch would be meaningless and her action would be ridiculous unless there was a roll of material back at the shop with which to cover the couch.

"That, of course, is precisely the lie the devil would like us to believe. He keeps saying to us, 'Oh, that swatch of hell is all there is.' But God is saying, 'The whole roll is waiting for you when you die.' Well, I would like to tell you something exciting. The Bible also makes plain that it's possible to have a little bit of heaven right here on earth. Wouldn't that be vastly better than a taste of hell? Let me tell you how."

If a person does not believe in God's justice and hell, you may proceed to show that the prophets Isaiah (Isaiah 57:21) and Ezekiel (Ezekiel 33:11), the apostles Peter (2 Peter 2:4, 6, 9) and Paul (Romans 2:4-5), and the Lord Jesus Himself (Mark 16:16; Luke 13:3; John 3:18) taught that God will assuredly punish sin.

K. UNIVERSALISM

Occasionally you will meet a universalist who will object, "Everyone will be saved." This is the same objection as "hell isn't real," only in a little different dress. Some Scripture that is useful in putting the lie to universalism is, "Then shall he say also unto them on the left hand, Depart from me, ye cursed, into everlasting fire, prepared for the devil and his angels. . . . These shall go away into everlasting punishment: but the righteous into life eternal" (Matthew 25:41, 46).

L. RELIGION IS A CRUTCH

Another objection often raised is that religion is a crutch for the weak, for those who are afraid to face life as it really is. They say that man, being afraid of the lightning, thunder, and the storms that sometimes beat upon us, has invented a god to whom he can flee for refuge. Is this really the case? Dr. R. C. Sproul in *The Psychology of Atheism*[5] has answered this objection very effectively. I paraphrased his answer recently in talking to an unbeliever who raised this objection.

I said: "Do you really believe that? Do you really believe that I am afraid of the lightning and thunder and storms? The truth is that I have been through a number of

[5]Dr. R. C. Sproul, *The Psychology of Atheism* (Minneapolis: Bethany Fellowship, Inc., 1974), 42ff.

hurricanes and actually enjoyed them! There is very little about the world in which we live today that really frightens modern man. The devil is a great liar, but I will tell you what the truth about this matter really is.

"Though there are many wonderfully appealing aspects to the Christian God—His love, His compassion, His mercy, His longsuffering, etc., there are also threatening aspects to the Christian God which make any earthly terror pale by comparison. There is His justice and the judgment to come. There is His anger against sin and the wrath that He has promised to pour out upon it. And there is the prospect of everlasting punishment in hell. Rightly, the Scripture concludes, 'It is a fearful thing to fall into the hands of the living God' (Hebrews 10:31). And Jesus declares that we should not fear him who is able to kill the body and after that there is nothing more he can do, but rather that we should fear Him (God) who is able to plunge both body and soul into hell. 'Yea,' says Christ, 'I say unto you, fear Him.' The truth of the matter, then, is that rather than the believer creating an imaginary God to whom he may flee, the unbeliever has created an imaginary world in which God does not exist in order to flee from a just God who is infinitely angry with him because of his sins. This is the truth of the matter, as every unbeliever knows deep down in his soul."

M. WHAT ABOUT ALL THE HYPOCRITES IN THE CHURCH?

"If Christianity is true," someone asks, "why are there so many hypocrites in the church? I know a man who is a deacon, but he . . ."

1. **Not everyone in the church is a true Christian.** Mark Twain once said that there is a difference between the right word and almost the right word, like "lightning" and "lightning bug." Likewise, it is important for us to distinguish between a true Christian and one who calls himself a Christian.

2. **Simply going to church doesn't make anyone a Christian** any more than being born in a barn makes someone a cow. You can lead a moral life, keep the Golden Rule, and still not be a Christian. In fact, Christ warned us to be careful to distinguish between wheat and tares, as well as between sheep and goats.

3. **Only truly valuable things have counterfeits.** Encountering counterfeit money, gold, or furs doesn't cause us to quit using those valuable commodities. It does make us more cautious so that we are never again deceived by counterfeits. Likewise, when we come upon counterfeit Christians—hypocrites—we should not reject the real thing. We should just be more careful that we never become a hypocrite.

4. **The Bible doesn't claim to produce perfect Christians** in an instant; we're only perfectly forgiven. Christians admit that they sin and need forgiveness. But just because we sin from time to time doesn't make us hypocrites. If everyone were perfectly healthy, we wouldn't need hospitals; likewise, if everyone were perfectly sinless, we wouldn't need churches. Because we do sin, we need the church and we need Christ.

5. **God disciplines Christians who are guilty of hypocrisy.** This is proof that we are

his sons and daughters (Hebrews 12:4-8). Great numbers of Christians live consistent lives without any sign of hypocrisy.

6. Don't let something you and Christ agree upon come between you. If you hate hypocrisy, remember that He hates it more than you do (Matthew 23:13-14). So if you agree with Him, don't let your common enemy—hypocrisy—come between you. Someone once said that if you let hypocrites stand between you and God, you're admitting that they are closer to God than you are.

7. Is hypocrisy the real problem? Or is it a smoke screen for rejecting Christ? Often people who don't sincerely want to turn to Christ are looking for an opportunity to shift the blame to someone else and make their rejection of Christ look reasonable. But they will still be held accountable regarding their own personal response to the Gospel.

N. WHY DOES GOD ALLOW SUFFERING?

Perhaps no other question has been asked more about God. It is not a hypothetical question but one that touches all of our families and friends—one that challenges the very character of God. Why do innocent people suffer? Why are babies born blind? Why is a promising young life suddenly snuffed out? Why are there earthquakes, tornados, wars in which thousands of harmless people are killed and children are burned beyond recognition or maimed for life? One-third of the world went to bed hungry last night; how does that square with God's love?

There are no easy answers to this profound question. It's a question that through the ages has been asked in different forms. Let me share with you five common forms of that question, together with some replies which have proven most helpful to me and to those with whom I've shared the Gospel.

1. Why did God create a world in which there would be suffering? The general tendency is to blame God for evil and suffering and to pass on all responsibility for it to Him. But we must never forget that when God created man, He created him innocent. Man was not created evil or with suffering as part of his lot on earth. Genesis 1:26-31 and 2:7-9 tell us that God put man in a beautiful garden with everything good. It was Paradise—heaven on earth—with no sin, pain, sorrow, or death. Then, through sin, man lost his trouble-free paradise. But God didn't leave man in this predicament forever. Revelation 21 and 22 describe for us a "paradise regained," which God is preparing for His redeemed people, where they will enjoy forever perfect bliss and eternal life free of any suffering. Revelation 21:4 states, "God shall wipe away all tears from their eyes; and there shall be no more death, neither sorrow, nor crying, neither shall there be any more pain: for the former things are passed away."

2. If God isn't responsible for all suffering, who is? The Bible states clearly that man himself, because of his sin, is the cause of human suffering. God created man innocent. He gave him the ability to obey or disobey. Had man obeyed, there would never have been a problem. He would, no doubt, have lived an unending life of fellowship with God and enjoyment of Him and His creation. Genesis 3 tells us that as a result of man's sin, suffering entered the world—man laboring by the sweat of his brow, and woman giving birth in great pain. The point we must keep in mind is that *man*—not God—through sin and rebellion, was responsible for bringing suffering into the world.

Not only that, but man is directly the cause of 85 percent of all the suffering in the world today. That is, he inflicts it upon himself—lung cancer, murder, rape, drunken driving accidents, robbery, poverty that arises out of laziness. According to statistics from the American Lung Association, an average of 70,000 people die every year from emphysema. Smokers make up 97 percent of those individuals. God doesn't inflict emphysema on smokers. It is a natural consequence of their bad choice.

While much of the suffering is caused directly by us or those around us, much suffering can only be explained by the fact that the world is in a fallen state. God's universe was without suffering until man sinned. Before that, babies would not have been born deformed, earthquakes and tidal waves would not have taken countless lives. But those tragedies occur because our world is in a fallen state. It is the result of man's sin.

3. Why did God create man with the ability to sin in the first place? To be sure, God could have made us so we couldn't sin, but if He had done so, we would no longer be humans, we would be machines. How would you like to be married to a robot that says, when you push a button, "I love you," or to a life-sized doll that is programmed to hug you and say, "You're wonderful!" There would never be any conflict or harsh words, but there would never be any spontaneous love, either. Love, to be love, must be voluntary—that is, love must be the result of a person's own choice. Adam's bad choice led to consequences, and those consequences included suffering.

4. Why doesn't God stop all the suffering? Because He is all-powerful, God could, in fact, stamp out all the suffering in the world in a split second! But let's consider what He would have to do. He'd have to do away with the consequences of our sin, but then there would be no choice, for consequences make choices significant. Then He'd have to do away with indicators that something is wrong. Pain can be to us like a warning light on the dashboard of a car telling us that something is wrong. And God often provides those indicators to get people's attention. It wouldn't be fair for God to give no indication that something is wrong and let people head unwittingly for ultimate suffering in hell. God would also have to do away with the other benefits that result from suffering, such as personal growth, purity, and other virtues which can be brought about through suffering.

5. What is God doing about the world's suffering? First, He sent His Son to suffer redemptively (Hebrews 2:18; 1 Peter 2:20-24). Second, He gives grace to us when we suffer (2 Corinthians 12:7-10). Third, He purifies through suffering when we mix it with faith (Romans 8:18, 28-29). Fourth, He uses *us* to help others face their suffering (James 1:27 and 5:14-16; 2 Cor. 1:3, 4).

O. WAS JESUS AN ACTUAL SPACE-TIME HISTORICAL PERSON?

There are some misinformed people who postulate that Jesus may never have existed at all and view Him as a mythical person patterned after the characters in the ancient mystery religions. Others accept a historical Jesus and interpret anything miraculous in mythical terms. Such positions are usually a blatant denial or misuse of the objective historical data available.

1. Well over a dozen non-Christian sources from ancient history mention Jesus. Even though the first century was not characterized by advanced communications, and there were, comparatively speaking, very few writers of ancient history, and though Jesus' background as a peasant from a humble carpenter family would not draw a great amount of attention, there are, nevertheless, a surprising number of non-Christian sources that do speak of Him.

For instance, there was Josephus (A.D. 37–97), a Jewish historian who had been born into a priestly family and became a Pharisee at age nineteen. After the destruction of Jerusalem in A.D. 70 he moved to Rome, where he became the court historian for Emperor Vespasian. Josephus makes two references to Jesus. The first simply refers to James as "the brother of Jesus, who was called Christ." The second is more detailed and is found in one of his major works called *Antiquities*:

> At this time there was a wise man who was called Jesus. And his conduct was good and he was known to be virtuous. And many people from among the Jews and other nations became his disciples. Pilate condemned him to be crucified and to die. And those who had become his disciples did not abandon his discipleship. They reported that he had appeared to them three days after his crucifixion and that he was alive; accordingly, he was perhaps the messiah concerning whom the prophets have recounted wonders.

Other writers, such as Tacitus, who was called the greatest historian of ancient Rome; Suetonius, chief secretary of Emperor Hadrian; Pliny the Younger, Roman author and administrator in Asia Minor who became known as one of the world's great letter writers, and many others made reference to Jesus Christ, the church, and Christians in their writings.

2. A number of early non–New Testament Christian writers produced volumes of important works that contain references to a historical Jesus. For instance, Ignatius, bishop of Antioch and a leader in the early church before his execution in Rome, wrote:

> Jesus Christ who was of the race of David, who was the son of Mary, who was truly born and ate and drank, was truly persecuted under Pontius Pilate, was truly crucified and died in the sight of those in heaven and on earth and those under the earth; who moreover was truly raised from the dead, His Father having raised Him, who in the like fashion will so raise us also who believe in Him.

Writers such as Clement, a leading elder in the church at Rome; Quadratus, one of the early apologists; Justin Martyr, a major Christian apologist; and others made reference to Christ as a space-time historical person.

3. Archaeological sources corroborate historical facts in the life of Jesus. The names of various governmental officials, the census that took place at the time of Jesus' birth, the crucifixion process recorded in the Gospels, etc., are corroborated by archaeological discoveries.

4. New Testament sources, to be absolutely fair, must be included. Oxford historian of antiquity A. M. Sherman-White points out that the same standards commonly applied to ancient secular history can also be applied to the New Testament records. He concludes that when such criteria are applied, there is undeniable evidence of Jesus Christ as an actual space-time historical person.

Concerning manuscript evidence, the New Testament is easily the best-attested ancient writing. Ancient classical works have comparatively few manuscripts, with twenty entire or partial copies being considered an excellent number. By comparison, the New Testament has over 5,000 manuscripts or partial copies. For most ancient classical works a gap of 700 to 1,400 years between the original and earliest copy is very common. By comparison, the Chester Beatty Papyri, containing most of the New Testament, are dated about 100 to 150 years after its completion. And while we have complete copies of all the New Testament books, it is not so with all the other ancient works. For instance, of the 142 books of Roman history written by Livy, 107 books have been lost.

The evidence is overwhelmingly supportive of the fact that Jesus Christ was born, lived, taught, died, and rose again. He was and is an actual person who lived in history.

P. GOD WOULDN'T ASK THAT

This is an objection that is sometimes raised to the second diagnostic question. I would recommend a response something like the following: "Well, I'm certain that God doesn't need me to write His script for him. That's why I used the word *suppose*. *Suppose* that you were to die and God were to say to you. . . . I think that question brings the whole matter into focus and is helpful for our thinking. Suppose He were to ask you that, what do you think you would say?"

If this answer does not suffice, then you might also say the following: "I am sure that I do not know exactly what questions God will ask us, but Jesus indicates in Matthew 7:22 some answers that people will be giving to a question asked them at the final Judgment. He says, 'Many will say to me in that day, Lord, Lord, have we not prophesied in thy name? and in thy name have cast out devils? and in thy name done many wonderful works?' Though the question they are answering is not explicitly stated, it certainly is implied that it is something like, 'Why should you be admitted?'"

Q. I HAVE ALWAYS BELIEVED THAT

This is the most common objection met in sharing the E.E. presentation. Quite often we will get to the point of explaining what saving faith truly is and the prospect will say something like, "That's what I said I was trusting in when you asked me." Obviously, you can't grab him by the lapels and cry, "Liar!"

This objection comes up so often that we must take special care to get an answer to the question: "Suppose that you were to die tonight and stand before God and He were to say to you, 'Why should I let you into My heaven?' What would you say?" Not only must we get an answer, we must also understand the answer and get our prospect to agree that we understand what he is saying. There is no harm, after getting the answer to the question, in saying, "Now let me see if I understand you. You're saying . . ." Then rephrase what he has just said. He will either acknowledge or deny that your understanding is correct.

This is particularly important when the prospect has been quite religious but has not understood the Gospel. This type of person is the type most likely to deny that he has the wrong answer. If you have sufficiently clarified the answer to the question, your prospect is unlikely to reverse himself at the end and say, "Oh, I've always trusted in Christ for salvation!"

If, in spite of all your efforts, you come to the end of the presentation and he still says, "Oh, I have always believed that," the following answer is recommended:

"I know that you have always believed in God and in Christ as His divine Son—that He was born of a virgin and died on the cross and rose again from the dead. And I'm sure that you have even trusted in Him for many temporal needs in your life, such as sickness, travel, etc., but when it came right down to what you were trusting in for your hope of eternal life, like myself and so many people, you were trusting in your own efforts to try to be good enough.

"Do you remember what you told me? You said, 'I try to follow the Golden Rule and keep the Ten Commandments and do the best I can.' Don't you think that it would be a good idea to place your trust for eternal salvation in this one in whom you have always intellectually believed and also trusted for many temporal things?"

What you have done in this answer is to give him credit for everything he has believed: for his intellectual assent to the historic facts of the Gospel and for his temporal faith. The reason this is important is because he may think you are denying he has ever believed in God or believed in Christ, even intellectually, or that he has ever trusted in Him for anything. And this confusion will lead to defensiveness or even hostility on his part if he thinks you are denying that he believes these things. Therefore, you give him credit for everything he has believed, but point out that the one crucial thing that is needful for his salvation he has not done—namely, to place his trust in Christ for his eternal salvation.

R. I BELIEVE WE ARE SAVED BY BOTH FAITH AND WORKS

It might help if we remember that ultimately there are only three possible religions: First, there is that religion wherein it is taught that a man will become acceptable to God by his own works, his own doings, keeping commandments, following certain rules of morality, piety, benevolence, etc. Second, there is that religion that teaches simply that man will be saved by faith in Christ. Third, there is that religion that teaches that a man will be saved by a combination of the two—both by faith and by works.

We might do well to identify those groups that hold to these various concepts: Most pagan religions believe that man will be saved by his works, by keeping some set of rules, whether it be the eightfold path of Buddha, the teachings of the Koran, or any of the others. Christianity teaches that man is saved by grace alone through faith. It is the teaching of most of the cults (such as Jehovah's Witnesses, Mormonism, etc.) that man is saved by faith and works.

1. Does James contradict Paul? It is interesting that the great literary man Ruskin said that there was only one book in the world that made it clear concerning faith alone and works and that was the Bible. Some people have said that the Bible contradicts itself at this point. They have specifically said that James contradicts Paul, for Paul is one of the major teachers of the concept of grace by faith, though it is taught throughout the New Testament.

On the surface these passages do appear to contradict each other. The apparent contradiction in James 2:14 states, "What doth it profit, my brethren, though a man say he hath faith, and have not works? can faith save him?" Further in verse 20: "But wilt thou know, O vain man, that faith without works is dead?" In verse 21: "Was not Abraham our father justified by works, when he had offered Isaac his son upon the altar?" And in verse 24, "Ye see then how that by works a man is justified, and not by faith only."

Now listen to Paul in Romans 3:28 where he gives this great conclusion of his fullest presentation of the Christian Gospel: "Therefore we conclude that a man is justified by faith without the deeds of the law." In Ephesians 2:8-9, he states, "For by grace are ye saved through faith; and that not of yourselves: it is the gift of God: Not of works, lest any man should boast." In fact, in Galatians 2:16 he says the same thing six different times: "Knowing that a man is not justified by the works of the law, but by the faith of Jesus Christ, even we have believed in Jesus Christ, that we might be justified by the faith of Christ, and not by the works of the law: for by the works of the law shall no flesh be justified." Both negatively and positively he asserts this truth six different times.

So, there is no question about the fact that there apparently is some contradiction! But is there, in reality, a contradiction? In seminary my Greek professor stated that he once thought there was a contradiction between James and Paul. However, after learning the Greek language and studying the passage in James in the original text, he found that the supposed contradiction evaporated.

2. Same truth defended. Let us see if there is indeed a contradiction, or if Ruskin is right and the Bible is, indeed, the only book that is absolutely clear on the subject of faith plus works. Are Paul and James defending two different truths? I believe a careful examination of the text and context will reveal that they are both defending the same truth against different errors or against a different set of antagonists.

An illustration might be of a seventeenth- or eighteenth-century damsel dressed in a white gown who is being attacked by two different bands of cutthroats. She is being defended by two heroes who have drawn their swords. Approaching from the north is one group of brigands and cutthroats who have set their hearts upon destroying this fair damsel, and one hero is fighting them while another hero has taken his stand at her other side and is fighting another group of cutthroats who are coming from the south. Though they are both defending the same truth, they are, in fact, fighting in opposite directions. And so are Paul and James.

3. Different errors fought. Let us look first at the people to whom they are speaking. Paul is addressing the Pharisees, or the heathen who would attempt to justify themselves by their own efforts. He is dealing with the legalist who is saying that by keeping some set of rules, whether it be the Ten Commandments of the Old Testament, or whether it be the laws of some heathen religion, he will obtain the favor of God. It is against this legalist that Paul is so adroitly fighting. James, on the other hand, is addressing the members of the Christian church—a particular portion of the members of the Christian church: the hypocrites therein. You have heard it said that there are too many hypocrites in the church. That is not a recent saying. James is saying the very same thing right here, for he is talking to the professing members of the church. These are the people who think they will be saved by professing the right faith in Jesus Christ, and they have come to the place where they say, "We see that a man is not saved by his good works. What we must do is profess our faith in Christ and hold to the right doctrines and be a part of a church which is sound in the faith." Yet there is absolutely nothing in their lives that would evidence the fact that a real faith exists.

Once, a lady became very distraught with me after I had told her the Gospel of Christ, of the free grace of God and the proffered gift of eternal life to those who would trust or believe in Jesus Christ. She sat up indignantly in her chair and said, "Do you mean to tell me that all I have to do is sit here and say I believe in Jesus Christ, and I will go to heaven?"

My answer was, "No ma'am, that's not what I said."

She asked, "Well, what did you say?"

And I replied, "If you will believe, or trust, in Jesus Christ, you will have eternal life as a free gift." She said, "You said it again! All I have to do is say that I believe, or trust, in Jesus Christ, and I'll go to heaven."

Again I answered, "No, ma'am, that's not what I said. I didn't say it now, I have never said it in the past under any circumstances, to anyone, anywhere, at any time. I have never made such a statement and never will because it is absolutely false."

She asked, "Well, what did you say?"

I said, "I did not say you would be saved by *saying* that you believed in Christ, but rather by *believing* in Him."

James says here: "What doth it profit, my brethren, though a man have faith and have not works? Will faith save him?" Is that what James said? It is not! He said:

"What doth it profit, my brethren, though a man *say* he hath faith, and have not works? can faith save him?"

Unfortunately the King James Version does not deal too accurately with the last part of that verse. If you examine the Greek text, the phrase is *hay pistis.* It uses the definite article and should be translated, "What doth it profit, my brethren, though a man say that he hath not works, can that faith save him?" In order to understand what James is saying, you have to know that throughout this whole chapter, when James talks about faith, he is talking about a *said* faith, a profession of faith. He never means "What shall it profit if a man have faith and not have works," because it is not possible that a man truly have real faith and not have works.

4. **Three key words.** There are three key words in this passage in James. The first one we have just mentioned. It is the word *say.* "Though a man *say* he hath faith" (verse 14); "Yea, a man may *say,* Thou hast faith, and I have works" (verse 18).

The second word is *show.* It is found in verse 18: "Shew me thy faith without thy works, and I will shew thee my faith by my works."

The third word is *see,* which is found in verses 22 and 24: "Seest thou how faith wrought with his works" and "Ye see then how that by works a man is justified."

5. **Self-righteous or barren orthodox.** Faith is invisible. A man may *say* he has faith, but you cannot see it, nor can you show it apart from works. There is absolutely no way anyone can know you have faith apart from your works. That is precisely why, at the Judgment, people are judged by their works. By their works they demonstrate the reality of their faith, though they are saved by faith. But the genuineness of that faith is shown to the world, and the world sees that that faith is real by the works that the people have done. So we see that Paul is dealing with the self-righteous, and James, on the other hand, is dealing with the barren orthodox—those who believe that by the correctness of their creed, they will be saved; those who may be expert on the confession, may argue it with great eloquence, may believe it in all of its details, may confess the Apostles' Creed and the Westminster Confession, yet they have no fruit, no joy, no love, no peace, no works, no service for Jesus Christ.

Paul is talking to those who would deny faith in the cross of Christ for salvation, and James is talking to those who would demean that faith and reduce it and diminish it to nothing other than a bare, naked mental assent. For Paul, faith is an act of the entire, the whole interior, being of man. It is an act of the mind that accepts the deity of Christ and His atoning act in His resurrection as true. It is the act of the affections that responds to the love of God and, in turn, loves God with all of the heart and mind, strength and soul. It is an act of the will that bows to the sovereignty of God and determines to follow Jesus Christ. Paul says that we are saved by faith, but he says it is a faith that works by love. Even in Ephesians 2:8-9 where it says that we are saved by faith apart from works, it goes on in the next verse to say that we are created in Christ Jesus *unto* good works, which God has prepared for us.

We also see that James and Paul are using the concept of works in a different sense. Paul is talking to those people who would do works in order to be saved—works which they believe would lead to salvation. James is telling people that they need those works that flow out of salvation and result in salvation. True faith reaches up to connect us to the dynamo of the universe, to the Holy Spirit of God, and it always results in a transformation of life by the surging of the power of God into our lives. A man may say he has faith, but if he does not demonstrate that transformation of life, then his faith is spurious. The importance of trusting in Christ alone for our salvation may be further explained as follows:

6. Faith and works boats: "Imagine that you are out in the middle of a lake, and there are two rowboats, and you are standing with one foot in each boat. One boat, however, is filled with holes and is sinking fast. It is obvious that unless you do something, you will soon be in the lake. The boat with the holes represents ourselves with all of the leaks caused by sin. The boat without holes represents Christ. It should be obvious that with one foot in each boat, we shall end up in the same place we would have ended up if we had had both feet in the boat marked *self*. The only safe place is to have both feet firmly planted in the boat marked *Christ*.

7. Rope or thread? "Or to change the picture, suppose you were trying to cross from one cliff to another one a hundred feet away. It is five thousand feet down to the rocks below. You have, however, a one-inch-thick piece of rope which is capable of holding up several tons. There is a difficulty, though, for you have only fifty feet of rope. I say, 'Do not worry! I have fifty feet of thread. We can tie my thread to your rope, and then tie that to trees on either cliff, and then you can go across.' You decline my offer, and I respond, 'What is the matter? Do you not trust the rope?' 'Yes,' you say, 'I trust the rope, but I do not trust the thread.'

"Then let's change the story and make it ninety feet of rope and only ten feet of thread. You're still not comfortable. Then suppose we make it ninety-nine feet of rope and only one foot of thread. One inch of thread? You see, if you have one inch of thread, you will be just as dead on the rocks below as if you tried to cross on a hundred feet of thread. The rope obviously represents what Christ has done, and the thread represents what we have done. We must trust in Christ alone. As Charles Spurgeon put it, 'If we have to put one stitch into the garment of our salvation, we shall ruin the whole thing.' "

S. I'LL DO IT LATER, NOT NOW

If a prospect responds, "No," or "Not yet," you may be able to discover the underlying cause for delay and deal with it by asking the following nonthreatening question: "I'd be interested to know, if you were to receive the gift of eternal life tonight, what problems would it create for you?" When he shares with you what underlying problem is keeping him from trusting Christ, you can tactfully, lovingly, deal with the problem, and then ask him again if he would like to receive the gift of eternal life.

Often one will hear the Gospel and agree to its truthfulness, but will not want to receive Christ at the moment. Of course, such an attitude is presumptive. The prospect assumes that he will have another opportunity to respond to God's gracious invitation. Probably he will; possibly he will not. The evangelist has a responsibility to press the urgency of the matter and persuade the prospect. Jesus warned of the fool who said, "Soul, thou hast much goods laid up for many years; take thine ease, eat, drink, and be merry," only to hear the frightful words, "Thou fool, this night thy soul shall be required of thee" (Luke 12:19-20). Paul echoed the same thought: "In the day of salvation have I succoured thee: behold, now is the accepted time; behold, now is the day of salvation" (2 Corinthians 6:2).

I once talked to a young man of about twenty-two who told me he would do it later. He said he believed in God and in Christ intellectually, and believed that the Bible was true, and he planned to accept Christ someday as his Savior. "But first," he said, "I've got a lot of living to do." I remonstrated with him for some time, but finally, when I saw that I could not persuade him, I let him go, reminding him that the Bible says that he who, being often reproved, hardens his neck, shall suddenly be cut off, and that without remedy (Proverbs 29:1). A week later, I heard that he was driving down the highway about seventy miles an hour when a truck stopped in front of him with its tailgate down. He was instantly decapitated. I remembered the words I had spoken to him: "He that hardens his neck shall suddenly be cut off, and that without remedy."

There are some situations in life where we face two options. But while we're considering which of these options to take, we're already in one of them. For example: Your car stalls on the railroad track; the train is coming. You have two options: to try to start the car and save both yourself and the car, or to get out and run, and at least save your life. While you are considering these two options, however, you are already in one of them. You are in the car, and the train is getting closer. So it is with God. You have two options: to accept Jesus Christ as your Savior, or not to accept Him. While you are making up your mind about that issue, you are already in one of the options. You have not accepted Him, and the moment of your death, which is uncertain, draws nearer, and eternity looms before you.

Thirteen

ADDING
ILLUSTRATIONS

Following are a number of illustrations we have found effective in illuminating the Gospel. The illustrations available for this purpose are limitless. Perhaps you will have good response with some other illustrations. Since all of life is an illustration of spiritual truth, every sermon, book, or even the commonplace occurrences of everyday life provide abundant illustrations of spiritual truth. It should be noted that most illustrations are designed to point out one significant truth.

TRUSTING IN CHRIST—JOHN WESLEY

The life of John Wesley, who started the Methodist Church, illustrates very clearly the importance of trusting in Jesus Christ alone for salvation. He went to Oxford Seminary for five years and then became a minister of the Church of England, where he served for about ten years. Toward the end of that time, in approximately 1735, he became a missionary from England to Georgia.

All of his life, he had been quite a failure in his ministry, though he was, as we would count men, very pious. He got up at four o'clock in the morning and prayed for two hours. He would then read the Bible for an hour before going to the jails, prisons, and hospitals to minister to all manner of people. He would teach, pray, and help others until late at night. He did this for years. In fact, the Methodist Church gets its name from the methodical life of piety that Wesley and his friends lived.

On the way back from America, there was a great storm at sea. The little ship on which they were sailing was about to sink. Huge waves broke over the ship's deck, and the wind shredded the sails. Wesley feared he was going to die that hour, and he was terrified. He had no assurance of what would happen to him when he died.

Despite all of his efforts to be good, death for him was a big, black, fearful question mark.

On the other side of the ship was a group of men who were singing hymns. He asked them, "How can you sing when this very night you are going to die?" They replied, "If this ship goes down, we will go up to be with the Lord forever."

Wesley went away shaking his head, thinking to himself, "How can they know that? What more have they done than I have done?" Then he added, "I came to convert the heathen. Ah, but who shall convert me?"

In the providence of God, the ship made it back to England. Wesley went to London and found his way to Aldersgate Street and a small chapel. There he heard a man reading a sermon that had been written two centuries earlier by Martin Luther, entitled "Luther's Preface to the Book of Romans." This sermon described what *real faith* was. It is *trusting only in Jesus Christ for salvation—and not in our own good works.*

Wesley suddenly realized that he had been on the wrong road all his life. That night he wrote these words in his journal: "About a quarter before nine, while he was describing the change which God works in the heart through faith in Christ, I felt my heart strangely warmed. I felt I did trust in Christ, Christ alone, for salvation; and an assurance was given me that he had taken away my sins, even mine, and saved me from the law of sin and death."

There it is. That is saving faith. *Repenting of his sins,* he trusted in Jesus Christ alone for salvation. Now, would you say that Wesley had not believed in Jesus Christ before this night? Of course, he had. He was a biblical scholar and had studied about Christ in English, Latin, Greek, and Hebrew. He had believed in Christ in all these languages. But he had trusted in John Wesley for his salvation.

After this, he became the greatest preacher of the eighteenth century. But it all began when he put his trust in Jesus Christ alone for his salvation and received Him as His Lord.

COMMITMENT—AFRICAN RIVER

In Africa there is a mighty river called the Zambezi. Imagine that you have fallen into this river and that you are heading downstream toward a huge waterfall. You are holding on to a small log that is barely keeping you afloat. Now, just before you reach the falls someone throws a rope to you from the shore. You have two options: ignore the rope and plunge over the falls to certain death; or let go of the log, grab the rope, and be pulled safely to the shore. That's a lot like our position with Christ. We hold on to whatever keeps us afloat and hope it will be enough when, in reality, we and our possessions will go over the falls. To live eternally we must be willing to let go of the "log"—whatever gives us false hope—and reach out to the rope—Christ—who alone is able to save us.

GOD'S HOLINESS—OUT-OF-TUNE INSTRUMENT

Imagine an orchestra playing in concert with one instrument out of tune. The conductor would not eliminate the entire orchestra; however, he would have to cast out the bad instrument. Spiritually, we are out of tune with God. He is righteous; we are unrighteous. He is perfect; we are imperfect. God is sinless; we are sinful. Just as it was necessary to cast out the discordant instrument for the orchestra to remain an orchestra, it was necessary for the one in perfect harmony with Himself to cast man out. God cannot exist with sin. He can have nothing to do with that which is other than He is, and He is absolutely perfect, holy, and righteous.

GOD'S HOLINESS—MISCARRIAGE

You can liken our relationship to God to that of a mother who has carried her baby almost full term and then has a miscarriage. The mother has grown to love the child; she anticipates the fellowship and the presence of the child. However, the child has something in his biological makeup that actually acts in opposition to the mother's own biological makeup. This is the way it is spiritually. Man is actually a creature of God. However, man worked against God and introduced discord. Now God must cast away His creature. He still loves man, but if man remained in union with God, it would destroy God's perfection, and God would no longer be God.

MAN'S INABILITY—BROAD JUMP

Let the sofa and the coffee table represent the two sides of an incredibly deep canyon. Say the width is one hundred feet. Now we can imagine all the men, women, and children who have ever lived or ever will be born on earth lined up on one side. They have to get to the other side, let's say, to save their lives from an impending danger. They will be lost if they don't make it. They have to jump. Now do you have any idea what the broad-jump record is? Between twenty-eight and thirty feet! How many people from the whole human race can jump the one-hundred-foot-wide canyon? None! That's exactly right! No one would make it, although some would do better than others. Some would jump way out—twenty feet or more. Some would only make it a few feet. Some would just stumble over the edge. But none would make it all the way! All would fall short of the mark. All would fall to their death.

This is the way it is spiritually. There is a gap between man and the kingdom of God. We try as hard as we can to jump the gap. We go to church, keep God's commandments, don't intentionally hurt anyone, and jump out as far as possible. That's the way I was in my own life—jumping hard! I had comfort from the fact that I was jumping farther than many. I figured God would accept those who jump the farthest. I knew no one was perfect, so I figured He would accept those who did the best. I thought God would lower His standard. But this would mean that God grades on the curve. He does not! I learned that this was wrong. He has only one standard:

perfection. Jesus said, "Be ye perfect even as your Father in heaven is perfect." I am not perfect. Suddenly, I recognized that those people I looked down on who were not doing as well as I in being good were no worse off than I. I knew we were all going to the same death. Regardless of how good we were, none were good enough to get across the canyon. We are all doomed to the same eternal death. We will all go to hell if we have to make ourselves good enough for heaven. There must be another way across, or there is no way at all.

MAN'S INABILITY—LEMON TREE

The reason we cannot keep God's commandments is that we do not have the nature to act according to His will. We have no inner ability to keep them. Imagine that you have a lemon tree in your yard. All it can produce is sour lemons. Now if you want to grow oranges, you may decide to pull off all the lemons from your tree and stick sweet, juicy oranges in their place. In a few minutes your tree could be covered with the sweetest oranges in town. Everyone will look and see your "orange" tree—but in reality, all you have is a lemon tree with dead oranges on it. You haven't changed the nature of the tree.

Our human nature is sour. Often we don't like it and we resolve to do better. We try to throw away the fruits of our sour nature. We get rid of the bottle, clean up our language, and try to better our family and business relationships. All we are really doing is picking off lemons and sticking on oranges. We get rid of bad habits and acquire good ones. However, this does not change the source of the stream of life. Our nature is untouched by our resolutions and reformations. We are as powerless to make our hearts good as we are to make a lemon tree into an orange tree. We need a new nature. The Bible says, "If any man be in Christ, he is a new creature" (2 Corinthians 5:17).

MAN'S INABILITY—CHINESE NATURE

If the Central Intelligence Agency wanted you to be an agent behind the bamboo curtain in China, you would be trained to talk, act, look, and think Chinese. You would go to school and learn the Chinese language so that you could speak it fluently without a trace of accent. After studying the mores of China and watching films of Chinese physical characteristics, you could duplicate their mannerisms. Perhaps you would undergo plastic surgery and have your face changed so that you would look Chinese. Then you could enter China and be welcomed as one of them. You would then do everything in the Chinese manner. No difference would be noticeable. As far as anyone in China would be concerned, you would be Chinese. Now let me ask you—would you be Chinese? No, not if you did not have Chinese parents. Nothing you can do will change your race.

Actually, it's the same way spiritually. You may talk and dress like a Christian. You may join Christian organizations and sing Christian songs, and in all ways act like a

Christian. However, none of these things will make you a Christian. You were born a sinful man and you have the nature of a sinful race. Nothing you can do outwardly can change this fact. Just as you would have to have been born of Chinese parents to be Chinese, so you need a new birth spiritually to be a Christian. It's impossible for you to become Chinese. However, with God all things are possible, and you can be born anew spiritually and become a child of God. Those who have been born again put their trust for eternal life in Jesus Christ alone.

CHRIST'S WORK—HUMAN PREDICAMENT EQUATION

You can take the human predicament and make an equation out of it. Man's sinfulness plus God's justice can equal only one thing: eternal hell for man. That is what we deserve. However, there is another factor in the equation. If we add to man's sinfulness and God's justice the factor of God's love, again one answer is possible: the cross of Christ. Because God loved His people with an everlasting love, it was necessary that Christ provide redemption through the blood of His cross.

GOD'S JUSTICE—AREOPAGITE

It is said that none ever could claim he was dealt with unjustly by the Areopagite in Athens. His sentence always proved to be upright. How much more is this true of the righteous judgment of God.

GOD'S MERCY—DYING THOMAS HOOKER

When Thomas Hooker lay dying, a friend said, "Brother, you are going to receive the reward of your labors." He humbly replied, "Brother, I am going to receive mercy." We need nothing but mercy, but mercy we must have or we are lost. Justice would give us what we deserve—hell. God in His infinite mercy and grace gives us heaven.

A huge crowd of people was watching the famous tightrope walker, Blondin, cross Niagara Falls one day in 1860. Blondin crossed the rope numerous times—a 1,000-foot trip, 160 feet above the raging water. The story is told that he spoke to the crowd, asking if they believed he could take one of them across. Of course, they all gave their assent. Then he approached a man and asked him to get on his back and go with him. The man who was invited refused to go. It is like that with Jesus Christ. Mental assent, or even verbal assent, is not enough. There must be trust   not strength—but trust in Christ alone.

FAITH—OBJECT DETERMINES VALUE

Have you ever considered what makes faith valuable? Some seem to think that faith has an intrinsic value and they say, "Have faith!" I submit that faith must be in a valuable object if the faith itself is to be valuable. Faith in the wrong object is not valuable—it is disastrous. You may have all the faith you can muster in the brakes of your car; however, if the fluid line is broken, your brakes will not stop the car, and neither will your faith. Suppose you awaken in the night with a headache and stumble into the dark bathroom and, in faith, take a tablet that you think to be aspirin. But unfortunately you've really taken a roach tablet. They may inscribe on your tombstone, "He died in faith," but your faith was in an object not worthy of your confidence. Many pregnant women took the mysterious drug thalidomide in the faith that it would make their pregnancy easier. Their faith did not prevent their bearing deformed children. Faith, to have any value, must be in a valuable object. When it comes to your eternal welfare, only Jesus Christ is worthy of your confidence and trust. To have faith in anyone else or in anything else is disastrous.

GOOD WORKS—PRICELESS CABINET

A famed cabinetmaker is very fond of you. He wants to surprise you with the greatest gift you'll ever receive. Unknown to you, he gathers all the money he has. He takes all his life's savings, and though he has to deny his own son the privileges that others have, he sells all that he has, cashes in stocks and bonds, and hunts the world over to find the best wood money can buy. The priceless unfinished wood is brought into his shop. Day and night he works to produce the most perfect, the most beautiful table the world has ever known. He goes without food, without sleep, and his health is neglected. Finally, the butting, the sawing, the gluing, the fitting, and the sanding are all done. He finishes this masterpiece by hand, polishing for hours. Finally, the last stroke is made with the cloth. The next day, he comes to your door with his men holding the table draped in cloth. You welcome him in, and he unveils the priceless gift. What will be your response? Let's say you run and grab a piece of sandpaper and make a move toward the table. This expert craftsman stops you short and exclaims, "It's finished!" It is like this with salvation. God paid a priceless sum in giving Jesus on the cross for us, who Himself cried out, "It is finished!" We can add nothing—not one thing! We have only to receive—undeserving as we are. To change anything about that gift of God is to refuse it. Where then are good works? They are in the honoring of the giver. Just as that table will be placed in the open for all to see, and just as all who see it will be told all about the glory and mercy of the man who made it, so we will, by the nature of our acceptance, lift up God in our lives and proclaim what He has done for us. And this will be evidenced in all that we do and say.

GOD'S ONLY FORGOTTEN SON

This is a powerful illustration that can be used at the end of a presentation if the person is hesitating about his willingness to place his trust in Christ. You might say . . .

"Suppose that the police were to break in to this room right now with guns drawn and take me away handcuffed to prison. You, of course, would be startled, and when you read in the newspaper that I was being tried for multiple murders and bank robberies, you would be even more surprised. After you heard that I had been convicted and sentenced to die in the electric chair, you would no doubt be amazed, indeed. Since, however, you know me and you are supposed to 'love your neighbor' even as you love yourself, you decide to try to do something to help me.

"You go down and speak to the judge and say, 'What can I do to help? I'll do anything at all. I will even be willing to give my life for him,' to which the judge replies, 'That would not be a sufficient sacrifice, for this man has killed many people. However, we would accept the life of your child. That would be an adequate sacrifice.'

"You go home and agonize. You have but one child—a lovely young daughter. You pray. You wrestle with your decision, and finally you decide that if you really are going to love me, even as yourself, you must do this. And so you bring your child down to the prison where you are told, '*You* must do it. *You* shave her head. *You* put her in the chair. *You* pull the switch.' And so, as your child looks pleadingly at you and says, 'Mommy, why have you forsaken me?' you cover her head and watch her writhe and die as you pull the switch. The guards inform me of what has been done by you in my behalf and say that because of that, I am free to go home.

"A few days later, you are sitting in a booth in a restaurant having dinner. I come in behind you with a friend and sit down, not seeing you. You overhear my friend say to me, 'According to the newspapers you had been condemned and were to die in the electric chair. What happened? How is it that you're free?'

"And to your astonishment you hear me reply, 'Oh, it was all a big mistake. When they looked at the record of my life, they saw that I was really a pretty nice fellow. There were a great many people I had not killed and numerous banks I had not robbed. Why, I had even put money in some banks, and helped several old ladies cross the street in years gone by. After weighing my whole life, they decided to let me go. Therefore, I am free.'

"As you listen to these incredible words, there flashes into your mind a picture of your daughter writhing in the electric chair. You know in your heart that the only reason I am walking around alive is because on the other side of town there's a new grave with your daughter's name on the marker. How do you feel about me now? I think that is the way God might feel about you if you had come before Him today and told Him all about your good works, without even a word about His Son who died on the cross.

A little boy in the first grade in Sunday school was reciting John 3:16, but he got it slightly mixed up, and I think he is a picture of many of us. He said, 'For God so loved the world that He gave His only *forgotten* Son.'"

Fourteen

SCREENING
CONTACTS

Jesus Christ commanded His followers to go and make disciples of all nations. The number of people on this planet in this year 1996 is approaching six billion. How is such an enormous group of people to be reached with the Gospel and discipled into a vital relationship with local congregations? The answer is clear. We must go where these people are. We must share with them the Gospel of Christ. And when we go with the Gospel, we must believe that the Holy Spirit goes before us and establishes divine appointments.

If we wait for people to come into our church buildings before we go to them with the Gospel, the task will never be done. In the great commission, our Lord commands us to *go!* The apostles set the pattern. They visited households (Acts 10). They went to the synagogues (Acts 17). But they also went to public places and even house to house (Acts 20:20).

One effective screening tool that has helped us go where people are, determine their spiritual interest, and reach them with the Gospel of Christ is the religious questionnaire. As a witnessing tool, the questionnaire provides opportunity for conversation on spiritual matters by asking questions about the individual's spiritual interests, his relation to religious organizations, the degree of involvement in these organizations, his assurance of eternal life, and the basis of that assurance. This raises the subject. If the contact shows interest in continuing the conversation, we go on to share our testimony and the Gospel and often lead the person to Christ.

This approach to personal-evangelism training is new to many people and raises several basic questions that need to be addressed.

I. WHY USE THE QUESTIONNAIRE APPROACH?

A. IT INCREASES THE NUMBER OF WITNESSING AND TRAINING OPPORTUNITIES

As the number of trained evangelists and people wanting to be trained increased at the Coral Ridge Presbyterian Church, a new challenge confronted us. How do you provide enough responsive contacts for the training? There were many first-time visitors each week at the worship services, but the growing number of people in the organized training-ministry became so large that it was impossible to provide enough good contacts for every team.

At first, we tried casual calling door-to-door and were able to get into many homes for a visit. But once we were inside the home, we found we had an even greater challenge. Many of the people who invited the teams into their homes were absolutely not interested in the Gospel. Our trainees were being exposed to one difficult situation after another, and this was discouraging. The questionnaire approach helped us solve this problem.

The assurance and religious questionnaires have become a main source of providing meaningful and responsive contacts for our evangelism and discipleship training ministry. Our trainees needed to see the basic presentation repeatedly shared with people who are spiritually open. Without this, they would never really learn how to share their faith.

The use of a questionnaire in the training ministry also helps equip a trainee to share the Gospel effectively. Once he has learned to present the Gospel in this manner effectively, he becomes better equipped to do so in his daily life.

So, with the church as the center of our evangelism training, we moved out in all directions. When our teams call on people who have first visited the church and the "first timers" are not home, the team uses a questionnaire and makes contact with someone else in the same community. This way, our trainees usually see the Gospel presented each week and spend less time traveling between calls. And—to their great delight—they find divine appointments everywhere!

B. IT SERVES AS A SCREENING DEVICE TO DISCOVER INTERESTED PERSONS

Wherever you go, you will find people who need Jesus Christ. The questionnaires are a means of discovering your divine appointments. You aren't limited to those who come to your church or those who ask you what they must do to be saved.

Many people who answer the questions will not be prospects for hearing the Gospel. Asking these questions helps to separate the prospects from the suspects and keeps trainees from exposure to too many difficult cases. At the same time, it helps you discover good prospects for sharing the Gospel. A prospect is someone who does not have eternal life but is interested in knowing how to receive it. He will be seeking or at least open.

As you talk with him, his need will be indicated by his spiritual interests, his religious affiliation or lack of it, and the basis for his hope of eternal life. And his attitude, reflected in the tone of his voice and his facial expressions as he responds to the questions, will let you know if he is looking for a faith.

C. IT HELPS YOU MEASURE THE SPIRITUAL CLIMATE OF A COMMUNITY

Each time you ask a prospect's religious affiliation, you will add data to your understanding of the community. After an extended use of the questionnaire approach, you can accurately estimate the predominant religions and denominations of an area and determine the best approach for reaching your target audience.

D. IT HELPS YOU DISCOVER DIVINE APPOINTMENTS

When we go with the Gospel, the Holy Spirit goes before us and establishes divine appointments. What He did with Philip and the Ethiopian eunuch (Acts 8:26-38), Peter and Cornelius (Acts 10), and for many, many others since then, He will do for you as you trust Him.

The Lord promised that when you go with the Gospel, He will go with you (Matthew 28:19-20). He cannot lie (Titus 1:2). He has all power and authority in heaven and on earth (Matthew 28:18), so nothing can keep Him away. You can be sure He is with you, even if you don't "feel" His presence, because He is faithful to His promise. He wants to use you to draw others to Himself. He will use you to accomplish His will in their lives, and He will use them to accomplish His will in your life. He will already be working in the life and circumstances of the individuals to whom He guides you (Acts 10:1-8).

He may use you to plant His Word in their hearts. He may use you to water the Word that has already been planted (1 Corinthians 3:6). But do not be satisfied with only planting and watering. You are commanded to make disciples. As you faithfully witness, He will give a harvest (Psalm 126:6).

A white-haired, eighty-four-year-old man sat alone on a bench in a shopping center in Atlanta, Georgia. Three people approached. One of the trio smiled and spoke to the elderly gentleman. "Hello, I'm John. This is Mary, and this is George. We are from First Church. We're trying to determine people's religious thinking and assist anyone looking for a faith. Would you help us by giving your thoughts in response to a few brief questions?"

The man looked up in astonishment. "I'm eighty-four years old. At least twenty times this year, people have told me that I should trust Christ as my Savior. They have told me that He is God clothed in human flesh. They have told me that if I put my faith in Him alone, He will give me eternal life and take me to heaven when I die. I think it's about time I did that. Can you tell me how to do it?" The team quickly explained how a person puts his trust in the living Christ. The aging patriarch found new life while sitting on a bench in a shopping center. *That was a divine appointment!*

It was a bright, sunny day. A handsome young man had nothing to do, so he was picking burrs out of his dog's hair in front of his apartment. Three young people walked up to him. A lady said, "Hi, I'm Dottie. Meet Fran and Jim. We're trying to determine people's religious thinking and to assist anyone looking for a faith. Would you help us by giving your thoughts in response to a few brief questions?"

He had not been in a church for a long time. He had not given too much serious thought to spiritual things. But in that moment, God moved upon his heart in an overwhelming fashion.

When the questionnaire was completed, Dottie asked if she could share how she came to know she had eternal life and how he could know it, too.

He was eager to listen. After the Gospel was presented, he prayed to receive the gift of eternal life.

A few weeks later, he entered the Evangelism Explosion Discipleship Training. Six months later, he was studying for the ministry. *That was a divine appointment!*

Divine appointments like this happen over and over wherever questionnaires are used. The names change, the places change, but the fact that God the Holy Spirit goes before His people and establishes divine appointments stays the same.

II. WHAT IS QUESTIONNAIRE EVANGELISM?

Questionnaire evangelism uses a simple printed list of questions to gather information and open the way for the evangelist to share the Gospel. Because this is a somewhat formal approach, it is best used with people with whom you have no opportunity to first cultivate a friendship or to relate to casually. It is best used in public places, door-to-door, or over the telephone. We offer two different questionnaires: the assurance questionnaire and the religious questionnaire.

The questionnaire is a small printed form containing introductory comments and questions, concluding comments, and various options for follow-through. At first, they were long and cumbersome. By regular review and revision, the questionnaires and the procedure for using them have been refined into the brief forms in this book. (See appendix A for sample questionnaires.)

A. IT IS NOT A SURVEY

A survey is a systematic, comprehensive study that, when completed, is announced or published with its findings. Unless you plan to do just that, you'd better be honest and refer to it as a questionnaire.

B. THE ASSURANCE QUESTIONNAIRE

The assurance questionnaire inquires about the person's denominational affiliation, local place of worship, and frequency of attendance. It then asks the two diagnostic questions and requests permission to share the Gospel.

C. THE RELIGIOUS QUESTIONNAIRE

The religious questionnaire takes a "softer" approach by asking the person if he is more interested in spiritual matters today than he was five years ago, if he perceives God as a supreme being who watches over him and to whom he will ultimately answer. Next, it asks if he prays at some time and in some way every day and if he attends a church, temple, or synagogue. Finally, it leads into the two diagnostic questions and uses the "Good News" transition to ask permission to share the Gospel.

III. HOW DO YOU USE THE QUESTIONNAIRE?

A. FOCUS ON DIFFERING TARGET AUDIENCES

Our church visits beaches, malls, airports, bus stations, parks, laundromats, apartment complexes, recreational areas, and residential sections for door-to-door personal evangelism using the questionnaire approach. Our visitation secretary provides maps with these locations marked for easy reference. Once we have visited someone in an apartment or home, we mark the maps accordingly to avoid duplication of visits.

B. KEEP LOW VISIBILITY

Whether witnessing in a public place or in residential areas, it is important to keep low visibility. Assign only one team per target area to avoid duplication. Do not send a team into a complex every week on the same day or time of day. Skip a week and, if possible, move to a different section of the complex. Otherwise, those who don't like Christians to witness will spread rumors. If this happens, people will be less willing to talk to you. Keep your questionnaire pad concealed until you are ready to use it in a public place or apartment building. Questionnaire pads should be visible only when using them and marking them. Be careful not to block traffic in hallways or shopping areas.

Don't blitz one house right after another in the same block, as the cults do. Rather use the "guerrilla approach" of striking and retreating. That is, drive up to the house, get out of the car, walk up to the door, and knock instead of using the sidewalk for going house to house. Get back in the car and drive for a block before approaching the next house.

One should dress appropriately for the target audience: coat and tie, if appropriate, for residential areas, casual attire for beaches and malls, modest and moderate clothing at all times so as not to draw attention to yourself. Your appearance either attracts or repels. Watch your facial expressions. The number one thing you should wear is a smile. It will attract, and it will usually cause others to be more interested in talking with you. If you are wearing sunglasses, take them off when talking to someone. Eye contact is important for good communication.

C. CHOOSE STRATEGIC LOCATIONS

Consider the best time for the contact. Some places are better at certain times than they are at others. In most places there are strategic locations. A good location will be close to the flow of traffic to allow you to watch the people go by. There you can pray for God to guide you to the person to whom you should speak. Ideally, your "good location" will also be a place where you can get out of the mainstream of traffic and have a degree of privacy as you talk. This will help the person not to feel embarrassed, especially when he prays to receive eternal life.

D. WATCH THE WEATHER

The weather is something else you need to watch. If it's wet or cold, be sure you pick a sheltered place. Some people are so eager to share the Gospel, they pay no attention to the circumstances around them. Cold or wet weather can work in favor of teams calling in homes. More people will usually be home, and they will be more inclined to invite you in.

E. TRAINER TAKE THE LEAD

Remember that you have been brought together by God to help each other learn to share the Gospel more effectively. The trainer is always in charge. Trainees are to rely on and follow the direction of the trainer.

These questionnaires are very brief and simple. Because they look so easy, eager trainees often want to use them too soon. While questionnaires may appear simple, the judgments that must be exercised in determining the course of action following the questionnaire are not so simple. Trainees are not usually qualified to make those judgments until near the end of a four-month training semester. With commendable zeal, they will sometimes rush in where angels fear to tread—and then panic. So, always be sure that an experienced trainer is in charge of the situation.

The trainer is to handle difficulties that may arise at any point in the contact. The trainer has experience, and the trainee can learn from the trainer how to deal with difficulties in the future. Until the trainee has mastered the variations and difficulties, he should depend on his trainer to handle them.

F. WATCH CAREFULLY THE INTERACTION BETWEEN TEAM AND PROSPECT

1. Groups. Avoid doing questionnaires with a group. If you approach three or more people and attempt to share the Gospel, you will find it extremely difficult. This is especially true with younger people. Most of the time there will be at least one who will try to argue. That will turn the situation into an argument rather than a presentation of the Gospel. Therefore, choose a person who is alone or with only one other person. If more people move into the situation after you have started the questionnaire and it turns into a debate, then politely leave as soon as you can. But if you are forced to share with two or more people at the same time, use a separate form for each person or put an *A* and *B* at the top of the column and mark each question twice according to each prospect's answer. Ask everyone being surveyed each question before going on to the next question.

When you come to the last question (God's "Why?") ask it first of the person who seems least likely to have a correct answer. This will avoid having someone give a correct answer that others will simply parrot. If a person replies: "I don't know," use the five-step procedure (suggested earlier) for obtaining an answer.

2. Gender. Usually it is best to pick someone of your own gender. When you witness to a member of the opposite sex who is about your own age, you will sometimes find that he or she may misunderstand your intentions or get more interested in you than in the Gospel. This is not a hard, fixed rule. Christ witnessed to women as well as to men. But whenever possible, the principle should be kept in mind. Having both men and women on the team will help keep this from being a problem.

3. Children. Be cautious about talking to young children. This is especially true if the child is of another race or the team is made up of all men. People tend to be protective, and if they see three men talking to a small child, sometimes they will stand by to see what is going on. They may even interrupt and try to find out what you are doing.

If you lead a child to Christ, before telling the parents what the child has done, try to discover the parents' spiritual condition. If they are not Christians and reject the Gospel, they may resent the child's spiritual interest and your involvement. If so, it may be best not to tell the parents what the child has done.

4. Residences. When visiting a residence, smile, and don't stand too close to the door or too near to the person. If speaking to more than one person, ask the diagnostic questions of the person who seems least likely to have the correct answer.

Position the team to include the prospect as part of a circle rather than three-on-one. Introduce your team by first names only, and don't ask the prospect's name until he begins to show a positive and friendly response. Just before the second diagnostic question is a good time to ask for his first name (only).

5. When not sharing, you should watch and pray—not with bowed heads, closed eyes, and folded hands, but with eyes open and wearing your most pleasant smile. Observe the presentation carefully so that your thoughts can be compared afterward. In that way, every member of the team will grow in understanding and ability to share the Gospel. Always look at the person who is talking. Don't stare at the prospect; he may become frightened and run away. Stay alert for opportunities to prevent disturbances. For example, notice if a crowd begins to gather, and let the presenter know.

6. Identify yourselves. Indicate clearly what church group you represent to distinguish your team from the cults. Communicate clearly your purpose as printed at the beginning of the questionnaire. Read the questionnaire, glancing up only briefly for the prospect's response. Move quickly through the questions with minimal "small talk," and during the questions, interact very little. Underline or write his answers clearly. Thank him after some of his responses and at appropriate places.

7. When people are resistant. Don't expect to share the Gospel with every person who is willing to answer the questionnaire. Many people are not ready for your witness. Knowing this will remove some of the pressure.

G. LISTEN CAREFULLY AND BE CAREFUL NOT TO REACT NEGATIVELY

If he says he doesn't believe in heaven, sidestep an argument by saying something like, "You believe in God, I suppose. Heaven is where God is." Or, "Let's suppose, for the sake of conversation, there is a heaven—wouldn't you like to go there?" And then ask him the assurance question.

If he says that your questions are too personal, volunteer to give him your answers, and use that as an opportunity to share a brief presentation of the Gospel in a testimony format.

If, in response to the second question, he says that he doesn't know, probe with the five steps E.E. teaches to obtain an answer. If he responds that he's not interested, thank him, give him an E.E. tract, and leave gracefully.

H. AVOID DIFFICULT CONTACTS

Remember to distinguish between "prospects" and "suspects." A prospect will not be argumentative or close-minded about the existence of God. A prospect will not be emotionally hostile or unreasonably antagonistic.

A suspect is the opposite of a prospect. He will sometimes be doctrinally difficult—like, for example, a Jehovah's Witness who goes to Kingdom Hall eight times a week. Even if the suspect wants to continue a discussion beyond the questionnaire, don't. Try to make a future appointment. When you approached him, you asked for permission to get his response to some questions. You are not under obligation to continue beyond that point unless you feel God wants you to.

Also, remember that we have no right to try to force somebody to submit to our presentation of the Gospel if he does not want to hear it. Jesus told us, "Lift up your eyes, and look on the fields; for they are white already to harvest" (John 4:35). Do not try to pluck green fruit.

I. KEEP RECORDS OF YOUR CONTACTS

Avoid overlapping or skipping homes. On the back of the form there is a place for the name and address of the prospect and the recording of attempted contacts. The name and address can be filled in before the contact is attempted. This information can be obtained from a city directory or a cross-reference telephone directory. In apartment complexes it can be obtained from the mailboxes. One form should be used for each apartment or residence. After the contact is completed, the form should be filled out and put away in your pocket or purse.

When contact is attempted but not completed, this should be noted. Note the day of the week and the time of day that the contact is attempted. Then the questionnaire should be placed back with the uncompleted contacts. When contact is unsuccessful on a particular day or time of day, the call should be rescheduled for a different day and time. If attempt at personal visit is repeatedly unsuccessful, contact should be attempted by telephone on various days and at different times.

IV. Assurance Questionnaire Outline

A. THE APPROACH

Fill in the blanks that are in the printed copy of the questionnaire, and say the following:

"Hi, I'm Jim. Meet Gladys and Jerry. We are from the (name of your church or group). We are trying to determine people's religious thinking and assist anyone looking for a faith." This helps the team relate more personally to the contact. It usually takes too long, initially, to give the first and last names of each team member. By mentioning the group you represent, you help to promote the ministry of that group in the community and you let the contact know that you are not a Jehovah's Witness or a member of some other radical cult.

Saying, "We are trying to determine people's religious thinking and to assist anyone looking for a faith" explains the purpose of the contact. First, you are trying to find out what the prospect's religious thinking is. You should have a genuine interest in this. Second, you are clearly and honestly saying that you are available to help anyone looking for a faith.

B. THE APPEAL

"Will you help us by giving your thoughts in response to a few brief questions?" Use these exact words. Asking for assistance puts us in the position of needing the contact person's help. Jesus used this approach when He talked to the woman at the well. He asked if she would give Him a drink (John 4:7). Asking for the person's response to a few brief questions lets him know you want only a small amount of time.

C. THE QUESTIONS

We ask about his spiritual interests and what religious group or church the person is a member of in order to discover his general religious background and orientation. We ask what local church he attends so that we may know if he has any local relationship. We ask him how often he attends to see the degree of his activity and involvement.

We ask if he knows for certain he would go to heaven to find out if he thinks he has eternal life. This does not tell us he knows for certain he has eternal life. You can rephrase this question for people under thirty in order to relate more effectively to them. People under thirty are concerned about dying, but they do not plan on doing it right away. So bring in the idea of accidental death. This is the number one cause of death among younger people. The reality of death is brought home to them more specifically with this idea. Rephrase the question in this way: "Have you come to the place in your thinking where you know for certain that you have eternal life? That is, if you were to be killed tonight in an accident, do you know that you would go to heaven?"

We ask what he would say if God asked why He should let him into heaven in order to discover the basis of his hope of heaven.

D. GENERAL PROCEDURE

Move through the questions quickly. Don't go off on tangents. Indicate the prospect's response to the question by underscoring the printed answer when it is on the form or by marking the square provided. Interact very little with the prospect. Ask the questions and record the answers without additional comments unless you find it necessary to do so briefly for additional rapport. Be sure that your comments are not judgmental when you do interact.

Don't react negatively to his answers by what you say, by the tone of your voice, or by facial expressions. That will cause him to react negatively to you. Stay very close to the wording on the questionnaire. Many generations of field-testing have proven it to be very effective.

E. THANKS

After you've received answers to the questions, express appreciation for his cooperation, and then determine your course of action for follow-through. Do not expect to share the Gospel with every person who is willing to answer the questionnaire. Many people who are willing to answer the questionnaire are not ready for you to share the Gospel.

After the interview is completed, the results of the conversation should be recorded as fully as possible on the back of the form for appropriate follow-through. Initial contact results reports should be filled out only if the person makes a profession or if there is to be some specific follow-through. Questionnaires should be handed in each week so that they can be tabulated and studied.

V. How Do You Share the Gospel?

A. USE THE GOOD NEWS TRANSITION INTO THE GOSPEL

For many years we transitioned from the questionnaire into the Gospel by simply saying, "This completes the questionnaire. Your answers are interesting. Thank you for your help. May I have a few more minutes of your time to share with you how I came to know that I have eternal life and how you can know it, too?" However, we are finding that more and more people today *think* they already have eternal life, so this approach doesn't get their attention or create a desire to hear more.

We have found that following the diagnostic questions, the "Good News" transition taught in the Conversational Introduction produces a much more open response on the part of prospects. That's because it *is* such tremendous news, because it is almost universally unknown among unregenerate people, because it is exciting and unexpected news, and because the enthusiastic manner in which you communicate the Good News transition precludes hostility.

Say something like this: "When I heard your answers to the earlier part of our questionnaire, I thought I had something great to share with you. And now, having heard your answers to these last two questions, I know we have something really fantastic to share with you. May we share that with you right now?" Or you might say, "You know, Bill, we have some very exciting news to share with you! In fact, I'm sure it's the very *best news* you will ever hear! May I take a few minutes to share it with you right now?"

B. TRY TO MOVE TO A QUIET LOCATION FREE FROM INTERRUPTIONS

If you are standing in front of an apartment door, you might say something like, "Would it be all right if we stepped inside for a few minutes?" Then, when you are seated, take just a minute before sharing the Gospel to build rapport by moving briefly through the Conversational Introduction. Remember, the more caring and personal association an evangelist has with a contact before the profession of faith, the easier the follow-up will be; and conversely, the less personal contact he has with the person before he shares the Gospel, the more difficult the follow-up will be.

If you are standing in a park or mall, you may spot a bench nearby where you can sit for a more relaxed presentation.

C. SHARE THE GOSPEL

If he gives permission to share the Gospel, proceed with a brief testimony (about one minute) before going into the Gospel. Personalize the presentation as much as you can. Share your testimony and the Gospel. Be sure, if there is a profession of faith, that you get the full name, address, and phone number for proper discipling of the new believer.

How long should the presentation be? When the Gospel is being presented in a public place or by telephone, it should be brief, clear, and to the point. Usually the testimony and presentation should be about ten minutes long. Remember that the qualifying question and the commitment question provide the opportunity to discover particular points of the Gospel that need to be expanded for the contact.

D. BE SENSITIVE TO THE PERSON'S TIME

Watch your prospect's body language and facial expression to determine how much time you have to share, and adjust the length of your Gospel presentation accordingly so that you can get to the commitment section for an unhurried conclusion. If the person seems restless, ask how much time the person has for you to share.

E. IF THE PERSON HAS A TIME PROBLEM OR IS UNWILLING FOR YOU TO SHARE

The time may not be right. The fruit may not yet be ripe. Simply respond, "If it's not convenient now, may we share with you at another time, over lunch or in your home?" Get their name, address, and phone number; establish a future appointment; obtain permission to phone or to send a letter. Ofttimes people who are hesitant to talk about spiritual matters in public will be open to visiting with you in their home or over the telephone.

If it's a difficult case, such as with a member of a cult or someone filled with objections, make an appointment to talk to him privately. Remember that you are in a training ministry and that too many such contacts can discourage your trainees at a time when they are struggling just to learn how to communicate the Gospel.

F. GIVE LITERATURE

Do not give literature as a substitute for talking to a person about the Gospel. Try to at least get in a brief presentation and then give the printed material. This gives the person something to read to reinforce what you have said. Whenever you give literature, put the title on the back of the questionnaire so you can keep a record of what has been given. Do not give literature until you have first read it yourself. The content of the printed piece should always speak to the need of the individual receiving it.

It is good to have your church name and address stamped on the back of each tract. Call it to the person's attention and issue an invitation, verbal or printed, to attend your services.

Two excellent pieces of literature you may want to leave with a person are *Do You Know For Sure?* or *Where Will You Spend Eternity?* These handsomely illustrated booklets give a thorough presentation of the Gospel, using the Bible's own words to explain each of the major headings of the Gospel presentation. They include a prayer to receive Christ, a decision card, and a brief explanation of how to begin growing as a Christian. The tracts can be obtained through Evangelism Explosion International.

It is good to always keep a tract under the second page of your questionnaire pad so it is handy to give to your prospect at a moment's notice. *Where Will You Spend Eternity?* is an excellent tract for this purpose.

A good supply of E.E.'s Gospel tract, *Do You Know for Sure?* should also be available for use with questionnaire evangelism. Sometimes, when a person shows interest but doesn't have much time, you can walk him through this tract page by page, briefly highlighting the important points. Be sure to call to his attention the commitment section and the prayer, suggesting that he can receive Christ in the quiet of his home later.

As you conclude your friendly encounter with the person, be sure to thank him for his time and interest.

G. MAKE A FUTURE APPOINTMENT

1. For the sake of the contact. Sometimes you should try to make a future appointment for the sake of the person being contacted. If the person you contact is pleasant, responsible, unsaved, and seeking but has no time to listen, try to make a future appointment for his or her sake. Such appointments should be in the regular witnessing schedule, if at all possible, to avoid overloading your trainees with too much work.

2. For the sake of the trainees. Other times you should try to make a future appointment for the sake of the trainees. If the contact is a militant member of a radical religious group, philosophically argumentative, or emotionally hostile, the trainer should try to make a future appointment to present the Gospel when the trainees are not along. Thus, trainers will shield trainees from especially difficult cases before they have gained some self-confidence and are more comfortable with the presentation.

It is wrong to simply drop difficult people. Sometimes they are seeking, but trainers must not run the risk of alarming their trainees with difficult situations. Future follow-through appointments for a difficult case would not be in the regular witnessing schedule. Set a time when you can go back with more experienced witnesses.

3. Setting up the appointment. If the contact agrees to an appointment, get his name, address, and phone number. Establish the location, the date, the day of the week, and the time of day when you will visit. It is wise, when possible, to phone the day before the appointment to verify the time and place. If he refuses a future follow-through appointment, you may try to gain permission to send him a letter or give him a phone call. You may also invite him to attend your fellowship group or your church, or give him printed material.

H. SEND A LETTER OR MAKE A PHONE CALL

Try to get permission to send a letter if the contact is hesitant to let you present the Gospel or is in a hurry. Be sure you get his name and address.

There are times when people are not willing to talk about religion in a public place, but they are willing to talk over the phone. If you feel this is the case, try to obtain permission to call later. Be sure to get the name, phone number, and the best day and time to call.

I. INVITE THE PROSPECT TO CHURCH OR FELLOWSHIP GROUP

Almost any time you make contact with someone, it is all right to invite him to church or to a fellowship group. If the person sounds antichurch, it would be wise to invite him to the fellowship group first. A printed invitation is very helpful. Members will invite more nonmembers to the church or fellowship group if they have a printed invitation to give. The impact of the invitation also has a longer-lasting influence when in printed form.

If it is possible to plan ahead and have specific topics printed on the invitation, even more invitations can be distributed. It can appear that a member is nagging a nonmember if he keeps giving a general invitation, but if there are different titles for each month or each week, there is always something new to invite nonmembers to attend.

VI. OTHER BASIC INFORMATION YOU SHOULD KNOW ABOUT THIS APPROACH

A. RESULTS

When using a questionnaire in public places and door-to-door, you will find two interesting phenomena. First, you will usually make more contacts, but there will be fewer professions per number of evangelistic contacts than when calling on church visitors. Second, you will find that fewer of those who make professions with a questionnaire will be discipled into vital, visible relation with the local church.

Don't let these facts throw you. Enlist prayer partners and ask them to pray that you will be led to prepared people who will be abiding fruit. As you pray, you will find that the number of presentations and genuine conversions will both increase.

Remember, also, that your primary objective is to train soul winners. Should only a few persons come to Christ or nobody at all, if you are training your people to witness, you are seeing the most important results. Your people, as they become more and more proficient in sharing their faith, will begin to witness to their friends, relatives, associates, and neighbors. And with God's enabling, they will bear lasting fruit for God's glory.

B. ATTITUDE

Give serious thought to your attitude toward the Lord—the most important part of the whole witnessing process. Your attitude should be one of loving obedience and trust. Jesus said, "If ye love me, keep my commandments" (John 14:15). He commanded us in the great commission, "Go ye into all the world" (Mark 16:15). We are to "go out into the highways and the hedges, and compel them to come in" (Luke 14:23).

C. TRUST

Trust expects the Lord to establish divine appointments and to go with you to keep them. Trust is willing to accept joyfully whatever role God gives in bringing others to him. Your faith is important for witnessing. Recall the story of the four men who brought the paralytic to Jesus Christ. They could not get through the crowd, so they climbed on the roof, tore a hole in it, and lowered their friend into the presence of Christ. Jesus said it was because He saw "their faith" that He healed the man (Mark 2:5). When you go out to share the Gospel, believe that God will use you to bring people to Him. He will honor your expectant faith.

Fifteen

DEVELOPING
LEADERS

I. A LIFELINE OF CONCERN AND COMMUNICATION

Picture an army composed only of generals and privates. As the general sits in his command tent studying strategy for the total battle, his field phone rings. The enemy is attacking on the western front. There are no officers in that sector—there are only privates. The general must leave his command tent and rush to the battle so he can lead his men.

When he arrives on the western front, hundreds of privates eagerly await his orders. But the enemy is attacking in full force! He cannot give personal orders to each private. Some wander around not knowing what to do, and before they are aware of what has happened, they are captured. Others, on their own, charge into the midst of the conflict. The general shouts, "Come back! The enemy has the high ground. He will slaughter you! Pull back to the ridges where you have sufficient cover. There we can hold the line."

Many of the troops do not hear the general. He is only one voice, and the battle is raging. Those who charge ahead are quickly cut down by enemy fire. There is great confusion, and in the attempt to run to safety, many wounded men are left unattended on the field. The soldiers who were closest to the general heard his command and took up positions on the ridges.

As the battle rages, a courier comes from headquarters to tell the general that the enemy is now attacking on the eastern front. He must immediately go there and lead the soldiers. What is he to do? The enemy is attacking on all fronts. Soldiers without direction are being wounded and killed. The enemy is overrunning his forces, and he cannot adequately defend his positions.

Any war fought like this will be lost in short order! Before the general can ever think of victory, he must take time in the command tent to develop strategy for offensive battle. He must have capable leaders on graduated levels in the organization.

The Christian church is an army doing battle against Satan and the forces of evil. This conflict is more intense and devastating than any military conflict has ever been. In this army, it is imperative that there be levels of leadership to function as a lifeline of concern and communication. They are a channel for the sharing of life within the body of Christ.

A. FOREWARNED IS FOREARMED

Every person has particular problems. But when you enter training to learn to share the Gospel, you can expect special and unique problems. Capable witnessing Christians are special targets for satanic attack. They are much more of a threat to Satan than the Christian who is satisfied merely to occupy a pew on Sunday.

Diabolical devices are used—especially on new trainees. If Satan can discourage and defeat you before you are able to share the Gospel, you will not be nearly so great a threat to him. If he can cripple you spiritually in your process of learning to share the Gospel, you will be very cautious about ever attempting it again. He will use the pressure of time, the slowness of mind to learn, the fear of confronting people in a face-to-face situation, family conflicts, physical health, and anything else to discourage and defeat you.

More often than not, laypeople are better equipped than the minister to help other laypeople with problems they encounter in the course of the training. The levels of leadership are designed to enable the more experienced to help the less experienced.

It is more than a cliché to say that a chain is no stronger than its weakest link. God says in His Word that when one member of the body suffers, all suffer. We generally agree that we are to bear one another's burdens. The problem is that more often than not, everyone's responsibility is no one's specific responsibility. The church cannot afford to be the only army that does not care for its wounded!

This lifeline of concern emphasizes the responsibility of the more experienced for the less experienced in the training—the responsibility of the more knowledgeable person in the ministry for the person with less knowledge. New trainees must feel free to share their fears and frustrations with trainers, and this means more than sharing the problems encountered in the learning process. It should also include sharing personal problems related to their spiritual growth. The sharing of personal problems should also take place between trainers and lieutenants, lieutenants and the staff director.

Sometimes this sharing is on a one-on-one basis. Other times it takes place in the visitation team of three; still other times it occurs in the lieutenant group of twelve. Of course, when anything of a personal, intimate nature is shared, it *must* be kept in Christian confidence.

As this communion of life grows, the unity within the body of Christ becomes more visibly evident. This will enable you to have more spiritual vitality for witnessing. It will also demonstrate the reality of Christ in the lives of His people and become a united witness to the truth of our faith (John 17:21).

This line of communication and leadership encourages new trainees to ask their trainers or lieutenants questions they might not ask the minister, because they are too shy or feel that the minister is too busy.

Our training ministry is constantly growing from the personal encounters that take place as the Gospel is shared. This line of communication enables trainers to effectively bring new ideas to the leadership so that all may benefit. It provides the minister with a personal line for communicating information to every person in the E.E. ministry.

B. GROWTH BRINGS DIFFICULTIES

As the size of your local E.E. group grows, body life becomes more difficult. To keep this vital, lieutenant groups of no more than twelve people are formed. At specified times during the semester, your lieutenant group will stay at the church during the time for on-the-job training to pray for the teams that are out calling. During this time, you may also share your personal needs and pray for one another. If there is time left before the report session, you can practice your E.E. material.

II. A PROCESS FOR DEVELOPING LEVELS OF LEADERSHIP

As the weak and the wounded are cared for, they become healthy and strong. When you seek to disciple someone to the place where you now are in your Christian life, you will grow, too. When your disciple arrives in his spiritual life to where you are now, you will no longer be there. You will have grown to a new level of maturity. It is through this process that the army of Christ develops ranks of leaders.

Let me emphasize again that levels of leadership constitute a lifeline of concern and communication. It is not to be strict military regimentation, but concern sometimes requires confrontation, and communication is not possible without honest praise and constructive criticism. Scripture says we are to submit ourselves one to another (Ephesians 5:21). We are to exhort and admonish one another. Human nature chafes against the shaping process of accountability, but if Christians really care about one another and desire to be made into the likeness of Christ, they will lovingly encounter one another and listen to the counsel of fellow members of the family of God.

Individuals in the Evangelism Explosion Discipleship Training Ministry are given additional responsibilities as they prove themselves able to perform them. As you extend yourself into new areas of ministry and responsibility, you will discover the gifts God has given you. There are many types of gifts needed in the ministry of Evangelism Explosion Discipleship Training. Behind and through the "gifts" there is a need for Christlike love for others in the family of God and especially for those who have yet to hear the Gospel.

III. LINKS IN THE CHAIN

The levels of leadership constitute a succession of equally strong links in a chain. Notice the reverse order in this chain of command. The staff director is not on top but on the bottom. The more experience and responsibility a person has, the more he is the servant of others (Mark 10:43). Now let's look at each of these links in the chain.

A. PRAYER PARTNERS

A prayer partner is a person who shares in your evangelistic activity as a trainer or trainee by praying for you and the people with whom you share the Gospel.

God has honored this ministry in a unique way. In the first training semester that prayer partners were required for all participants at the Coral Ridge Presbyterian Church, the number of professions of faith increased more than 100 percent over the previous training semester. Churches using the prayer-partner ministry have discovered that trainers and trainees with faithful prayer partners are more fruitful and less likely to become discouraged and drop out of the training.

Potential prayer partners should read the *Partners in Praying* booklet. Then, if they desire to enter into this ministry of intercession, they should complete the commitment card attached to the back cover.

You should have at least two prayer partners. You can enlist more, but do not have more prayer partners than you can contact and pray with each week. Your prayer partners should be adult Christians, usually over eighteen years of age. They should be members or regular attenders of your local church. They should *not* be members of your immediate family.

They should *not* be present trainees or trainers in the E.E. ministry of your church. Selecting adults *not* in E.E. helps increase the flow of general information of the ministry to your congregation. It also gives the wider sense of participation that is necessary for a concerted effort in evangelizing your community.

Preferably, your two basic prayer partners should be a man and a woman. A married couple is excellent. They can intercede together for you and the people with whom you share the Gospel. If you enlist a prayer partner who is married and of the opposite sex, exercise caution not to leave any wrong impression about your weekly contact. This is especially true if either of you is married to an unbeliever. Intercessory prayer should become a vital part of your prayer partner's family devotions. This can have a deep impact on their children's lives, also.

A prayer partner must be seeking to walk with Christ and must believe that God answers prayer. He must desire to pray intelligently for you, the people with whom you share the Gospel, and the worldwide ministry of Evangelism Explosion. Therefore, he must be willing to talk with you each week so you can give requests and reports on answered prayer. If possible, this weekly contact should be in person. Your prayer partner may come to the church and pray while your team is out calling, or may attend only the report session. This will give him an opportunity to hear firsthand what God has done in response to his prayers and gain information for further prayer. If your prayer partner cannot come to the church, then you can have a brief personal contact at another time. Information can be communicated by telephone.

The time for sharing answered prayers and giving new requests should usually not exceed fifteen minutes a week. Remember, you should see that your prayer partner hears what happened with your team and knows the results of the total calling effort for the week. Be sure to pray for your prayer partner's needs, also.

Use only the first names of the people contacted. Any matter shared with you in confidence in the calling situation *must not* be shared with anyone else! Be sure to regularly remind your prayer partner that all requests you can share *must* be kept confidential.

Pray with your prayer partner each week. After you have reported answered prayers and given new requests, lead in audible prayer. Your prayer partner might not feel comfortable praying aloud, so do not pressure, but do give an opportunity each week. Pray together each week even if the contact is by phone.

One of the purposes of the prayer-partner ministry is to bring Christians who are in the same church together in new relationship for a meaningful ministry of intercession. Therefore, it is important that each participant enlist new prayer partners each training semester. Do not keep the same prayer partners two semesters in a row.

There are many benefits in the prayer-partner ministry. It provides intercessory prayer for the lost and for you as you participate on a witnessing team. It gives effectiveness to follow-up. It provides a personal line of communication about the outreach ministry of your church to those who are not participating in it. The evangelism discipleship training group must not become a closed clique—an elite group of Pharisees. The prayer-partner ministry provides opportunity for meaningful involvement in the evangelistic activity of the church for other members who are otherwise not able to participate due to physical or mental handicaps.

Though many who begin praying for this ministry will participate as trainees, the prayer-partner ministry must not become merely a gimmick to draw them into the calling force. The ministry of intercessory prayer is vital for accomplishing God's work in this world.

B. TRAINEES

A trainee is one who is seeking to master the content of the Gospel and the basic procedure for sharing it with others. He is responsible for attending all classes and on-the-job training sessions unless God prevents him. He commits himself to completing all homework assignments before class each week. He is responsible for praying regularly with and for his trainer. He is responsible for enlisting at least two prayer partners and contacting and praying with them each week. He functions at least as an enlistment scout seeking to find others in the church who are good candidates to be trainees in the next discipleship training semester. (Further qualifi-cations and responsibilities for trainees are discussed in this book in chapter 11, "Enlisting and Enlarging.")

C. JUNIOR TRAINERS (ALSO CALLED ASSOCIATE TRAINERS)

A junior, or associate, trainer is a person who has gone through at least one semester of E.E. discipleship training. He may have the basic content of the Gospel and some ability to communicate it but needs more experience in actually sharing the Gospel. Like the trainee, he is responsible for attending all the basic classes. He generally attends the Level 2 advanced training class if the church offers it. He is responsible for participating in on-the-job training. The homework is to be completed each week before class. Prayer partners are to be enlisted, contacted, and prayed with each week. Each is to pray for and with his trainer. In consultation with his trainer, he will present the Gospel from the beginning of the training semester, as he is able to do it well. He will enlist trainees for the next semester.

D. TRAINERS

The trainer is one who has knowledge of the content of the Gospel and the ability to share it. He is responsible for attending all classes (Level 3 classes) and on-the-job training sessions for the semester unless God prevents him. Homework assignments are to be completed before class each week. He is responsible for giving personal attention to the trainee or junior trainer working with him. He is to pray for and with them regularly. He is to assist them with any personal or learning problems. If necessary, he can call on his lieutenant or the teacher/trainer to help. When his trainee or junior trainer is absent, he is to check and find out why and supply him with the assignment and any information from the class he might need.

He is to report to his lieutenant whenever a member of his team is absent. When a trainer knows he is going to be absent, he should contact his trainees or junior trainers and let them know so they won't be caught off guard by his absence. A trainer should also notify his lieutenant if he is not going to be present.

A trainer should regularly check with his team members to see how they are progressing. This can be done going to and from calls, after report sessions, at another time convenient to both, or over the telephone at a later time. The best trainers make it a point to meet for about one hour of private tutoring with their trainees between class sessions. This can be a family affair that brings all of the families involved together rather than fragmenting them. Some use a potluck dinner once a week for this purpose. If this is done, be sure you do not let it deteriorate into an extended time of fellowship with no tutoring. Each week, the trainer has his trainee or junior trainer recite the memory work.

When the contact during the calling session turns out to be a Christian, and it is time for the trainee or the junior trainer to present the Gospel, the trainer should ask the contact if he would like to know what the church believes about the Gospel and then turn the presentation over to the other team members.

The trainer should encourage his trainee/junior trainer to stay for the report session. When personal contact is not made with a prospect during the calling time, the trainer should use this time to have the trainee/junior trainer practice his presentation, share any personal problems or questions, and then have a time of prayer. The trainer should set an example of consistent witnessing in his daily life and encourage his trainee/junior trainer to do likewise. Trainers are to enlist trainees for the next training semester for their own teams and for other teams, as well.

Before a person functions as a trainer, he or she must satisfactorily meet minimum standards. This is where certification with E.E. International comes in. Trainer certification in Evangelism Explosion is *not* certification to be a witness. Rather, it is certification in this specific training ministry to train others. All Christians are commanded by Christ to witness, so it would be presumptuous for any group to claim the authority to certify a Christian as a witness.

Certification is a way of establishing minimum standards of excellence so we can give God our best evangelistic effort. God deserves nothing less than our best. The sacrificial lamb in the Old Testament was to be closely observed for a period of time to see if it had any blemish or tear in its skin. If it was not perfect, it was not acceptable. God wants the best we can give Him. None of us is absolutely perfect, therefore no method of evangelism put together by men is going to be perfect. But as we are obedient to the great commission and go forth with the Gospel, the resurrected Christ, by His Holy Spirit, goes with us. In actual witnessing situations, He gives insights that are never received in the classroom. As these insights are shared, every person in the local training is made more effective. As those insights are shared with E.E. International and then communicated to others throughout the world, lay evangelists become more effective, and the quantity and quality of the spiritual harvest is greatly increased.

For a person to be certified as a trainer in a local Evangelism Explosion ministry, he must meet minimum standards agreed upon by E.E. International and his local church. These standards include:

1. A basic ability to verbalize the Gospel as demonstrated by making a thirty-minute Gospel presentation to another person. This presentation is evaluated by a standard oral presentation checklist.
2. An understanding of the basic concepts of the Gospel. This is tested by a final written checkup.
3. An understanding of the basic principles of communicating the Gospel. This also is evaluated on the basis of the final written checkup.
4. Experience in actually sharing the Gospel. This is evaluated from the participation report form.

No one should seek to be certified until he has completed at least ten actual visitation experiences over a period of not less than two months. No one is to be certified as a trainer unless he is functioning as a trainer. If you want to give some kind of diploma to people who complete level one training, fine; but don't certify them as trainers until they actually serve as trainers. Certified trainers in the local church must realize that their training does not qualify them to function as a teacher/trainer, leadership clinic administrator, or leadership clinic teacher. Further instruction and training of a different nature are required for these responsibilities.

Once a person becomes a certified trainer, he can function as a missionary trainer in certified-leadership clinics. He can also minister on a short-term or long-term basis in certified E.E. ministries in different parts of his own country or other parts of the world. *For detailed suggestions on how to be an effective trainer see Appendix B.* Specific requirements for trainer certification and information concerning leadership clinics are available though E.E. International.

E. LIEUTENANTS

Trainers who demonstrate faithfulness and fruitfulness in the discipleship training over a period of time may be given the responsibility of working with up to three trainers. By *faithfulness* we mean that they have been consistent in their attendance and the use of the content and concepts of Evangelism Explosion Discipleship Training. By *fruitfulness* we mean that they have led others to profess faith in Christ and to become vital members of their local church, enlisting trainees and discipling them to become trainers.

Lieutenants are to attend all classes and on-the-job-training sessions unless prevented by God. They are to complete any homework assignments given them. They are to pray regularly for and with those in their charge. They are to enlist prayer partners and contact and pray with them each week. They may alternate on their trainers' teams for on-the-job training. This is especially important for people functioning as trainers for the first time. The lieutenant can monitor their performance in the field and affirm what they are doing correctly and give suggestions to improve other aspects of their witnessing and training activities.

Lieutenants are to check with their trainers to see that prayer partners are contacted and prayed with by both trainers and trainees. They are to check with their trainers after each calling experience and help with any problems or questions that may have arisen. If trainers in their group are absent, the lieutenant is responsible to check and see why and share any information with them they need from the class. If a trainer from the lieutenant's group is absent, the lieutenant should check with the other members of the trainer's team to see what happened in his on-the-job training. If a trainee is regularly absent, the trainer and lieutenant should seek to make personal contact to help and encourage in any way possible.

When the lieutenant encounters any problem or question he cannot handle, he should share this with the staff director. If the lieutenant is not able to make contact with his trainers before or after the report session, he should contact them in person or by phone during the week. The lieutenant should work with his trainers to encourage and implement enlistment of new trainees in the next semester. Progress on this enlistment should be reported to the church office.

F. ASSISTANT LAY TEACHERS/TRAINERS

Assistant lay teachers/trainers must be faithful and fruitful. These terms are defined for assistant lay teachers/trainers in the same way as for lieutenants. The assistant lay teacher/trainer must be respected by the other members in the E.E. fellowship. He must have the ability to communicate to a group in public. He must have the ability to receive and act on constructive criticism. He is responsible to attend the teachers' meeting with the certified teacher/trainer. Usually it is best for these to be monthly meetings. He is to teach under the supervision of the teacher/trainer as assigned.

He is to participate regularly in on-the-job training and to disciple one trainee. He is to complete all homework assignments related to his particular responsibilities. When he has completed one semester as assistant lay teacher/trainer, his work is to be evaluated by the responsible person from the recognized leadership of the local church. If it is acceptable, he is then to attend a certified leadership clinic for Evangelism Explosion training to become a certified lay teacher/trainer.

Both staff and lay teachers/trainers are certified *only* in leadership clinics. Valuable training procedures and strategies are provided in leadership clinics that are not usually available in local churches. This information is essential for the proper leading and teaching of Evangelism Explosion in the local church. Attending a leadership clinic gives opportunity for fellowship with Christians of like heart and vision from various parts of one's nation and the world. To properly lead a local E.E. ministry, it is essential that the leader have a vision for world evangelization. This is provided in the leadership clinics.

G. TEACHERS/TRAINERS (LAY AND STAFF)

Lay teacher/trainer is a part-time volunteer position. A layman becomes a lay teacher/trainer by first functioning as a trainee, trainer, lieutenant, assistant lay teacher/trainer, and then, after being recommended, attending a certified leadership clinic.

Staff teachers/trainers are usually theologically trained, ordained persons. However, some are laypeople who have gone through the full E.E. process (trainee, trainer, lieutenant, assistant lay teacher/trainer, certified lay teacher/trainer) and then have accepted a full-time staff position. If a person does not have formal theological training, it is essential that he have this minimum four-semester experience in Evangelism Explosion before he is given this full-time staff responsibility.

Many certified teachers/trainers are functioning in local churches throughout the world. Two-way lines of communication between the local churches, and the International Center of Evangelism Explosion in Fort Lauderdale make it possible to increase evangelistic skills, to inform for specific intercessory prayer, and to enlist for missionary work on a short-term or long-term basis throughout the world. With mutually agreed-upon minimum standards, it is possible for certified trainers from one part of the world to move into an E.E. work in another part of the world and help bring in the harvest.

As people trained in Evangelism Explosion share the Gospel, they gain new insights into ways of being more effective. As these are shared with the International Center and field-tested, they are then first made available to other certified teachers/trainers. Maximum information on this evangelistic ministry is provided to those who relate in this reciprocal fashion. We try to provide service for those who need help and to gain information from those who are doing well so that this may be shared with others to improve the quality of evangelistic activity across the world.

As indicated previously, information for all levels of certification with E.E. International may be obtained by pastors upon request.

H. LEADERSHIP-CLINIC ADMINISTRATORS

Leadership clinics are conducted in model churches in various parts of the world. A model church usually has a minimum of forty active certified trainers. Its E.E. ministry must be properly related to a total balanced ministry of worship, education, stewardship, leadership training, etc. A ten-year growth history is studied along with the specific strategy for effectively ministering to and evangelizing the community around the church. In the United States, the church is usually in a community of approximately 100,000 people, but some clinics in smaller churches and smaller communities effectively minister to pastors of smaller churches.

When these factors exist, the certified teacher/trainer goes to the E.E. International headquarters, together with a layperson, to take leadership clinic administrative training. This consists of approximately fourteen hours of instruction. Clinics are analyzed in detail so that the administrators will understand what they are putting together in their own church. Not until the administrators have been trained is a date established for an area clinic to be conducted in their church. E.E. International provides the teacher(s) for the clinic, and the local teacher/trainer and leadership clinic administrator are responsible for the administrative aspects of the clinic.

I. LEADERSHIP-CLINIC TEACHERS

An increasing number of certified teachers/trainers are demonstrating an ability to teach not only laypeople in their local church, but church leaders in leadership clinics, as well. E.E. International is constantly seeking to develop more properly certified teachers to conduct clinics in their own churches and in churches other than their own.

IV. TEN MILLION FULL-TIME LAY EVANGELISTS!

Through the ministry of E.E. International, new resources for world evangelization are being mobilized. As a fellowship begins in a local church and people are equipped to share their faith, something happens to them. From within the fellowship, God lays His hand on a few and gives them a *holy restlessness*. They are not content to function as they did before. They lift up their eyes and see the whitened harvest field. Then, as they are guided by the Spirit to move out, they have behind them strong prayer and financial support. In many cases, they have been able to relocate in other parts of the world in an E.E. program in their own denominational group. Thus, they are able to move from country to country and be used of God in a significant way.

Will you join us in praying that God will mobilize a mighty army of at least 10 million full-time lay evangelists in the very near future?

Sixteen

DISCIPLING
ALL NATIONS

God has done something wonderful and unheard of. Something unique in the history of the world. He told us to go into all the world and make disciples of every nation. E.E. has done just that! We have obeyed His great commission and established our friendship/evangelism/discipleship ministry in every nation of the world.

How did this all happen? Well, here's a brief summary of the milestones that led up to this phenomenal event.

1959

My wife and I arrived in Fort Lauderdale, Florida, to pastor our first church. Meeting in a school, we saw our congregation's attendance during the first nine months decline from forty-five to seventeen persons.

1960

Pastor Kennedy Smartt invited me to hold revival meetings in Atlanta, and I learned from him how to do personal evangelism.

1962

I taught evangelism and gave my first trainees—Anne Kennedy, Victor Wierman, and Freeman Springer—on-the-job training. Anne, Victor, and Freeman led their first souls to Christ, and Evangelism Explosion was born!

1967

E.E.'s first leadership training clinic was held in Fort Lauderdale with 36 pastors attending.

1970

The first edition of the E.E. textbook was published, and E.E. was incorporated as a separate corporation from the church.

1971

Interest in E.E. skyrocketed as 1,500 pastors and lay leaders registered for the February E.E. leadership clinic.

1972

A board of directors was elected, and E.E. spread to other locations. Philadelphia and Chicago hosted E.E. clinics.

1973

Crossing the border into Canada, E.E. was implemented at a seminary in Regina, Saskatchewan.

1974

Spreading to Europe, E.E. was launched in Great Britain, Germany, and Scandinavia.

1975

Continuing its worldwide impact, E.E. was implemented in South Africa, Zimbabwe, and Australia.

1978

The first Asian E.E. clinic was held in Hong Kong, and from there moved rapidly to other nations on that continent.

1983

E.E. next spread quickly across South America, Central America, and Mexico.

1987

To conserve results and maintain E.E.'s worldwide growth, vice presidents were appointed over every continent.

1988

Not content that E.E. was in only 66 nations, I challenged the continental vice presidents to take the E.E. ministry to **every nation** by the year 1995.

1989

The vice presidents rose to the challenge, and by the end of 1989 reported that E.E. had entered a total of 89 nations.

1990

In one year, the total number of nations implementing E.E. rose dramatically to 103.

1991

During another incredible year, E.E. continued to grow, adding 17 new lands, for a total of 120 nations.

1992

Russia, closed for so many years to any evangelistic thrust, suddenly opened to E.E., and the new total of nations rose to 141.

1993

Entering many other difficult lands, E.E.'s ministry expanded to a total of 160 nations.

1994

The dramatic story of E.E.'s worldwide impact continued for another year, and the nation total stretched to 174.

1995

In one year alone, E.E. had entered an all-time, one-year high of 36 new nations! It had been considered humanly impossible to enter some of those lands. But, praise God, by the end of the year we had entered every nation but one—North Korea.

1996

E.E. entered North Korea and reached our goal of *all* 211 of the world's nations!

To the best of our knowledge no other Christian ministry has, heretofore, reached all the nations of the world. Multitudes of people prayed. Scores of workers sacrificed. And the result? To God's glory—a milestone in church history.

So significant was this milestone that we invited at least one official E.E. delegate from each of the nations in the world to join us here in Fort Lauderdale for four great days of joyous *celebration*. First, we worshiped our heavenly Father who made it all possible. Then, after four days of worship, fellowship, workshops, and strategic planning for the future, we capped our celebration with a great inspirational banquet.

But, thankfully, no one viewed that great celebration as any kind of a conclusion. Rather, it was just a beginning, a beachhead, a launching pad for a far wider, deeper, stronger thrust into every one of those already-reached nations!

As we look to the future, God has given us a vision of equipping the body of Christ worldwide to reach all of the unreached people of the world through the E.E. ministry. To accomplish this, we need to do the following:

- We need to establish E.E. ministries around the world which are *indigenous* and therefore self-sustaining and "sending" ministries.
- We need to bring to *full development* all existing E.E. ministries throughout the world.
- We need to provide the staff, resources, and organization required to *sustain* healthy, indigenous E.E. ministries.
- We need to *reposition* E.E. in today's society and the Christian world for more effective and relevant communication.
- We need to define and implement the E.E. ministry throughout the world with *consistent* process, policy, principles, and procedures.

Jesus Christ said that His Gospel of the kingdom would be preached in all the world for a witness until "the end." Evangelism Explosion, until that great day arrives, will continue equipping His body worldwide for friendship, evangelism, discipleship, and healthy growth.

According to James F. Engle, author of the book *What's Gone Wrong with the Harvest?* E.E. is doing an outstanding job of training pastors and laypeople for evangelism and discipleship. In the December 16, 1991, issue of *Christianity Today*, which features evangelism in the '90s, Engle asks, "Who's really doing evangelism?" He answers this question by analyzing the responses of 1,500 *Christianity Today* readers to a survey. The survey's findings provide much-needed data that churches in America cannot ignore. Just under 40 percent of those surveyed have some form of evangelism training.

When the persons were asked about how they learned to share the Good News, several of the best-known training programs were cited. One important finding in the survey was that first place in the training/equipping process went to Evangelism Explosion. That is, the survey found that E.E. leads all other ministries in evangelism training of both staff and laity.

Evangelism Explosion is also proving to be increasingly fruitful overseas—even in relatively resistant cultures. In one African country, Muslims represent 99.8 percent of the population, and the government refuses to recognize the legality or the existence of the church. Renaming its clinics "picnics" for security reasons, E.E. celebrated a recent training clinic where 25 of the 400 known Christians in the country attended and were equipped to share their faith and train others to do the same.

In one Asian country, considered to be one of the least evangelized on earth and where missionaries have not been permitted, the government continues to enforce allegiance to Islam. Despite the fact that there are no Christian radio programs and no Scriptures in the local language and that all incoming mail is examined to screen out Bibles and religious literature, an E.E. teacher/trainer from a neighboring country visited the country and met and trained five expatriate Christians who, in turn, trained five others.

In Haiti, where Voodooism is officially recognized and practiced, E.E. instructors trained 41 Haitians in on-site clinics. As a result, over 260 of their fellow Haitians became Christians.

In Wales, where churches are often in a state of decline, one pastor, applying E.E.'s biblical strategy, has seen his congregation grow by 600 percent.

In Minsk, Belarus, formerly part of the Soviet Union, one church reports that 20 persons recently completed E.E. training, with 790 persons professing faith in Christ during the training.

E.E. is reaching and impacting some of the most remote islands as well. Our E.E. director in Fiji writes, "Yahreta was a seminary student and was placed on my E.E. team during the E.E. clinic in Kiribati. His first comment to me was, 'Where is heaven? I can't see it so I don't believe it exists.'

"I mumbled something to him about heaven being where God is and thought to myself that this was going to be an interesting team. Yahreta seemed really interested in the clinic and so did most of the other seminary students, ten of whom said they received eternal life at the clinic. I'm certain that some of the other 30 clinicians did, too.

"Eight months later I returned to Kiribati, and Yahreta heard I was there. He came to see me and said that he now knows there is a heaven, that he is going there, and that he can tell you how to go there, too. He added that over the holidays he and a fellow seminary student named Benedict went back to their home island. They called all the people on the island into the large meetinghouse. Then he and Benedict shared the Gospel and led the whole island to Christ. Even the pastor on the island thought this was the best news he had ever heard!

"Yahreta said that before the E.E. clinic on Kiribati, many of the students had 'borrowed' things without returning them to the owner. But the clinic had such an impact upon them that they took all of the borrowed items back. When asked why they had done that, they replied, 'In the E.E. clinic we learned that God won't use us unless we are clean vessels, and we want God to use us.'"

In closing, let me encourage all of you who are reading this:

- If your church is not yet involved in E.E., commit yourself to pray and do everything possible to enlist your pastor, church leaders, and congregation to launch a vibrant, fruitful E.E. ministry in the very near future.
- Commit yourself to regular and lifetime involvement in your local church's E.E. ministry.
- Commit yourself to walk in the Spirit, mature in Christ, and grow in your ability to present the Gospel.
- Commit yourself to faithfully pray for a genuine explosion of evangelism worldwide.
- Commit yourself to incorporate friendship, evangelism, and discipleship into your life as a daily practice and lifestyle.
- Commit yourself—over and above what you give to your local church—to support, as God enables you, the worldwide ministries of Evangelism Explosion.
- Commit yourself to encourage and enlist your congregation to support regularly—as part of your church's missions or benevolent giving—the worldwide ministries of Evangelism Explosion.
- Commit yourself to do everything possible to participate with us here at Evangelism Explosion International as we purpose to glorify God by equipping the body of Christ worldwide for friendship, evangelism, discipleship, and healthy growth.

Recently, a charter member of our church reminded me of something I said back in 1960 to about fifteen of our faithful members who were gathered in a Fort Lauderdale schoolroom for our weekly Sunday evening service. After reading from the Old Testament God's promise to the prophet, "Call unto me, and I will answer thee, and shew thee great and mighty things, which thou knowest not" (Jeremiah 33:3), I closed my Bible and looked out over the small congregation and said full of faith and enthusiasm, "You know what?—I believe we can change the world!"

Thirty-six years have passed since that very humble Sunday evening gathering. By faith in God and His faithfulness, through the untiring efforts of E.E. people here in Fort Lauderdale, across North America, and around the world, we have seen some of those great and mighty things the prophet spoke about. All praise to our wonderful God! But the job is not finished yet.

Not long ago an unbelieving, rather sarcastic secular reporter said to me, "Dr. Kennedy, it sounds to me like you aim to Christianize America!"

"No, sir, I'm not aiming to Christianize America," I replied with a smile. "I'm aiming to Christianize the *world!*"

Friend, isn't that what Christ commanded us to do? Didn't He commission us to make disciples of all nations? Will you, as it says in Jeremiah, call unto Him to show us great and mighty things such as we have never known? Will you join me in believing God for an explosion of evangelism and discipleship that will far surpass our world's exploding population and impact dramatically for time and eternity every nation of the world? *Thank you and may God bless you richly!*

Amen.

APPENDIX A

Assurance Questionnaire Form

Copyright 1996. Not to be reproduced without written permission.
Exvangelism Explosion, Inc. P.O. Box 23820, Ft. Lauderdale, Florida 33307.

I am _____ of _____

We're trying to determine people's religious thinking and assist anyone looking for a faith.

I.   Will you help us by giving your thoughts in response to five brief questions?
     (1) Yes   (2) No

II. Of what religious group or church are you a member?

(01) Baptist   (08) Lutheran
(02) Catholic   (09) Mormon
(03) Christian Church   (10) Methodist
(04) Christian Science   (11) Presbyterian
(05) Congregational   (12) None
(06) Episcopal   (13) Other
(07) Jewish

_____
(Please print name of "other" group)

III. What local church do you attend?

(1) _____
      (Please print name of local church)
(2) None

IV. How often do you attend?
     (1) Weekly (2) Often (3) Seldom (4) Never

V.   Have you come to the place in your spiritual life where you know that you have eternal life – that is, do you know for certain that if you were to die today you would go to heaven or is that something you're still working on?

     (1) Yes   (2) Hope So   (3) No

VI. If you were to die today and stand before God and He said to you, "Why should I let you into My heaven?" what would you say?

_____
(Print person's actual words.)
_____
_____
_____

When you answered the first few questions, I thought I had some good news to share with you. But now that I've heard your answer to the last question, I know I have some really fantastic news.

_____

May I have a few minutes to share this news with you?   ☐   ☐
                                                                  Yes   No

If "No" then ask: Would you be open to discussing spiritual matters over lunch or in your home?
                                                                  ☐   ☐
                                                                  Yes   No

Date _____

Team members _____

☐ Visit   ☐ Gospel Presented
☐ Christian   ☐ Profession
☐ Not Ready   ☐ Left Literature
☐ Invitation to Church
☐ Appointment: Place _____

                     Date _____
                     Time _____

Name _____
Address _____
City/State/Zip _____
Phone _____

Comments _____
_____
_____
_____
_____
_____
_____
_____
_____
_____

RELIGIOUS QUESTIONNAIRE

I am _____ and this is

_____ and _____

We're from_____

We're in the community doing a questionnaire to determine people's religious thinking.

Would you help us by giving your
thoughts in answer to a few brief   ☐   ☐
questions?   Yes   No

According to a recent survey, there
is today a rise of interest in religion.
Are you more interested in
spiritual matters than you were   ☐   ☐
five years ago?   Yes   No

Do you perceive God as a Supreme
Being who watches over you and to   ☐   ☐
whom you ultimately answer?   Yes   No

Do you at some time and in some   ☐   ☐
way pray every day?   Yes   No

Do you have a church, temple, or   ☐   ☐
synagogue that you attend?   Yes   No

_____
(Name of church, etc.)

Most people think that one of the
things a church should do is help
people discover eternal life – that is,   ☐   ☐
how to get to heaven? Do you agree?   Yes   No

Have you come to the place in your
spiritual life where you know for
certain that you have eternal life –
that is, if you were to die today,   ☐   ☐
you would go to be with God in   Yes   No
heaven or is that something you're   ☐
still working on?   Hope So

(continued on reverse side)

If you were to die today and stand before God and He were to ask you, "Why should I let you into My heaven?" what would you say?
(person's actual words) _____

_____

_____

_____

When you answered the first few questions, I thought I had some good news to share with you. But now that I've heard your answer to the last question, I know I have some really fantastic news.

May I have a few minutes to share this news with
you?   ☐   ☐
                                          Yes   No
If "No" then ask: Would you be open to discussing
spiritual matters over lunch or in your home?
                                          ☐   ☐
                                          Yes   No

Date_____

Team members _____

☐ Visit   ☐ Gospel Presented
☐ Christian   ☐ Profession
☐ Not Ready   ☐ Left Literature
☐ Invitation to Church
☐ Appointment: Place _____

          Date _____

          Time _____

Name _____

Address _____

City/State/Zip_____

Phone_____

Comments _____

_____

_____

_____

_____

_____

_____

930301

APPENDIX B

Suggestions for Trainers

1. Effective prayer and effective evangelism cannot be separated. Have each team member pray sentence prayers in the car before you leave for your visit. Ask the Lord for safety, wisdom, open hearts, and divine appointments. When your team returns to the church after the contact, you should have a time of prayer together. Each member of the team should pray briefly. Express gratitude to God for the great things He has done. Needs of the Gospel presenters to be more effective in sharing in the future should be brought to the Lord. Intercede for the person contacted and those related to him.

2. Senior trainers are in charge of the team. Even though you may not feel superconfident, it is important that you exert your leadership in example, prayer, and instruction. Set an example of enthusiasm and excitement as you lead your team.

3. Associate trainers are to assist the senior trainer. From time to time, let them check the audit outline for the trainee. Early in the semester, assign specific parts of the presentation for your associate trainer to share with the prospects during on-the-job training.

4. Faithfully come to class five to ten minutes early each week. Get your visitation packet; check the cards for location; study the map, if needed; and plan the sequence of your visits in an orderly time-saving manner.

5. Start working with your team members promptly, even if only one of them is present. Use the time allotted to go over assignments, and listen to them recite the unit's memory assignment. It is good to have one team member recite the assigned portion of the presentation to the other while you listen and mark the audit outline. This is important because all three of you are involved and learning by listening as well as reciting.

6. Try not to interrupt the one reciting or prompt too often. Mark his audit outline appropriately, and then go over it with him when he has finished reciting. Tell him what he did right and what he might do better.

7. Collect your trainees' yellow audit outlines each week after On-the-Job Training (OJT) and check to see that they have done their assignment and filled in their OJT experience. Remember, people do what you *inspect,* not what you *expect,* so be "tough and tender" and help them to keep up with their work.

8. Follow your weekly schedule closely, going to the various levels of classes on time and out on your OJT visitation on time. Try to return for the report session on time and let your team members go home on time.

9. Use your travel time to talk about Evangelism Explosion. Keep a positive attitude. Remind the lady team member that she is to stand close to the door for easy visibility. Give instructions as to who will do what and who will share what parts of the presentation. Assure your trainees that if their mind goes blank or they forget something, you will be there to step in and help them. Remind your team members to stay on track with the presentation and to look at the person speaking.

10. If prospects are not home, leave a note on the door. Write their names ("Dear Bill and Sue") on the note. Go immediately to the next home; however, it is usually best not to approach any home after 8:45 P.M. When it begins to get late, you might want to do questionnaires at a public place like a park, supermarket, mall, beach, laundromat, or bus station.

11. Remember, it's important that your trainees see and hear a presentation every week. For OJT, you might also visit one of your team's prayer partners for an E.E. enlistment visit and Gospel presentation. Or you might return to the church and role-play the presentation for them.

12. During the first few weeks of OJT, you will do most of the sharing, so encourage your trainees to participate in the introduction. Share with them the kinds of questions you would like them to ask. Remember that fear comes from the unknown, so every week of OJT, let them know what you expect from them and what they can expect from you. Build their confidence by affirming and encouraging them constantly.

13. When a prospect gives strong evidence of already being a Christian by answering the diagnostic questions correctly and giving you a clear testimony of the new birth, you may still have a good opportunity to do OJT. Follow carefully the instructions in chapter 5, "Asking Diagnostic Questions," for what to do when prospects give the right answers. Remember, your first priority for visitation is to provide OJT opportunities for your trainees.

14. On your way back to the church, evaluate the visit. Ask your trainees if they saw clearly the outline, recognized the illustrations, and saw how you applied the Scriptures. Ask them what you did right and what you could have done better. Make yourself vulnerable to their evaluation and encourage them to be frank. This will make it easier for you to evaluate them with their presentation. Also analyze what happened by answering these questions:

   • What did we learn that will help us minister in the future to the person with whom we shared?
   • What did we learn that will help us be more effective in evangelizing in the future?
   • What did we learn that will be helpful or encouraging to other people in the discipleship training program?
   • What specific prayer needs arise from this contact? These will be for the team members' ability to share the Gospel as well as requests for the person contacted. Some needs will be confidential and must be kept among the team members. Others should be shared in the public report time and/or with prayer partners.

15. From the first OJT, begin evaluating your trainees. Be positive, affirming, noticing the little things they do right: "I noticed the way you looked at whoever was speaking. I appreciated your smile and the way you took part in the conversation. I liked the way you passed the presentation to me when your mind went blank," etc.

16. If prospects are not home, fill in your team's names and the date on the report form. When three or four attempts have been made with no one home, give the card to the E.E. administrator to telephone for an appointment.

17. If you are unable to find an address, indicate so on the card and give it to the E.E. administrator to call for an appointment. The prospect may have a genuine interest in the Gospel or in identifying with your church.

18. When a visit is completed, indicate that clearly on the card, and fill in all of the information requested. Names of children, ages, responses to the two questions, results, etc., will help the church staff follow through properly and minister appropriately to the prospect. Return the card to the place designated by your E.E. administrator.

19. When there is a profession of faith, indicate so clearly on the card. Be sure to record all the information necessary for a good seven-day-callback visit and for the church to be able to follow through with appropriate pastoral care.

20. Leave all other cards in your packet so the administrator will be able to find them. Indicate clearly any appointments you have for the following week so the administrator will assign that card to your team.

21. Record complete information on the report board, and show your team members how to do this. As time passes, assign that task and other record-keeping tasks to your team members, remembering that you are training them to function properly as trainers in the future.

22. If you have had opportunity to share the presentation, report orally, using first names only for your team and the prospects you have visited. Follow closely your teacher/trainer or administrator's instructions, procedures, and time restrictions. Try to incorporate inspiration, instruction, and intercession into each report. It's good for the whole team to stand at the front as you report, because it enhances team spirit and prepares the trainees for when their turn comes to report.

23. Before you leave the church, assign appropriate follow-up assignments, phone calls, and correspondence to your team members. Use church stationery for thank-you or follow-up notes to your prospects.

24. Contact your associate trainer and trainees during the week to encourage them and to see how they are progressing. If they are encountering difficulties, spend extra time with them between classes. Encourage them to study a little each day rather than doing all of their study at one time the night before or the day of the class.

25. Share with your teacher/trainer or group leader if you are having problems with a trainee. They are prepared to help you, and your asking them to do so might help keep someone in the training.

26. Constantly keep before your associate trainer and trainees the goal of becoming a trainer in the future. Say to them, "I'm so glad I've had the privilege of training you. I want you to have the same joy with someone else. May I help you enlist them?"

APPENDIX C

EVANGELISM EXPLOSION—Public Report Board Layout

Suggested format for a chalkboard to be used during report sessions to record results of calling for the week.

Place the total *number* of each appropriate item in the proper boxes.

TOTAL TEAMS CALLING _____

TEAM MEMBERS' NAMES	Category										
TYPE OF CONTACT	Church visitor										
	Ques.—Public										
	Ques.—Door-to-door										
	Other										
	Referral										
	Family/friend										
	Sunday school										
	Personal										
	Total attempted										
	Total completed										
GOSPEL PRESENTED	How many times										
	To how many people										
	For trainee										
	Profession										
	No decision										
	Christian										
	For assurance										
GOSPEL NOT PRESENTED	Not admitted										
	Already Christian										
	Only questionnaire										
	Only friendly visit										
	Only pers. testimony										
FOLLOW-UP	Immed. full										
	Immed. abbrev.										
	Appt. for 7-Day										
	7-Day Call Back										

ABOUT
THE AUTHOR

Dr. D. James Kennedy was born in Augusta, Georgia, was reared in Chicago, and has spent most of his adult life in Florida. He received his bachelor's degree from the University of Tampa, his Master of Divinity, *cum laude*, from Columbia Theological Seminary, and his Master of Theology, *summa cum laude*, from the Chicago Graduate School of Theology. He received the Doctor of Divinity degree from Trinity College and Trinity Evangelical Divinity School, and his Ph.D. from New York University.

Dr. Kennedy has lectured and taught in dozens of seminaries, colleges, and countries and at the general assemblies of a number of denominations. He has spoken to over 100,000 ministers and seminary students on the subject of lay evangelism, and he has been a regular member of the faculty of the Billy Graham schools of evangelism.

The Results of This Ministry

The Evangelism Explosion ministry has been in continuous operation in the Coral Ridge Presbyterian Church of Fort Lauderdale, Florida, for the past 33 years. Up to 700 people have gone out weekly to share the Good News of Christ with others. God's gracious working through this effort has been exciting to observe. The church has grown from 17 to about 9,000 members and from one minister to 19. Of more importance than membership figures is the actual attendance on Sundays. The attendance has reached more than 12,000 on a peak Sunday morning. In the area of stewardship, the church has gone from home-mission support to a budget of more than $30 million. Approximately 150 families from the church have gone into full-time Christian service. Coral Ridge now telecasts its services to some 25,000 cities and communities and 35 countries. But Evangelism Explosion isn't confined to Coral Ridge Presbyterian Church in Ft. Lauderdale, Florida. Pastors have been trained in every nation on every continent and have returned to equip their laypeople for personal evangelism and discipleship, and the Evangelism Explosion ministry has been planted in every nation of the world.